I0222908

GLOBAL
DIMENSIONS
IN HOUSING
APPROACHES IN
DESIGN AND THEORY
FROM EUROPE TO
THE PACIFIC RIM

GLOBAL
DIMENSIONS
IN HOUSING
APPROACHES IN
DESIGN AND THEORY
FROM EUROPE TO
THE PACIFIC RIM

SERIES EDITOR
GRAHAM CAIRNS

EDITORS
KIRSTEN DAY

First published in 2018 by Green Frigate Books

Green Frigate is an imprint of Libri Publishing

Copyright © Libri Publishing Ltd.

Authors retain the rights to individual chapters.

ISBN: 978-1-911451-05-1

The right of Kirsten Day and Graham Cairns to be identified as the editors of this work has been asserted in accordance with the Copyright, Designs and Patents Act, 1988. All rights reserved. No part of this publication may be reproduced, stored in any retrieval system or transmitted in any form or by any means, electronic, mechanical, photocopying, recording or otherwise, without the prior written permission of the copyright holder for which application should be addressed in the first instance to the publishers. No liability shall be attached to the author, the copyright holder or the publishers for loss or damage of any nature suffered as a result of reliance on the reproduction of any of the contents of this publication or any errors or omissions in its contents.

A CIP catalogue record for this book is available from The British Library

Book and Cover design Carnegie Publishing

Cover image: The cityscape of Hong Kong (Francesco Rossini)

Printed in the UK by Lightning Source

Libri Publishing
Brunel House
Volunteer Way
Faringdon
Oxfordshire
SN7 7YR

Tel: +44 (0)845 873 3837

www.libripublishing.co.uk

CONTENTS

GRAHAM CAIRNS

FOREWORD

HOUSING – CRITICAL FUTURES

In the first books of the Libri Publishing series Housing the Future, the context for the whole publishing endeavour was described as one characterised by complexity and diversity. More specifically it was laid out as follows: in London, a leading capital of global finance, there is a chronic shortage of affordable housing for those that service the 'service' sector. The crisis is at levels not seen since World War II. In Beijing, capital of the twenty-first century's political powerhouse, the displacement of long-standing communities is a daily occurrence. In Mumbai, the biggest health risk faced by the city today has been identified as overcrowded housing, while in São Paulo, football's 2014 World Cup took place against a backdrop of community unrest and the chronic living conditions of the poor. The private sector, the state and residents themselves are searching for solutions. Whether housing refugees in conflict areas, providing safe water to the households in the developing world or ensuring key workers can live in the cities they support in the West, the question of housing is not only global, but critical.

This book, the third and final in the series, is inspired by the same set of issues as the first: the need to deal with a critical issue at a critical time – the provision of affordable and decent housing. However, it also draws on the idea of critical regionalism, universalised some thirty years ago through the writings of Kenneth Frampton – an awareness of how global forces play out regionally. Taking this dual perspective of 'the critical' – the absolute need to deal with a real issue on the one hand, and the link between the global and the regional on the other – this book, the Libri Publishing series of which it forms part and the broader research programme that overarches both seek to draw in perspectives from across the world on ways to improve housing provision globally. Whilst the focus of the series has been on design approaches, it will become clear in reading the diverse contributions to be found in these pages that design cannot, and perhaps should not, be isolated from the social, economic, political and cultural issues that are inevitably in play when we discuss housing.

On that basis we will see in this book arguments that the provision of adequate housing is one of the most important political issues today: an issue played out against a background of disparate policy interventions, resistances and conflicting aspirations; an issue involving architects, planners, developers, sociologists, artists, housing associations, community representatives, policy makers and more. We will also see that it is a question that affects both our private and public housing stock; the south and the global north; and both pre- and post-World War II housing across the world. We will see the differences in approaches manifest in countries experiencing rapid growth and unprecedented urbanisation, placed alongside approaches seen as applicable to countries dealing with an ageing population, immigration and shrinking cities. We will see that while some governments are struggling with the environmental implications of such changes in housing needs, others are employing technologically advanced initiatives to improve quality and levels of participation.

What this book captures then, is the complexity and variety of issues we need to contend with when we think of the design of housing in a global context. Obviously, it does not seek to offer a fully comprehensive overview of those issues but rather, presents us with a snapshot of approaches. Despite this synoptic character, it does offer one more component of the fuller Libri series, which consists of two other books: Housing the Future – Alternative Approaches for Tomorrow (2015) and Housing Solutions through Design (2017). Both these books sought to bring together the work of academics and their students concerned with using the academy as a place for not only preparing the next generation of architects to tackle housing as a major issue, but also academics and practitioners seeking to use the freedom of the academy to foster new and alternative ideas. Both of these books also interlaced these forward-thinking ideas from academia with the thoughts and works of some of the world's leading architects in issues of housing. Amongst them were Nicholas Grimshaw, UN Habitat Award winner Avi Friedman and RIBA Gold Medal winner Herman Hertzberger. This book does the same sort of thing, combining the work of academics, their students and practitioners. Not only does this continue the template of Libri's Housing the Future Series thematically, it continues its attempt to underline the importance of housing to students as the next generation of architects, designers and planners, and to function as a platform that fosters their engagement with it as a 'critical problem'.

When placed in the context of this broader book series then, the synoptic character of this book forms part of something more comprehensive: a global perspective on design as a contributory factor in solving the global housing crisis in its variegated forms across the world. Whilst that effort remains a drop in the ocean if seen in isolation, this book should also be considered in the even larger context of the broader research programme it sits in, the Housing Critical Futures initiative of the research organisation AMPS (Architecture, Media, Politics, Society). As a non-profit, AMPS has published various articles in its scholarly journal Architecture_MPS over the past five years and collaborated with scholars in universities from across the world in multiple conferences, film screenings, debates and research projects. Amongst these institutions one finds the Cyprus Institute, the University of Derby, the University of Liverpool, the University of

Seville, the University of the West of England, the University of Cyprus, Liverpool John Moores University, Abu Dhabi University, Swinburne University and more.

The book should also be read alongside works, debates, talks and papers written by, and in collaboration with, a whole series of other partners on the Housing Critical Futures programme including the Commission of Architecture and the Built Environment, the Royal Institute of British Architects, the Faculty of Public Health, Defend Council Housing, the Turner Prize Winning Art and Architecture Collective, Assemble, the UN Habitat University Initiative, the Royal Town Planning Institute, the European Council of Spatial Planners, the Centre for Alternative Technologies, Architects Without Frontiers, the Centre for Design Innovation, Bluecoat Chambers Art, the Public Health Film Society, the film director Ken Loach and many more.

This range of collaborators gives a sense of the reach and variety of the activities this book is included in. It is within this diverse framework that we have to think about this book's contribution to debates about housing, which in this instance oscillate along two axes. Firstly, the contributors here come predominantly from two global regions, Europe and the Pacific Rim. Secondly, the authors are concerned with either developed economies and the problems associated with housing there, or the developing world where a very different set of imperatives come to the fore. We should add to this that the book takes three approaches, each reflected in its tripartite structure. The first part examines housing design and supply in the urban conditions of developed economies today. This current concern is contextualised however by an introductory historical chapter considering the twentieth-century European legacy of Modernism in housing. The second collects together a number of student–professor engagements with housing in both developed and developing contexts, whilst the final part continues its dual geographical focus but places attention primarily on participatory design practices geared towards engaging communities in their own housing solutions. This community focus is underlined by a final stand-alone chapter that returns the reader to historical questions and forms a counterpoint to the design-focused, Euro-centric chapter used as an introduction to the book. Whilst being design focused then, this book accepts that design is only one aspect of a much more complex problem that, in what follows, will be explored via reference to politics, social issues, cultural difference, and artistic and creative workshops as a method of critical thinking. In this, and in many other regards, it forms a fitting contribution to this Libri Publishing series, Housing the Future, and the broader set of initiatives that series itself forms part of.

KIRSTEN DAY

INTRODUCTION

STRATEGIES FOR SUSTAINABLE FUTURE HABITATION

Ensuring an active community when issues of housing are at stake, it is argued in this book, will empower communities. This consistent theme sits alongside that of providing affordable, sustainable habitation for a world in flux – not just the developed world, but also the worlds of desperate hardship where urgency is commonplace and human survival the central issue. From Australia and the Asian region to Europe, the problems of contemporary accommodation presented here are compelling. Its affordability, function, suitability and availability are all questioned in the context of predicted future scenarios for population growth, particularly in urban areas. The arguments put forward are generally the product of design thinking, offering solutions based on imagination, developing innovative ideas rather than manufacturing a proposition of strategies to solve problems (with a cogent set of rules as a guide).

Most authors offer aspirational concepts and some reflect on history as a means of guiding us to a more positive future. Attention is often directed to innovative models for housing, room sizes, functions, spatial qualities and community participation in their construction, which is designed to attract a sense of ownership, pride and accomplishment for its inhabitants. There is also a broad focus on empowerment, self-managed housing models in Brussels, participatory design strategies in Scotland, collectives operating in Hong Kong and self-generation of habitation, for example. Other more damaged parts of the world are also drawn into the debate, however, with a number of examples discussed in which the provision of habitat is an emergency issue. This means provision of protective cover, privacy, security and 'place' is seen as a vital imperative, with life being tested for its most fundamental needs. In this context, emergency and temporary shelter are discussed in their diversity, from 1800s colonial housing for an indigenous Australian population, to concepts for living in nature reserves in Thailand and emergency shelter tactics in Indonesia. Echoing through all of these stories is a common thread of positive humanitarianism, even optimism, for the future, if these types of policies – and more – are developed.

Looking specifically at these themes by author, Kirsten Day documents work by Loc Tran and Thi Vo to show a depth of respect for traditional places and the human condition. The work she examines is concerned that basic values should not be replaced by 'others', but rather determined by the characteristics of living in a dense Asian city. Recycling inadequate housing in Vietnam's major cities – Hanoi and Ho Chi Minh City – is the primary focus along with conditioning buildings to the people, the climate, histories and local expectations that inhabit and inform them. The recycled market she documents retains the community values of the existing Tan Dinh market in Hon Chi Minh City, by maintaining the underpinning strengths of the place, its social interactivity and a central role as the communal meeting place, while continuing is main function as a thriving place of trade. It is thus a chapter that provides a template for sustainable future growth without the stigma of an inappropriate gentrification process or, worse, creating a picturesque theme park out of a genuine community resource.

Similar things can be said of Chiara Monterumisi and Alessandro Porotto who explore schemes in Stockholm and Vienna, where traditional community values provide a reciprocity for the citizens living in quiet and populous courtyard block housing estates that are multi-storey, but not high rise. Evidence of their viability appears in the housing having a direct access to open, green spaces which are relatively private, protected and secure, and in which families can meet and play, rest and enjoy. The figures provided by the authors make the point: 50 per cent of the land is open space and site density is just 2–3 per cent.

By contrast, the urbanity Francesco Rossini describes in Hong Kong, which must almost hold the record for most densely populated world city, is all about verticality: 7.5 million people packed into 1,100 square metres of land, resulting in a density of 6,800 people per square kilometre. Indications are that Hong Kong, which is now an SAR (Special Administration Region) of China, will continue to grow vertically whilst simultaneously increasing its land mass by land reclamation into the iconic Victoria Harbour and beyond in the New Territories. In this context, Hwang and Rossini consider options for place-making by speculating on a model for collective housing. They suggest lower densities than existing high-rise models. Driving the design is a plan to create 'place' rather than space for Hong Kong. Their three models contain communal shared facilities and integrated gardens as part of the housing.

Sadanu Sukkasame concentrates on strategies for emergency shelter in Indonesia, focusing attention on simplicity in mobility systems to allow best access to damaged parts of the world. In this scenario, houses are made using direct methods of supply, erection and containment – if only for a short period of time. Sukkasame's research is located in a Thai National Park that is both traditional land for the local Karen peoples and a refugee hot spot located near the southern border between Myanmar and Thailand. The traditional values of these hill tribes inform the work and suggest schemes for participatory designing processes.

Jaqueline Power's chapter recounts the lethal conflict of the colonial settlement of Tasmania, in southern Australia, where the indigenous population was eventually eradicated, but where a refugee settlement called Wybalenna (meaning 'black man's houses') had been established on the adjacent Flinders Island in a vain attempt to avert total genocide. She notes the resistance to settlement mounted by people who were denied their traditional places to live and roam. It is a set of circumstances that obliges Power to question how much of Wybalenna was a protected habitat and how much of it was a prison. The question echoes shamefully over the years when we consider recent Australian government options for 'housing' asylum-seeking boat-people refugees at prisons on the Pacific islands of Nauru and Manis.

By contrast to the focus outlined above, Catja De Haas's chapter, 'The Giant Dolls' House Project', investigates providing housing for the homeless. Uniquely, it is done through a collaborative project dealing with miniaturisation and rituals that is designed to draw attention to the issues of habitat. It is a project that has been modelled in a number of locations in and around London and Dubai. The models focus community minds on the abstract notion of 'house', which is represented by a small-scale model, but the invitation is for people to embed themselves into the models and imagine future scenarios for living.

Other writers have studied issues of self-managed housing in Brussels and community participation in Scotland. The work in Brussels by Anna Ternon and Gérald Ledent outlines issues of production as a means of taking up the slack in affordable housing provision. It draws attention to the widening gap between those with a house and others without, and the developing social and cultural inequities that develop from that scenario. They note especially the changing needs for housing, from that of a 'traditional' nuclear family to other paradigms such as blended families, transiting folk, singles, cross-genders and more. Within this context, one issue they bring up that demands understanding is a 2017 law prohibiting squatting. This law was enacted in reaction to the continued use of a building located at 123 rue Royale, Brussels, which functioned as unauthorised housing and provided a place for permanent and temporary dwellers for years. This building's potential as an alternative model has now been prohibited by law.

Nadia Bertolino and Sandra Costa Santos examine Claremont Court in Edinburgh, which is effectively Modern social housing dating from the 1960s, to describe how a socialised development can be produced using various design tactics. In this case they argue that the variety of issues contributed to the provision of liveable housing, despite its mass; building types; the controlling of various means of entry, egress and movement through the construction; choices of internal planning; and the creation of communal resources and so forth. Their conclusion is that planned housing estates can work and survive; however, they recognise the need for communal consultation and involvement to underpin this desired outcome.

British examples of mass-produced housing investigated by Tobias Vokuhl and Dr Mark Austin focus attention on the interim realm between urban density and a relative suburban emptiness, which they call 'sub-urbanism'. Their concern is the amount of space provided via mass production and its usefulness. They have interviewed a number of residents for their chapter to shed light on the actual experience of living in these places and their appropriateness to the task. The team from the Queensland College of Art at Griffith University led by Petra Perolini looks at similar concerns for spatial functionality and fitness for purpose. The concept they put forward is that rapid human population growth creates urban massing, which leads to housing shortages once the momentum to build cannot be maintained. As a result, they suggest, social, cultural and economic problems all emerge. The research project they document involved developing a model for 'smaller' footprint houses by recycling a standard single occupancy two-bedroom living unit into two apartments using the same floor area – which they call 'small living'.

Two other chapters explore the means of production of housing, one using digital technologies as a way of enticing participation in the design process and the other by adapting education in architecture to assemble teams of designers that can work in the field. Sally Stone, Laura Sanderson and John Lee describe their notion for 'continuity in architecture', which develops from their educational experience in an architecture school. Their aim is to close the gaps between propositions made in academia and the construction of actual buildings located in real communities. Their hope is that policy makers will reflect on the process and place value on participatory approaches as viable options for solving community housing needs. Lo Tian Tian, Marc Aurel Schnabel and Tane Moleta from Victoria University of Wellington propose a digital creative process to participatory housing design. They do not do this as simply a means to an end – the creation of create new housing – but as a means to entice participation in the creative process of designing. Their research focusses on digital tools that can enable freedom of expression about design issues, encourage the sharing of ideas, focus on matters of importance to do with needs, and produce visual exchanges that will captivate and engage participants.

These diverse chapters are, for purposes of coherence and clarity, divided in the structure of this book along three major axes. Firstly in Part One, the chapters that deal with issues of planning and policy in developed urban contexts are collated together. These include aligning works from Europe with others from the Pacific Rim as well as aligning essays on the social politics of housing with others that are more design focused. It starts with Monterumisi and Porotto's examination of an example from European housing history. This sets the framework for subsequent chapters dealing with issues and actions taking place right now in both Europe and the Pacific region. Part Three centres on what we may define as participatory and community practices in design developed by activists, educators and architects seeking to fully embed the communities they design for in the design and planning process. A large number of these essays are drawn from the academy and, in that sense, reflect what has been said before in this book, that academia offers those of us interested in new approaches the creative scope to think beyond the boundaries of contemporary established practice. To balance Part One, it ends with another engagement with historical precedent, in this case Jacqueline Power's critique of Palawa resistance. Interspersed between these two main sections are a short number of student projects or, more precisely, educational projects in which students have worked closely with professors to develop new ideas about housing design and related issues in close proximity to communities and real world problems.

Whilst this division into three parts helps us frame the diversity of this book, it should not detract from it. Despite this division, the scope of these chapters and the research underpinning them suggest an agreement of sorts across a wide range of scholars and practitioners as to how best to provide suitable habitation for the hugely expanding world population. Apart from issues of emergency and desperate need, the necessity of ensuring communal involvement in the creation and construction of housing – including strategies for participation and sustainable plans for shared decision making – is obvious throughout this book. Ensuring an active community when issues of housing are at stake, it is argued, will empower communities to own their places and, in turn, provide a lasting sense of pride in, and respect for, our housing stock. What can be discerned throughout this book then, is an outline belief that, if obtained, empowerment bestows on the built environment higher levels of security, privacy and respect for the most important habitation we use – our house.

PART ONE

CHAPTER ONE

CHIARA MONTERUMISI AND ALESSANDRO POROTTO

École Polytecnique Fédérale de Lausanne, Switzerland

WHY CAN'T WE LIVE TOGETHER? STOCKHOLM AND VIENNA'S LARGE COURTYARD BLOCKS

INTRODUCTION

The aim of this chapter is to look back on some valuable accomplishments of metropolitan housing districts built at the beginning of the twentieth century in Stockholm (1916–1930) and Vienna (1919–1933). Far from revising the narratives of modern history, those first attempts demonstrate how housing turned into a core-concern from that time, unlike the historians take as a starting point all those examples employing radical and functionalist models. The apt motto "from the block to the bar" marked out this transition.[1] On the occasion of the *IFHTP – International Federation for Housing and Town Planning* in Vienna (1926) and later the first *CIAM – Congrès Internationaux d'Architecture Moderne* (1928) in Switzerland, there emerged a worldwide effort of theory and policy to respond to a serious housing shortage. Two contrasting urban and typological models animated the debate: the large courtyard block and the north–south oriented bars. Nevertheless, leading avant-garde figures mostly shifted their attention away from the densely built-up block of the nineteenth-century city in favour of green settlements and housing estates.

The goal of this contribution is hence to examine in greater detail the large courtyard block through two case studies, one from Stockholm and one from Vienna. This type of building

---

1   See: Gropius, Walter. "Die Wohnformen: Flach-, Mittel- oder Hochbau?". *Das Neue Berlin*, 4 (1929), 74–80. May, Ernst. "Fünf Jahre Wohnungsbautätigkeit in Frankfurt am Main". *Das Neue Frankfurt*, 2–3, Febr-März (1930), 21–55.

was defined by Gropius and May as a mere intermediate step in the evolution,[2] but in actual fact it presented remarkable architectural qualities of morphology and spatial sequences. The large courtyard block was a convincing achievement in the process of reforming the urban perimeter block and it was a dominant and long-lasting model in some European cities. Such modern housing policies significantly influenced the history and structure of cities, as may be seen in the urban layout of Stockholm and Vienna today.

Housing started to become a public utility, part of a wider and multifaceted social vision. At the turn of the twentieth century, the response to accelerated metropolitan growth,[3] an acute housing shortage and increased building costs came first in the form of continuous fabrics of high-density multi-storey or provisional barrack quarters in the city outskirts. These were speculative buildings (*Hyrekasern* in Swedish and *Mietkasernen* in German) in the sense that, until the First World War, private construction was struck down and construction costs rose sharply due to material shortages and rationing. The flats were overcrowded and received limited sunlight due to the considerably reduced size of the courtyards. Sanitary conditions were terrible: no bathrooms, no water and lighting, and no facilities. Later, a favourable political and cultural milieu in both cities paved the way for approval of effective land policies and strategic urban plans allocating copious dwelling complexes equipped with improved sanitary conditions and many more facilities. The attention and the responsibility of planners, architects, cooperatives and politicians focused on "the families [that] are the foundation upon which the society is built",[4] as well as on "large masses of population".[5] In Sweden, town planners of the municipality liaised with housing cooperatives in conducting these programmes, whereas in Vienna the municipality was solely responsible.[6]

---

2   Gropius presented three schemes starting from a condensed block, later a regular large courtyard block and a bar settlement. May added an additional step to the three diagrams. The same three schemes were also reproduced in the Swedish functionalist manifesto *acceptera* (1931) by Uno Åhrén, Erik Gunnar Asplund, Wolter Gahn, Sven Markelius, Gregor Paulsson and Eskil Sundahl.

3   From 1850 to 1930 Stockholm's population increased from 93,000 to 502,200 inhabitants, while Vienna shows a growth from 551,300 to 1,935,881 inhabitants. As the data show, Vienna is four times larger than the Swedish capital.

4   See Sven Wallander, "Våra arbetsuppgifter", *Vår bostad*, 1 (1924): 1–3.

5   See Gemeinde Wien, *Die Wohnungspolitik der Gemeinde Wien* (Wien: Gesellschafts- und Wirtschaftmuseum, 1929). Vienna municipality promoted its two housing programmes through promotional booklets.

6   Vienna municipality built 58,353 flats in the timespan 1923–1933. See Hans Hautmann and Rudolf Hautmann, *Die Gemeindebauten des Roten Wien 1919–1934* (Wien: Schönbrunn, 1980). About Stockholm, the data are somewhat less precise in the sense that most case surveys were conducted on a national basis. For example, between 1916 and 1929, 129,800 housing units were built in 280 Swedish towns (See Catherine Bauer, *Modern Housing* (Boston: Houghton Mifflin, 1934)) of which approximately 70,452 were in Stockholm and its suburbs (See USK – Stockholms stad. *Bostäder i Stockholm 1893–1985* (Stockholm: USK, 1989)).

In comparing the case studies – Humleboet in Stockholm and Fuchsenfeldhof in Vienna – one will recognise some formal and spatial analogies behind the attempt to reform the layout of the city and the conditions of living together. These large courtyards, carefully designed as a fine balance between green and no-green areas, formed an appropriate living space for the community. The analysis is here carried out from a careful study of original photos and drawings that the authors consulted in the archives.[7] Starting from these items, the aim is to produce analytical re-drawings of the plans (typological assemblages and courtyard layout) as well as to calculate design parameters (Table 1), which allows the strengths and weakness of the examples examined to be effectively verified. Of the numerous residential districts built in the form of large courtyard blocks, the choice went to Humleboet and Fuchsenfeldhof because they present sequences of three collective spaces, likewise land lot surfaces and the novelty of as much as 50 per cent of the plot being reserved for courtyards.[8] Curiously, the two projects are also linked by an article published in the Swedish magazine *Vår bostad* in 1927[9] dealing with the extremely impressive Viennese effort, in particular that of municipal authorities, in order to increase housing and to create something new, something of value,[10] as in the case of the Fuchsenfeldhof, which is displayed in the article.

STOCKHOLM

Humleboet belongs to a wider housing complex called *Röda Bergen* (Red Mountains). It is an extensive hilly area in the north-west part of the unbuilt outskirts. The peculiar features of the area interrupted the orthogonal east–west oriented grid-plan, *Lindhagenplanen* (1866), causing radical changes to the pattern of streets and building lots.

The layout of today's site plan does not entirely correspond with the first urban plan (1907–1909) drawn up by the urban planner Per Olof Hallman.[11] He was the first to introduce Raymond Unwin and Camillo Sitte's theories in Sweden, planners with whom he also had a close relation. Hallman tackled the irregular lie of the land by designing large partially opened courtyard blocks and buildings for the community (e.g. kindergarten, church and school). The picturesque result was a peculiar conflation of the two planning sources of reference previously mentioned, with which it presents some points in common. Before World War One, an extensive portion of the south

---

7   In Stockholm *Arkitektur –ochdesigncentrum*, *Stadsbyggnadsexpeditionen* and *Stadsarkivet*, while in Vienna *Baupolizei MA37-West*.

8   Otto Grimlund, "Det nya Wien. Ett storartat kommunalt nybyggnadsarbete för lindrandet av bostadsnöden". *Vår bostad*, 4 (1927): 12–14.

9   The magazine was the promoting and critical platform of the housing cooperative HSB.

10   Grimlund, "Det nya Wien", 12.

11   He took part in the first Town Planning Conference (London, 1910) and together with Albert Lilienberg arranged the first *IFHTP* exhibition and seminar in Göteborg (1923). Hallman was also expert member of the Stockholm town planning committee, of which he later became director.

blocks, particularly those buildings facing onto the wide alley, were built. After the war, the urban plan was slightly revised by architects Sven Wallander and Sigurd Lewerentz who stressed symmetry and regularity more than before. However, the separation between traffic-bearing roads and residential streets remained. The merging of two topographically different areas – the two halves of the hexagon – by means of two main orthogonal axes was kept as well: the regular straight north–south alley was enlarged, and the east–west axis presented some changes in its irregular widenings and narrowings affecting the sequence of collective spaces.

What radically changed was the dwelling type employed: they replaced semi-detached houses with multi-storey mass-buildings, whose ground floors were frequently used as shops, ateliers or common utilities. Wallander and Lewerentz captured the real needs of the Swedish population, seeking functional solutions for allocating families, especially elderly and low-income people. *Röda Bergen* presents an irregular hexagon shape formed by ten large courtyard blocks. Humleboet is situated in the eastern entry side of the district along one of the two main street axes. It consists of seven blocks of different shapes and sizes due to the cadastral system. In 1924–1927, Wallander built three big blocks while Gustaf Laurelius, Sam Kjellberg, Paul Hedqvist and Theodor Kjellgren designed the other four blocks of the district (Figure 1). The housing cooperative HSB – *Hyresgästernas sparkasse – och byggnadsförening* (Savings and Construction Association of the Tenants)[12] – was responsible for numerous large courtyard blocks in *Röda Bergen*. In Humleboet only two blocks do not belong to HSB and they are in the east wing of the regular and stretchered courtyard.

The layout of *Röda Bergen* comprises a series of interconnected spaces largely consisting of partially open courtyard blocks, stairways and right-angled or curving streets. Apart from the two large ones in the north, the remaining courtyards are usually not completely enclosed by building blocks, but open to the street and the park. One should note that there were courtyards shared by inhabitants of all the quarter and others exclusively accessible to people living in the blocks facing the courtyard. All these design choices reveal a decisive improvement in the spatial and collective qualities of the large courtyard block. One clearly feels Sitte's ambition for the "city as unitary expression of the collective identity"[13] where artistic and civic needs "do necessarily not run contrary to the dictates of modern living".[14] The irregularities are actively exploited, which meant following the lie of the land with its ever-changing prospects. The Swedish hybridisation of residential spatial features –

---

12   Wallander was the leading figure of the HSB cooperative, which was founded in 1923.
13   Heleni Porfyriou, 'Scandinavian Town Planning 1900–1930 and the contribution of Camillo Sitte' (PhD diss., Bartlett School of Architecture and Planning, University College London, 1990), 103.
14   George R. Collins and Christiane C. Collins, *Camillo Sitte: The Birth of Modern City Planning* (New York: Rizzoli, 1986 [1965]), 92. This book contains the English translation of the Sitte's masterpiece *Der Städtebau nach seinen künstlerischen Grundsätzen* (1889).

such as the 'closes', 'cul-de-sacs' and 'quadrangles' that Unwin carefully illustrated in *Town Planning in Practice* (1909) – made this possible. As he commented, the state of cities at that time showed that any sort of "amenities of life" were neglected.[15] Beyond improving sanitary conditions, "there is also needed the vivifying touch of art, which would give completeness and increase their value tenfold; there is needed just that imaginative treatment which could transform the whole".[16]

Like *Röda Bergen's* other large courtyard blocks, Humleboet is a combination of modest-scale buildings and extensive areas of parkland and countryside.[17] In the first layout, Hallman gave particular care in distinguishing private greeneries from collective ones. Later, he actively participated in the debate about increasing green areas into the courtyards and reducing the separating walls, features of the high-dense perimeter blocks. The practice of erecting walls was the result of the speculative construction of tenement buildings. Conceiving the neighbourhood as a whole in terms of land laws and design principles also permitted the interactions between the inhabitants, who started to appreciate living together.[18]

The revised urban plan stipulated a medium density corresponding to three-to-four-storey apartment buildings. Most of Humleboet's blocks respect this rule, except for the buildings along the eastern perimeter, which are seven storeys. The five architects built 389 dwelling units: most of them are one room plus kitchen/kitchenette and toilette; in the cases where showers were not included in the apartment, they were in the basement as a communal utility.

The case study is characterised by three green courtyards differing in size, geometry and usage. On the east side towards the roundabout and nearby the symmetrical urban staircase that permits to reach the housing complex, the head of Humleboet has a rectangular green area in common with the facing block that is similar in shape and symmetrical with respect to the two-line planted alley. Initially, Lewerentz conceived the centre of this area as a fit place for a small kindergarten, plus two small children's play places, but the building was never built. To a certain extent, the function has been kept to the present: there are planted and gravel paved areas equipped with facilities for a playground. Strolling down the two-lane planted alley of the cul-de-sac, one passes the ground-floor archway-passage – accessible to vehicles and pedestrians – that divides the T-shape block from the U-shape ones. The one-way street that runs along one of

---

15   Raymond Unwin, *Town Planning in Practice* (London: Adelphi Terrace, 1909), 4.

16   Ibid., 4.

17   Parallel to Hallman, one should also mention the prominent role of some members of the Social Democrat party sitting on Stockholm City Council, like Anna Lindhagen. She was a driving force in introducing "allotment gardens" and stressing how important carefully designed and equipped gardens are in urban housing developments.

18   Anna Lindhagen, *Koloniträdgårdar och planterade gårdar* (Stockholm: Norstedt & Söner, 1916), 52–3. Some of her analysis and design suggestions were also supported by a Hallman speech dated 1916.

the two parallel bars is delimited, on the right, by an irregular trapezoidal plot which follows the slope of the terrain (Figure 2). Here, the topography of site was cleverly used in the design process. Moving toward two of the blocks designed by Wallander there is still a 10-metre strip of private gardens with drying racks, benches, flowerpots and pergolas. The gardening sheds and tiny vegetable gardens no longer exist. There is still the same elliptical playground area, rather more fully equipped than in the 1920s. Even though the size of the open area is generous, the overall impression is of intimacy, provided by the protective ring of three-to-four-storey blocks. Lastly, the rectangular courtyard between two parallel blocks – designed for the private use of the inhabitants of the four facing buildings by the Swedish landscape architect Ester Claesson – was conceived as a series of green spaces that gave an overall impression of cosiness and harmony. She introduced some rooms for seating arrangements with pergolas contoured by hedges and some others for vegetable gardens. The original layout has been modified, but the purpose is still for socialising and cultivating.

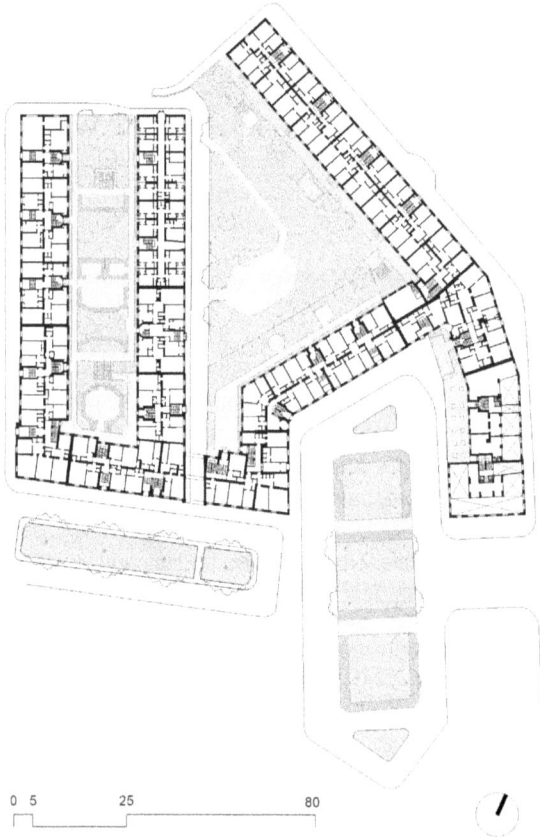

Figure 1. Humleboet ground floor plan. Image Chiara Monterumisi (2017)

Figure 2. Humleboet, trapezoidal sloping courtyard: from the collective space and private gardens (Digitala Stadsmuseet, 1928) to the communal green area and playground. Image: Chiara Monterumisi (2016)

VIENNA

In 1922–1925, Heinrich Schmid and Hermann Aichinger designed the Fuchsenfeldhof,[19] which was the first building entirely conceived as a *Hof* according to the city's planning guidelines for communal housing blocks.[20] Although scheduled for 1919, it was the first building to be built with the *Wohnbausteuer* of the first municipal program

---

19   See Gustav A. Fuchs, *Der Fuchsenfeldhof* (Wien: Wiener Magistrat, 1923).
20   On how the English-speaking world received the policies and guidelines of the Viennese municipality, see Charles Hardy, *The Housing Program of the City of Vienna* (Washington, D.C.: The Brookings Institution, 1934).

in 1923.[21] It can therefore be considered one of the first interventions of Viennese housing policy.[22]

The building site is in the Meidling (12th *Bezirk*), one of Vienna's suburban districts that became industrialised through the nineteenth century. Brickworks, textile and metalwork factories were located there, leading to the speculative building of tenement blocks. Thus, the urban plot of Fuchsenfeldhof had been partially built upon before the city acquired it in 1922.[23] The complex was erected in two phases. The first began in 1922 and included 212 apartments, several shops and workshops, the city's cooperative stores, a child-care facility, a central steam-powered laundry and communal baths. These functions were grouped in a six-storey building around one courtyard, which occupied only the eastern side of the trapezoidal city block. In the second phase (1923–1924), it grew to encompass the entirety of the city block, integrating two pre-war apartment buildings in the southwest corner. Grouped around three courtyards, the project added 267 apartments, four shops, two workshops, an instructional workshop, a kindergarten, a reading room, additional laundry and bathing facilities, playgrounds, a water pool and a new monumental entrance to the largest of the new courtyards. Two architects designed 481 apartments in the six- and seven-storey buildings around a sequence of four collective courtyards.

The block shows a rational layout in its spatial organisation and relationship with the urban fabric. The building considers the perimeter streets as limits. Tafuri stated that Fuchsenfeldhof conveys the stiffness of the urban form, because it is not able to modify the rigid plot shape.[24] This critical observation can be also interpreted differently: the rigidity of the urban form shows the ability of the block type to build new dwellings into the urban fabric without modifying the pre-existing general plan.[25] This feature allows

---

21 The first drawings of the first phase of the Fuchsenfeldhof project dated back to 1919. The start to building was conditioned by acquisition of land and financing. For more information about the economic and administrative system, see the text of the first housing program Karl Honey, *Die Wohnungspolitik der Gemeinde Wien* (Deutsch-Österr. Städtebund, 1926).

22 Usually, the *Metzleinstalerhof* is considered the first *Hof* of the Viennese experience. The courtyard block consists of a part designed by Robert Kalesa in 1919–1920 and a second one in 1923–1924 by Hubert Gessner. However, the *Metzleinstalerhof* was not yet included in the 1923 housing program.

23 Eve Blau, *The Architecture of Red Vienna 1919–1934* (Cambridge, Massachusetts: The MIT Press, 1999), 234.

24 Manfredo Tafuri, *Vienna Rossa. La politica residenziale nella Vienna socialista 1919–1933* (Milano: Electa, 1980), 152.

25 The *Höfe* are predominantly located in workers' areas where the urban fabric showed the signs of nineteenth-century housing speculation. Their construction was based on the general urban plan of 1893, without any modifications to the urban structure as shown by Emilio Battisti, *Architettura ideologia e scienza. Teoria e pratica nelle discipline di progetto* (Milano: Feltrinelli Editore, 1975), 87–91.

the *Höfe* to interweave intricately with the historic city. It is no coincidence that Werner Hegemann appreciated the Viennese complexes, stating they were "typically urban in character... Note, however, the pleasing variety of detail in each group, and the ingenious way in which the plans of the blocks are related to existing streets and open spaces".[26] In particular, the four enclosed courtyards of the Fuchsenfeldhof present valuable design solutions. Each is characterised by a different shape and volume variations. The relationship between the building and the size of the courtyard space is the special feature of the architects' handling of the collective programme.

The model of the large courtyard block has a long tradition in Vienna's history[27] and achieved a precise theoretical frame in two masters of Viennese architecture and town planning from the late nineteenth century: Camillo Sitte and Otto Wagner. Sitte theorised the large garden court in *Greenery within the City* (1900):[28] "The *sanitary greenery* should not be found amidst the dust and noise of the streets, but rather in the sheltered interior of large blocks of buildings, surrounded on all sides".[29] According to this idea, the courtyards contain recreational greenery that could be used for many other functions, like playgrounds and even markets. "What Sitte proposed here was nothing less than opening the formerly private ground of the urban block to the public – a strategy which later became important for the large *Höfe* of Red Vienna".[30] In his lecture on *The Metropolis* at the Urban Design Conference in New York (1910), Otto Wagner presented apartment blocks as the only appropriate housing typology for modern life, as opposed to suburban detached houses:[31]

> The longed-for detached house in the still more longed-for garden city can never satisfy the popular need, since as a result of the pressure of economy in living expenses, of the increase and decrease in the size of families, of change of occupation and position in life, there must be constant shifting and change in the desires of the masses. The needs which arise from such changing conditions can be satisfied only by rented apartment dwellings, and never by individual houses.[32]

---

26 Werner Hegemann, *City Planning Housing*. Vol. III (New York: Architectural Book Publishing Company, 1938), 93.

27 See Hans Bobek and Elisabeth Lichtenberger, *Wien. Bauliche Gestalt und Entwicklung seit der Mitte des 19. Jahrhunderts* (Graz-Köln: Hermann Böhlaus Nachf, 1966).

28 This article appeared in 1900 in *Der Lotse: Hamburgische Wochenschrift für deutsche Kultur*. It was printed as an appendix in the German edition of 1909 of *Der Städtebau nach seinen künstlerischen Grundsätzen*. The English translation was published in Collins and Collins, *Camillo Sitte*, 303–21.

29 Ibid., 319.

30 Wolfgang Sonne, 'Dwelling in the metropolis: Reformed urban blocks 1890–1940 as a model for the sustainable compact city', *Progress in Planning*, 72, 2, (2009): 77.

31 In 1911, Otto Wagner also showed his urban vision of Vienna in *Die Grossstadt*. The site plan and aerial perspective for the 22nd Vienna Municipal District project presented uniform residential blocks interspersed with monumental public buildings arranged along a central axis of green spaces.

32 Otto Wagner, 'The development of a great city'. *Architectural Record* 31 (1912): 498.

This statement is important, considering that architects of some of the largest and most significant Red Vienna buildings were students at the Wagner Academy.[33] In their turn, Schmid and Aichinger, the architects of the Fuchsenfeldhof, belonged to the so-called *Wagner Schule*.[34] On the one hand, Sitte stresses the multifunctional spatial quality of the courtyard; on the other, Wagner focuses on the urban features of the housing block type. Both principles coherently blended together in the socialist housing programme:

> In the communal buildings, at least 50% of the surface of the courtyard (*Hof*) is generally not built. ... Careful attention is paid to making large courtyards in a way that they can provide ornamental gardens and that the sun can reach all the rooms as much as possible. The courtyard garden of the communal buildings guarantees lighting and ventilation of the houses, as well as, no less importantly, it offers playgrounds for children and rest areas for people.[35]

The ground floor of Fuchsenfeldhof features a fully integrated combination of garden areas, public entryways, access to collective facilities, circulation paths and apartments (Figure 3). The block emerges as an interaction between public, collective and private spaces, accommodating many facilities and functions. The building "is in fact both public and private, domestic and civic, its courtyard spaces are both open to the city and enclosed within its walls".[36] The sequence of four linked courtyards enhanced the size and the communal amenities; it also improved the urban character through two monumental gateways connecting the street to the internal public space. Despite using the well-established *Hof* typology, Fuchsenfeldhof introduced in an innovative way a new spatial and functional quality into the urban district by incorporating public elements into the residential fabric. The spatial dimensions and the facilities in its courtyards made a key contribution to building practice in Vienna, demonstrating that Vienna's large courtyard blocks could embody Sitte and Wagner's urban theories and the social vision of 'collective living', as stated in the housing programme. In recent years, Fuchsenfeldhof has been renovated, adapting easily to contemporary living requirements. Most of the facilities and common equipment in the courtyard have been preserved. Although the water pool is nowadays used as a playground, the transformed elements have not altered the collective character after all (Figure 4).

33   Some famous architects, such as Josef Hoffmann, Josef Plečnik and Max Fabiani, also attended the Otto Wagner Academy. See Marco Pozzetto, *Die Schule Otto Wagners* (Wien-München: Verlag Anton Schroll, 1979).
34   See Monika Wenzl-Bachmayer (ed.), *Die Wagner Schule Rotes Wien. Architektur als soziale Utopie* (Wien: Wagner-Werk Museum Postsparkasse, 2010).
35   Gemeinde Wien, *Die Wohnungspolitik*, 44.
36   Blau, *Red Vienna*, 238.

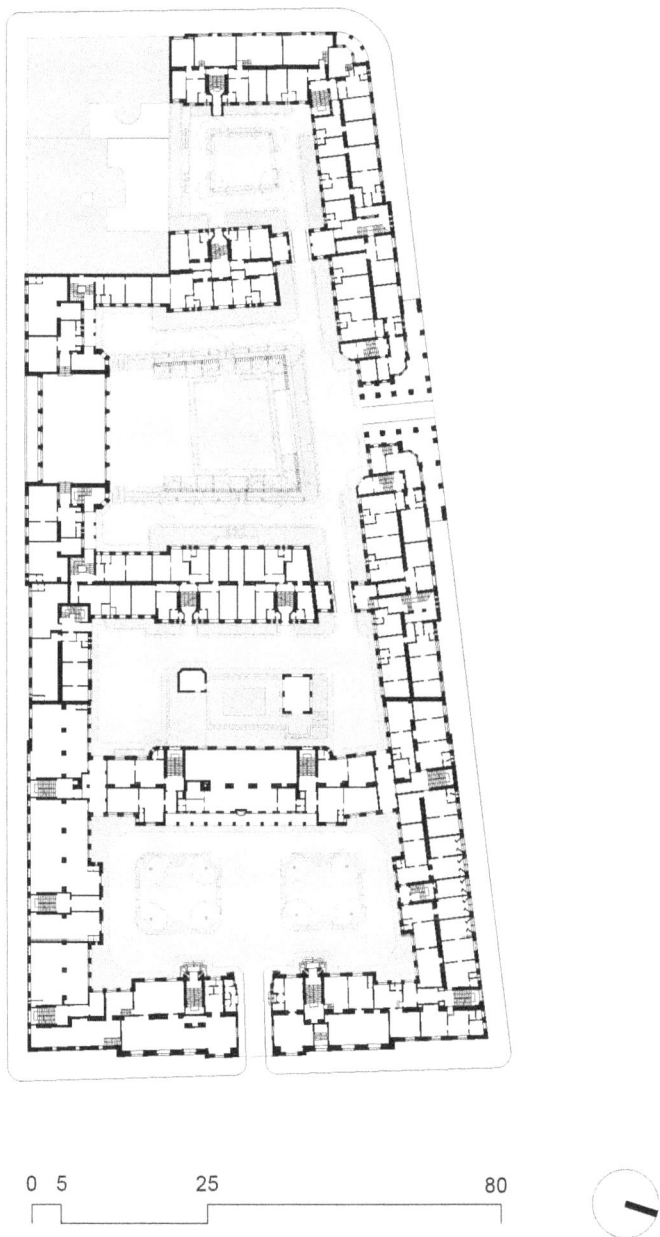

0 5   25   80

Figure 3. Fuchsenfeldhof, ground floor plan. Image Alessandro Porotto (2017)

Figure 4. Fuchsenfeldhof, the main courtyard: from the swimming pool (WStLA, 1920) to the collective garden area. Image: Alessandro Porotto (2016)

CONCLUSION

Investigating Humleboet and Fuchsenfeldhof has shown how they still offer key suggestions for conceiving the collective space of the courtyard. Their legacy is all the more important nowadays since housing is such a central topic. They can be considered as models – if properly adapted – for contemporary architectural practice. The authors' re-drawings (figures 1 and 3) highlight the peculiar features of the outdoor spaces, and these are also summarised by the chart data (Table 1).

Humleboet *Stockholm*		Fuchsenfeldhof *Vienna*
389	Number of dwellings	481
3, 4 and 7	Number of storeys	6 and 7
10,869 m²	Total land lot surface	10,680 m²
2,685 m²	Green areas	1,008 m²
1,564 m²	'No green' areas (stone pavers, asphalt and gravel permeable pavers)	3,371 m²
0.56 (56%)	Land occupancy rate	0.59 (59%)
2.38	Site residential density	3.22

Table 1. Comparative data between the two case studies

Although each of the two case studies describes a similar plot surface, the density is significantly lower in the Humleboet due to the greater quantity of storeys in the Fuchsenfeldhof. Differences also concern the building features and the architectural layout of the courtyards as illustrated in the pictures. The percentage of green-paved areas is also interesting: in Stockholm, natural features are prominent, the unusual topography becoming an integral part of the project, whereas in Vienna the layout of the outdoor spaces is the result of careful design control. The comparison between old and recent pictures shows how in these courtyards certain common ground-floor facilities and outdoor equipment are still available for daily use. From a typological point of view, the dwellings designed at that time show great flexibility and a capacity for adapting to current living standards, which generally amounted to merging two or three of them together by a few operations.

Although they were designed almost one hundred years ago, they still lump together many individuals and families low on the social ladder into a large block with a shared courtyard, achieving a novel architectural urban unit. Recently, Secchi viewed such European examples of large courtyard blocks as common ground in the search for adequate forms of living together and the expression of democratic ideals.[37] Today, the Viennese dwellings have been allocated to elderly people, members of the poorer class and immigrants, to all of whom the municipality still guarantees a low rent. In Stockholm, the inhabitants' backgrounds vary, as in the beginning: elderly people, lower- and medium-class families, single workers and single parents share those blocks. What is more, the skilful design of the two developments has prevented the buildings from deterioration and, on a larger scale, from the urban decline sadly affecting so many neighbourhoods of big European cities.

To some extent, Stockholm and Vienna mass-housing complexes demonstrate surprisingly valuable features as they are suitable to be adapted especially to the progressive changes in the social structure of the last century. The globalisation

37   Bernardo Secchi, *La città dei ricchi e la città dei poveri* (Roma-Bari: Laterza, 2013), 65.

process emphasises separation between groups and negatively influences the coexistence between people, who feel they belong to a more individualistic society. As a natural consequence, this strengthens the crisis of the collective dimension of the city and common living. As Bauman pointed out, nowadays people seek safety in the insecure world by expressing the desire for community.[38] In line with this, architects must similarly tackle housing issues. The song 'Why Can't We Live Together?' written by Timmy Thomas in 1972 was conceived to inspire a return to "living together" and, here, it is matched with the two housing experiences of the twenties that were designed with the same community goal in mind.

BIBLIOGRAPHY

Battisti, Emilio. *Architettura ideologia e scienza. Teoria e pratica nelle discipline di progetto*. Milano: Feltrinelli Editore, 1975.

Bauer, Catherine. *Modern housing*. Boston: Houghton Mifflin, 1934.

Blau, Eve. *The Architecture of Red Vienna 1919–1934*. Cambridge, Massachusetts: The MIT Press, 1999.

Bobek, Hans, and Lichtenberger, Elisabeth. *Wien. Bauliche Gestalt und Entwicklung seit der Mitte des 19. Jahrhunderts*. Graz-Köln: Verlag Hermann Böhlaus Nachf, 1966.

Collins, George R., and Collins, Christiane C. *Camillo Sitte: The Birth of Modern City Planning*. New York: Rizzoli, 1986 [1965].

Elmlund, Peter, and Mårtelius, Johan, ed. *Swedish Grace: The Forgotten Modern*. Stockholm: Axel and Margaret Ax:son Johnson Foundation, 2015.

Fabbri, Gianni. *Vienna. Città capitale del XIX secolo*. Roma: Officina Edizioni, 1986.

Forsell, Håkan. *Property, Tenancy and Urban Growth in Stockholm and Berlin, 1850–1920*. Aldershot: Ashgate, 2006.

Fuchs, Gustav A. *Der Fuchsenfeldhof*. Wien: Wiener Magistrat, 1923.

Gemeinde Wien. *Die Wohnungspolitik der Gemeinde Wien*. Wien: Gesellschafts- und Wirtschaftsmuseum, 1929.

Graham, John. *Housing in Scandinavia. Urban and rural*. Chapel Hill: University of North Carolina Press, 1940.

Hall, Thomas. *Planning and Urban Growth in the Nordic Countries*. New York: Taylor & Francis, 2011.

Hardy, Charles. *The Housing Program of the City of Vienna*. Washington, D.C.: The Brookings Institution, 1934.

Hautmann, Hans, and Hautmann, Rudolf. *Die Gemeindebauten des Roten Wien 1919–1934*. Wien: Schönbrunn, 1980.

Hegemann, Werner. *City Planning Housing*. Vol. III, New York: Architectural Book Publishing Company, 1938.

Honey, Karl. *Die Wohnungspolitik der Gemeinde Wien*. Wien: Deutsch-Österr. Städtebund, 1926.

---

38   See Zygmunt Bauman, *Community. Seeking Safety in an Insecure World* (Cambridge: Polity Press, 2001).

Kähler, Gert. *Wohnung und Stadt. Hamburg, Frankfurt, Wien. Modelle sozialen Wohnens in den zwanziger Jahren*. Braunschweig: Vieweg, 1985.

Lindhagen, Anna. *Koloniträdgårdar och planterade gårdar*. Stockholm: Norstedt & Söner, 1916.

Linn, Björn. *Storgårdskvarteret. Ett bebyggelsemönsters bakgrund och karaktär*. Stockholm: Statens institut för byggnadsforskning, 1974.

Lundevall, Owe. *HSB och bostadspolitiken – 1920-talet*. Stockholm: HSB:s riksförb., 1992.

Öhngren, Bo, 'The urbanisation in Sweden 1840–1920'. In *Patterns of European Urbanisation Since 1500*, edited by H. Schmal, 181–228, London: Redwood burn, 1981.

Paulsson, Thomas. *Den glömda staden. Svensk stadsplanering under 1900-talets början med särskild hänsyn till Stockholm*. Stockholm: Stockholmia, 1994 [1959].

Porfyriou, Heleni. 'Scandinavian Town Planning 1900–1930 and the contribution of Camillo Sitte'. PhD diss., Bartlett School of Architecture and Planning, University College London, 1990.

Pozzetto, Marco. *Die Schule Otto Wagners*. Wien-München: Verlag Anton Schroll, 1979.

Riboldazzi, Renzo. *Un'altra modernità l'Ifhtp e la cultura urbanistica tra le due guerre, 1923–1939*. Roma: Gangemi, 2009.

Secchi, Bernardo. *La città dei ricchi e la città dei poveri*. Roma-Bari: Laterza, 2013.

Silk, Leonard. *Sweden Plans for Better Housing*. Durham, N.C.: Duke University Press, 1948.

Sonne, Wolfgang. 'Dwelling in the metropolis: Reformed urban blocks 1890–1940 as a model for the sustainable compact city'. *Progress in Planning* 72 (2009): 53–149.

Stadt Wien-Wiener Wohnen. *Gemeinde baut. Wiener Wohnbau 1920–2020*. Wien: Holzhausen, 2016.

Strömberg, Thord. 'Sweden'. In *Housing strategies in Europe 1880–1930*, edited by Colin G Pooley, 11–39. London: Leicester University Press, 1992.

Tafuri, Manfredo, ed. *Vienna Rossa. La politica residenziale nella Vienna socialista 1919–1933*. Milano: Electa, 1980.

Unwin, Raymond. *Town Planning in Practice,* London: Adelphi Terrace, 1909.

USK – Stockholms stad. *Bostäder i Stockholm 1893–1985*. Stockholm: USK, 1989

Wagner, Otto. 'The development of a great city'. *Architectural Record* 31 (1912): 485–500.

Wenzl-Bachmayer, Monika, ed. *Die Wagner Schule Rotes Wien. Architektur als soziale Utopie*. Wien: Wagner-Werk Museum Postsparkasse, 2010.

CHAPTER TWO

TOBIAS VOKUHL AND DR MARK AUSTIN

Oxford Brookes University, United Kingdom

ROOM TO SWING A KID? AN EXPLORATORY STUDY INTO END-USER ENGAGEMENT WITH 'SPATIALLY CONSTRAINED' UK FAMILY HOMES

INTRODUCTION

CONTEXT

Despite the continued fall in UK residential construction (Figure 1) there is now a renewed emphasis on large-scale sub-urbanism, last witnessed during the post-war housing boom, which invites reflection on the nature of the domestic built environment currently being produced. In our view, the key question is this: does the currently mass-constructed housing stock actually facilitate the desired sustainable communities?

Figure 1. UK house building, permanent dwellings completed financial years 1970–71 to 2013–14, Source: ONS 2014, DCLG live table 209[1]

---

1   Office for National Statistics (2014). *Live tables on house building: new build dwellings. Table 209*

Sustainability in the built environment is commonly defined by three aspects: ecological, economical and social.[2] Whilst economic and ecological aspects of housing procurement and construction in the UK are well understood and quantified, the authors feel that significant research gaps remain in relation to social sustainability. We are, for example, producing the smallest new homes in Europe on small plots.[3] Space within homes is a factor that has significant impacts on the inhabitants' lives, shaping the cultural and social practices of today's and tomorrow's generations.

Research presented within this chapter complements recent academic work on space within homes[4,5,6] and sheds light on the way families engage with space-constrained UK family homes. Fieldwork includes the narrative interviewing of ten home-owning couples with young children in Oxford, arguably the most "unaffordable" city in the UK.[7] Through these interviews 'spatial concerns' do emerge within the sample group, as cultural and social practices such as the pursuit of pastimes and entertaining suffer. Individuals express frustrations with space limitations, but also demonstrate individual agency, creativity and pragmatism, and offer a different and arguably more sustainable vision of a flexible family home, a vision that allows for a staged spatial expansion of the building envelope, as needs arise and finances allow.

MASS PRODUCED HOUSING AND THE HOUSEBUILDING INDUSTRY

Current industry-led mass housing developments are far from being universally praised, with plot sizes having been shrunk to allow higher-density developments and tight internal layouts.[8] Value-engineered methods of construction have led to attic spaces dissected by braces, rendering future conversion of attic spaces impossible. These 'space and flexibility' limitations of common new homes are well recognised.[9] With little choice for the consumer, the Commission for Architecture and the Built Environment (CABE), in 2005, drew attention to discrepancies between desired

---

2   Sourani, Amr; and Sohail, Muhammad. 'Enabling sustainable construction in UK public procurement'. *Proceedings of the ICE – Management, Procurement and Law*, 166(6) (2013): 297–312.

3   Evans, Alan W.; and Hartwich, Oliver M. *Unaffordable Housing: Fables and Myths*. London: Policy Exchange, 2005.

4   CABE. 'Summary'. *Space in New Homes: What Residents Think*. London: CABE, 2009.

5   RIBA 2013, *Housing Standards and Satisfaction: What the Public Wants, Ipsos Mori and RIBA survey results*.

6   Carmona, M.; Gallent, N.; and Sarkar, R. *Space Standards: The Benefits*. CABE, 2010.

7   Lloyds. *Lloyds Bank Affordable Cities Review*. 2014.

8   Forde, N. (2009) *Space for Growth? The Modern Domestic Garden: Smaller Gardens, Fewer Benefits: Some Implications of Recent Planning Policies*. Thesis (MSc) Oxford Brookes University.

9   Morgan, M.; and Cruikshank, H. 'Quantifying the extent of space shortages: English dwellings'. *Building Research & Information*, 42(6) (2014): 710–24.

housing type and industry provision.[10] Other studies highlight concerns about quality of build, small bedrooms, storage and lack of light.[11,12,13] Considering the political and economic power held by commercial stakeholders and legislative bodies, Bone and O'Reilly summarise the dangers of the market-driven housing policy and warn of potential sociological consequences of homes unfit for purpose.[14]

MASS PRODUCED HOUSING AND SPACE

Within the last ten years an increasing amount of research has been published on the perceived lack of internal space within new homes. Evans and Hartwich, in a seminal piece of work on the subject, named newly built British homes the smallest in Europe (Figure 2),[15] whilst others employ terms such as "Rabbit hutches on postage stamps" to critique not only house, but also plot sizes, associated with new housing developments.[16] The 2011 RIBA report, *The Case for Space*, provided quantitative data on 1,159 one-bedroom flats and 3,418 three-bedroom homes, and found a significant lack of space in either category compared to space standards recently adopted locally by the Greater London Authority (GLA).[17]

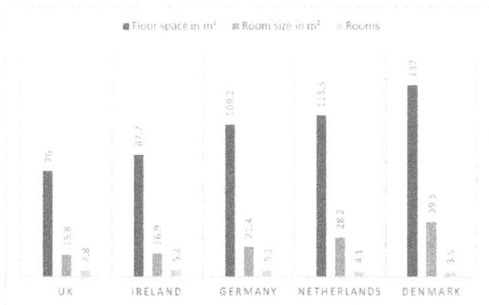

Figure 2. Average new dwelling size, room size and number of rooms in different European countries, Source: Table based on data from Evans and Hartwich (2005, p.8)[18]

---

10   Commission for Architecture and the Built Environment. *What Home Buyers Want: Attitudes and Decision Making among Consumers*. CABE, 2005.

11   CABE. 'Summary'. *Space in New Homes: What Residents Think*. London: CABE, 2009.

12   CABE. *Improving the Quality of New Housing, Technical Background Paper*. London: CABE, 2010.

13   RIBA 2013, *Housing Standards and Satisfaction: What the Public Wants, Ipsos Mori and RIBA survey results*.

14   Bone, J.; and O'Reilly, K. 'No place called home: the causes and social consequences of the UK housing "bubble"'. *British Journal of Sociology*, 61 (2010): 231–55.

15   Evans and Hartwich, 2005, op. cit.

16   Alan Evans. *Rabbit Hutches on Postage Stamps: Economics, Planning and Development in the 1990s*. Virginia: Granta Editions, 1990: 1.

17   Roberts Hughes, R. *The Case for Space: The Size of England's New Homes*. RIBA, 2011.

18   Evans and Hartwich, 2005, op. cit.

MASS-PRODUCED HOUSING AND SPACE STANDARDS

The growing amount of empirical evidence submitted by prominent institutions such as CABE, RIBA and the RICS recently led to consideration of a Nationally Described Space Standards (NDSS) for potential incorporation into UK Building Regulations (Figure 3). Internal space standards, employed nationally within the inter-war period in the shape of the Tudor Walters standards, and between 1969 and 1980 in the form of the Parker Morris standards for publicly funded housing, provided a precedent and the NDSS was consulted on during 2014–15, receiving positive reviews. However, unlike aspects of the Code for Sustainable Homes, the NDSS was not incorporated into the Building Regulation revision of 2015.

number of bedrooms	number of bedspaces	1 storey dwellings	2 storey dwellings	3 storey dwellings	built-in storage
studio	1p	39 (37)*			1.0
1b	2p	50	58		1.5
2b	3p	61	70		
	4p	70	79		2.0
3b	4p	74	84	90	
	5p	86	93	99	2.5
	6p	95	102	108	
4b	5p	90	97	103	
	6p	99	106	112	
	7p	108	115	121	3.0
	8p	117	124	130	
5b	6p	103	110	116	
	7p	112	119	125	3.5
	8p	121	128	134	
6b	7p	116	123	129	
	8p	125	132	138	4.0

Figure 3. Nationally Described Space Standard (Consultation Stage in September 2014) showing minimum gross internal floor area and storage (m²), Source: DCLG (2014, p.4)[19]

Given the above, Morgan and Cruikshank, in looking at the quantity of under-sized homes in England, recently highlighted the scale of the issue, finding that a significant percentage of the 16,000-strong housing sample failed the benchmark adopted by the Greater London Authority.[20]

MASS PRODUCED HOUSING AND THE FAMILY END-USER

Twenty-eight per cent of households consist of families with dependent children.[21] Political interest in understanding families remains high, as changes in family forms

---

19   Department for Communities and Local Government. *Nationally Described Space Standard – Technical Requirements, Consultation Draft, September 2014*. 2014.

20   Morgan, M.; and Cruikshank, H. 'Quantifying the extent of space shortages: English dwellings'. *Building Research & Information*, 42(6) (2014): 710–24.

21   Office for National Statistics. *Measuring National Well-being: Households and Families 2012*. ONS: 2012.

and functions are of significance to policy makers and government agencies.[22] The house-building sector also recognises the demographic and the 'family home' label is commonly applied to three- to five-bedroom homes.[23] The family user's interaction with the 'product' or a succession of 'products' will shape the social lives of the inhabitants. This raises questions about the extent to which small homes remain fit for purpose as occupant numbers change. Cole and Lorch elaborate on the consumer position:

> Whatever the prevailing norms, most building users have to accept what they find as 'givens'. This is why their behaviour, with the occasional exception is 'coping' or 'satisficing'. They make the best they can out of things because they are rarely able to create conditions which optimally suit them.[24]

Figure 4 shows occupier reasons for dissatisfaction with their home from a 2013 Ipsos MORI poll for RIBA of over seven-hundred participants. Lack of space is the second-highest-rated factor.[25]

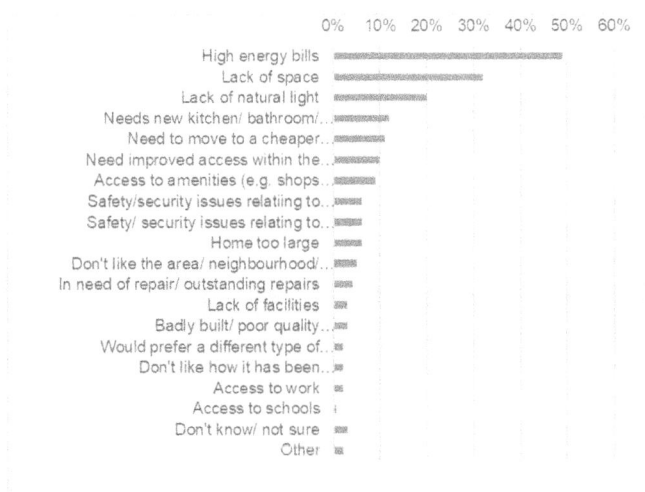

Figure 4. Occupier reasons for dissatisfaction with their home in a 2013 Ipsos MORI poll of 702 occupants, Source: Ipsos MORI for RIBA (2013)

Notably, the occupier is the only stakeholder with direct and prolonged interrelationship with their home. This was explored by different professional bodies, such as RIBA,

---

22 Giddens, A. *Anthony Giddens Sociology. Sixth edition*. Cambridge: Polity Press, 2009.

23 Bovis Homes. *Cranbrook Family Home Gets Set for the Family!* 2015.

24 Cole, Raymond J. (ed.); and Lorch, Richard. *Buildings, Culture and Environment: Informing Local and Global Practices*. Oxford: Wiley-Blackwell, 2003.

25 RIBA 2013, *Housing Standards and Satisfaction: What the Public Wants*, Ipsos Mori and RIBA survey results.

CABE, Design for Homes, Good Homes Alliance and the Joseph Rowntree Foundation. In highlighting financial pressures on home ownership, the latter recently demonstrated that filtering up into a larger property was becoming unaffordable for many.[26] Some also identify recent stamp-duty increases as an additional obstacle to upsizing and downsizing.[27]

RESEARCH METHODS

TRANS-DISCIPLINARY THINKING

Undertaking a qualitative exploration of issues relating to space within homes, a combination of research methods was employed in this study through an iterative process of data capture, based on Max-Neef's promotion of not only interdisciplinary, but trans-disciplinary thinking.[28] Home is thus recognised as a place of cultural, financial and sociological significance. Such inter-relationship is expressed profoundly by Oliver,[29] when representing Rapoport's significant contribution to vernacular architecture studies: "an understanding of behavioural patterns is 'essential to the understanding of built form' and that 'forms, once built, affect behaviour and the way of life'".[30]

NARRATIVE INTERVIEWING AND ANALYSIS

Through snowballing, and the extensive use of personal and social networks, a sample group of ten local home-owning couples with young children was established. Interviews were conducted in the participants' homes and audio recorded.[31,32] The expectation was of co-created data[33] and the interviews themselves lasted from twenty-six minutes to forty-nine minutes; overall, six hours of audio recorded data was generated. Fieldwork notes and reflections were used to ensure reflexivity and to document decisions made along the way. A synopsis was carried out for all interview material and one verbatim transcript coded for analysis. Emerging themes and data derived from an accompanying questionnaire, designed to establish subject descriptors

---

26 Wilcox, Steve. *The Geography of Affordable and Unaffordable Housing and the Ability of Younger Working Households to Become Home Owners.* York: J.R.F., 2005.

27 Cantrell, Mark. 'Stamp duty cost puts home owning pensioners off downsizing, claims survey'. *Housing,* 2016.

28 Max-Neef, Manfred A. 'Foundations of Transdisciplinarity'. *Ecological Economics,* 52 (2005): 5–16.

29 Oliver, Paul. *Built to Meet Needs, Cultural Issues in Vernacular Architecture.* Oxford: Elsevier, 2006: 50.

30 Rapoport, Amos. *House Form and Culture.* London: Prentice Hall, 1969.

31 Gillham, Bill. *Research Interviewing: The Range of Techniques.* Maidenhead: OUP, 2005.

32 Silverman, David. *Interpreting Qualitative Data.* Fourth edition. London: Sage, 2011: 153.

33 Gubrium, Jaber F.; and Holstein, James A. *Postmodern Interviewing.* London: Sage, 2003: 128.

and some basic quantitative data on the sample homes and owner perception, were evaluated within an Excel spreadsheet. In integrating quantitative questionnaire derived data and the qualitative interview data with relevant theory, cross-disciplinary theorising and hypothesising became possible.

FINDINGS

TRADE-OFF

One of the first emerging insights was the recognition of a trade-off scenario affecting end-users. Eric, father of one, summarises this neatly:

> Everywhere in Oxford is going to be a trade-off, unless you are incredibly rich.

(Eric, 2014)

In line with RIBA's findings,[34] internal space is part of a complex trade-off between different fit for purpose factors, and at times is knowingly sacrificed for the achievement of other culturally or socially beneficial factors. These include characterful building design, garden, school catchment area, location of friends and family, or work, with a unique trade-off scenario emerging for every couple (Figure 5).

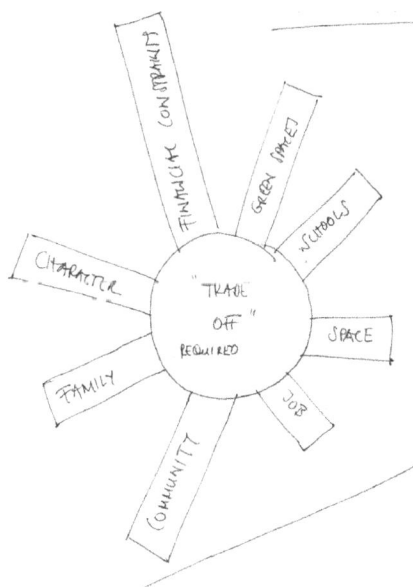

Figure 5. Requirement for 'trade-off'. Source: Fieldwork notes DR1, 2014

---

34   RIBA 2013, *Housing Standards and Satisfaction: What the Public Wants, Ipsos Mori and RIBA survey results.*

In line with RIBA's 2013 emphasis on strong occupant desire for more space,[35] this study highlights the tension experienced in rationalising space within a trade-off context.

EXPERIENCING SPACE

In rationalising space and lifestyle, Euan and Natasha comment on some of the day-to-day impacts:

> We can fit the buggy in, but it is difficult to open the door when it's in the hallway.

> (Euan, 2014)

> When we have got people coming 'round we put it [the buggy] in the garage or in the car, to get it out of the way.

> (Natasha, 2014)

Tracy, a young mum of two, reflects on the inability to provide a proper guest bed to overnight visitors, asking guests to utilise mattresses on the floor:

> We just tend to make things work. It is where you live and it is not necessarily about if you have the ideal space to do something… friends stay because they want to spend time with you, not because they are coming to a luxurious hotel.

> (Tracy, 2014)

Natasha admits to being self-conscious about hosting within the space of her inter-war semi:

> I do feel a bit embarrassed sometimes when lots of people are here… I feel I have to say to people "It'll be a bit of a squish"… but nobody minds… but I feel I just need to warn them.

> (Natasha, 2014).

Natasha is obviously conscious that she cannot provide the standard of hospitality that her parents (in a large Edwardian house) may have been able to give. Tensions with culturally coded room use become apparent, as individuals express frustrations with space limitations, whilst trying to demonstrate individual agency, creativity and pragmatism.

QUANTIFYING SPATIAL CAPITAL

Interestingly, a numerical assessment of worth linked to table capacity became evident:

> I would love to have a proper dining room table [rather than a multi-purpose table].

> (Eve, 2014)

---

35   RIBA 2013, *Housing Standards and Satisfaction: What the Public Wants*, *Ipsos Mori and RIBA survey results*.

When we have our parents to visit as well... We can have seven around the table.

(Peter, 2014)

In here we had a lovely old table with six chairs, and we had to downsize [the table] to a four-chair... [space-saving table].

(Ben, 2014)

Peter, Ben and Natasha are putting a numerical value against their ability to host. In a more extreme scenario, Tracy and Darren reflect on their own situation:

Tracy: We are more likely to have one or two friends over.

Darren: We're never going to entertain large numbers.

Tracy: His brother has a larger house and he tends to host the larger social occasions... his dining-room table can seat sort of 16 people.

Darren: It is our dream that when we have this extension built we can have this family with their six kids round for a meal... Four or five, four, I think that is the maximum we can have for dinner.

Here, table seating capacity appears to affect social positioning. The dining room table size (e.g. "seats six") is used to place a numerical value on the home owners' hosting capability. Such hosting capability index might then categorise an individual as host or hostee, a measure of objectified capital, quantified through the seating capacity of the table.

FICTIVE KIN AND THE INTER-USE OF SPACE

As individuals are socially placed within the wider family and friendship networks, the home's internal space is placed within the immediate neighbourhood and spatial proximity to support systems are sought, whether to kin or fictive kin.

A significant percentage of the research participants do not have close family nearby. This societal shift towards geographical separation from siblings and parents is widely recognised within the literature,[36,37] and the emergence of 'fictive kin' and highly permeable family boundaries are recognised as hallmarks of the present developments in evolving family definition. McKie and Callan refer to a "spatial embeddedness" of relationships within physical communities and neighbourhoods.[38] Darren remembers:

One Christmas your mum came over and she stayed at a friend's house, they were away for Christmas and because it is a good community the friends said "here are the keys... just watch out for the dodgy fridge door".

(Darren, 2014)

---

36   Giddens, Anthony. *Anthony Giddens Sociology.* Sixth edition. Cambridge: Polity, 2009.
37   Hollows, Joanne. *Domestic Cultures.* Maidenhead: Open University Press, 2008.
38   McKie, Linda; and Callan, Samantha. *Understanding Families: A Global Introduction.* London: Sage, 2012.

This inter-use of privately owned spaces reduces pressure on individuals to provide culturally appropriate guest accommodation within their own property. Again, available space within the home has the potential to endow individuals with spatial capital.

FUTUREPROOFING SPACE

Traditionally there is an expectation of filtering up to better housing. Naomi, Claire and Irene, however, express concerns:

> Moving is expensive, it is emotionally draining, it is one of the top five stressful events in life, so we didn't kind of want to do it too many times.

(Naomi, 2014)

> We worked out that extending, at this point, would save us about £40,000 on moving.

(Claire, 2014)

> But it also dawned on me that replanting ourselves would mean starting from scratch with regards to socialising and school.

(Irene, 2014)

In fact, eight out of the ten couples reference extending as an alternative to relocating. Sue reflects on her childhood home:

> Well my dad extended twice on our family home, 'cause it was just a little three-bed semi and there was three of us.

(Sue, 2014)

Natasha comments on the timing of a likely extension:

> We expect we can probably do it [extending] when the kids are at school. Then we can release the money from the childcare, release that money... then there would be the cash.

(Natasha, 2014)

Peter, from the outset, specifically looked for an older property:

> These houses here were built specifically smaller than their plot of land. To give the sense of space. So everybody has extended. And this was one, which had the right plot of land to be extended.

(Peter, 2014)

Overall, a significant amount of consideration was given to the thought of acquiring a house with capacity to extend. Participants actively observe neighbourhoods for signs of extension potential when house hunting. Expected rewards of the extension or loft conversion, when completed, are described as the realisation of the kitchen-diner space, enabling improved flexibility, communality and hosting, the creation of a separate downstairs adult space and the ability to better cater for overnight guests.

LIMITATIONS, PRACTICAL IMPLICATIONS AND FUTURE RESEARCH

The study drew on a limited number of participants to allow for depth and detail within the data. Specifically, the main sample group consisted of ten, mostly ethnically 'white', almost exclusively middle-class, home-owning couples, with an above-national-average household income, living in the most unaffordable city in the UK. However, the following relevant questions have been raised.

Firstly, do we fully understand the level of overlap between current industry interpretation and end-user perception of a 'fit for purpose' family home? Presuming that filtering up is increasingly unaffordable and strong locational ties are being established at the early family life stage, it could be argued that a fit for purpose family home should be built with a modest spatial offering at purchase, but positioned on a reasonably sized plot and designed with growth in mind, which would be reflected within a more 'conversion friendly' roof structure and upper-storey layout, as well as a designed-to-extend concept in building envelope design. This would allow the building user to extend when occupant density (e.g. through childbirth) reaches a critical level and finances allow, offering a more sustainable alternative to relocating and upsizing.

Secondly, the desire for hosting and the hosting capability limit imposed on the user by the property deserve further exploration. Considering the social implications of either being considered a host or hostee, the built form has the power to significantly shape the social positioning of the occupant in this respect.

Thirdly, further research might help to establish how, within the garden cities of tomorrow, the generation of spatial capital can be facilitated within reasonably dense residential areas. Given a suspected likelihood of continued internal spatial constraints, should local provision be made for the 'outsourcing' of social events, visitors and storage? Exploration also beckons of the extent to which the inter-use of privately owned spaces within spatially constrained neighbourhoods is practised and whether, as part of locally achievable social and cultural capitals, it has a place within the current models of social sustainability.

CONCLUSION

The interconnected nature of house and occupant cannot be denied. Houses shape cultural and social practices and we re-shape our houses as cultural practices change. This could not be exemplified more clearly than by the thousands of altered or extended inter-war semi-detached properties still functioning as family homes in the UK today. To be equally sustainable, modern family homes need to be fit for purpose for today's occupiers. This requires government and industry to take note of the impact of spatial constraints on the primary stakeholder. Emerging from this Oxford-based study is an insight from the family building user, which challenges the current industry model of providing small inflexible houses with dense internal layouts, on small plots. Research participants offer a different and arguably more sustainable vision of a family home, which allows for staged spatial expansion, taking into account financial position, personal taste and suitable timing, and fosters the longer-term integration of individuals within a 'locale', allowing the development of vibrant local communities. Should the above findings be shown to be more widely representative of this section of society, the question arises of who would be the driving force for flexible family housing that grows with the occupants – housing with room to swing a kid.

BIBLIOGRAPHY

Ball, Michael. *Housing Supply and Planning Controls: The Impact of Planning Control Processing Times on Housing Housing Supply in England*. National Housing and Planning Advise Unit. Fareham: NHPAU.

Bourdieu, Pierre. 'The forms of Capital'. In: J. Richardson, ed., *Handbook of Theory and Research for the Sociology of Education*, 241–58. New York: Greenwood, 1986.

____. 'On the family as a realised category'. *Theory, Culture and Society*, 13(3) (1996): 19–26

____. *The Social Structures of the Economy*. Cambridge: Polity, 2005.

Bryman, Alan. *Social Research Methods*. Second edition. Oxford: OUP, 2002.

Byrne, D. *Applying Social Science: The Role of Social Research in Politics, Policy and Practice*. Bristol: Policy Press, 2011.

CABE. 'Summary'. *Space in New Homes: What Residents Think*. London: CABE, 2009.

Charmaz, Kathy. *Constructing Grounded Theory*. Second edition. London: Sage, 2014.

Clements-Croome, Derek. *Intelligent Buildings*. Second edition. London: ICE, 2013.

Cooper, I. 'Transgressing discipline boundaries: is BEQUEST an example of "the new production of knowledge"?' *Building Research & Information*, 30(2) (2002): 116–29. xxvii.

Creswell, John W. *Research Design: Qualitative, Quantitative, and Mixed Method Approaches*. Third edition. London: Sage, 2008.

Dent, Peter; Patrick, Michael; and Ye, Xu. *Real Estate: Property Markets and Sustainable Behaviour*. Abingdon: Routledge, 2012.

Department for Communities and Local Government. *Attitudes to housing, Findings from the Ipsos MORI Public Affairs Monitor Omnibus Survey (England)*. London: Crown, 2009.

____. *Policy paper: Creating the conditions for a more integrated society*. London: Crown, 2012.

____. *Housing Standards Review, Consultation*, 2013.

____. *Nationally Described Space Standard – Technical Requirements, Consultation Draft September 2014*. 2014.

Evans, Alan. *Rabbit Hutches on Postage Stamps: Economics, Planning and Development in the 1990s*, Virginia: Granta Editions, 1990.

Evans, Alan W.; and Hartwich, Oliver M. *Unaffordable Housing: Fables and Myths*. London: Policy Exchange, 2005.

Fulcher, James. *Sociology*. Third edition. Oxford: Oxford University Press, 2007.

Garcia-Mira, Ricardo; Uzzell, David L.; Real, J. Eugenio; and Romay, Jose, eds. *Housing Space and Quality of Life*. Aldershot: Ashgate, 2005.

Gee, James. *An Introduction to Discourse Analysis Theory and Method*. London: Routledge, 1999.

Giddens, Anthony. *The Construction of Society*. California: UCP, 1984.

Glaser, Barney G.; and Strauss, Anselm L. *The Discovery of Grounded Theory: Strategies for Qualitative Research*. New York: Transaction Publishers, 1967.

Goodhart, Pippa; and Sharratt, Nick. *You Choose*. London: Random House, 2004.

Goodier, Chris; and Pan, Wei. *The Future of UK Housebuilding. RICS Research Report*. London: RICS, 2010.

Greater London Authority. *Housing for a Compact City*. London: GLA, 2003.

____. *Housing Space Standards: A Report by HATC Limited for the Greater London Authority*. London: GLA, 2006.

Groak, Steven. *The Idea of Building*. London: Spon, 2002.

Gubrium, Jaber F.; and Holstein, James A. *Postmodern Interviewing*. London: Sage, 2003.

Handel, Gerald, and Whitchurch, Gail. *The Psychosocial Interior of the Family*. Fourth edition. Aldine Transaction, 1994.

HM Government. *The Building Regulations 2010, Conservation of Fuel and Power in New Dwellings, Approved Document L1a*. 2010.

Hofstede, Geert. *Culture's Consequences in Work Related Values*. Beverly Hills: Sage, 1984.

Jackson, Alecia Y.; and Mazzei, Lisa. R *Thinking with Theory in Qualitative Research, Viewing Data Cross Multiple Disciplines*. Abingdon: Routledge, 2012.

Jonker, Jan; and Pennink, Bartjan. *The Essence of Research Methodology: A Concise Guide for Master and PhD Students in Management Science*. Berlin Heidelberg: Springer, 2010.

Kohler-Rissman, Catherine. *Narrative Methods for the Human Sciences*. London: Sage, 2008.

Marsh, Ian; Campbell, Rosie; and Keating, Mike. *Classic and Contemporary Readings in Sociology*. Abingdon: Routledge, 1998.

Miller, Tina. *Making Sense of Motherhood: A Narrative Approach*. Cambridge: Cambridge University Press, 2005.

____. *Making Sense of Fatherhood: Gender, Caring and Work*. Cambridge: Cambridge University Press, 2011.

Miller, Tina; Jessop, Julie; Birch, Maxine; and Mauthner, Melanie eds. *Ethics in Qualitative Research*. London: Sage, 2012.

Ministry of Housing and Local Government. *Homes for Today and Tomorrow (Report of the Parker Morris Committee)*. HMSO: London, 1961.

Monroe, Moira; and Madigan, Ruth. 'Negotiating Space in the Family Home'. In: Cieraad, ed. *At Home: An Anthropology of Domestic Space*. New York: Syracuse, 1999.

Muthesius, Stefan. *The English Terraced House*. New Haven; London: Yale University Press, 1982, xxxi.

Naoum, Shamil. *Dissertation Research and Writing for Construction Students*. Oxford: Butterworth-Heinemann, 1998.

National Housing and Planning Advice Unit. *Housing Requirement and the impact of recent economic and demographic change*. Fareham: NHPAU, 2009.

Office for National Statistics. *Home Ownership and Renting in England and Wales – Detailed Characteristics*, 2013.

____. *Guide to Social Capital*. 2014.

Oxford Brookes University. *Ethical Standards for Research Involving Human Participants – Code of Practice*. 2014.

Oxford City Council. *Sites and Housing DPD Background Paper 12, Living Conditions*. 2012.

____. *Local Development Framework, Annual Monitoring Report April 2013–March 2014*. Planning Policy City Development, 2014.

Patricios, N. 'The Neighbourhood Concept: A Retrospective of Physical Design and Social Interactions'. *Journal of Architecture and Planning Research*, 19:1 (2002): 70–90.

Portes, A. 'Social Capital: Origins and Applications'. *Annual Review of Sociology*, 24 (1998): 1–24.

Rosen, Andrew. *The Transformation of British life 1950–2000: A Social History*. Manchester: Manchester University Press, 2005.

Scott, Peter. *The Making of the Modern British Home*. Oxford: OUP, 2013.

Silva. 'Gender, home and family in cultural capital theory'. *British Journal of Sociology*, 56(1) (2005): 83–103.

Silverman, D. *Interpreting Qualitative Data*. Fourth edition. London: Sage, 2011.

Sourani, Amr; and Sohail, Muhammad. 'Enabling sustainable construction in UK public procurement'. *Proceedings of the ICE – Management, Procurement and Law*, 166(6) (2013): 297–312.

Straus, Anselm; and Corbin, Juliet M. *Basics of Qualitative research: Techniques and Procedures for Developing Grounded Theory*. Second edition. London: Sage, 1998.

Taylor, E.; and Cen, N. *Public Attitudes to Housing*. DCLG, London: HMSO, 2011.

Tourangeau, Roger; Rips, Lance; and Rasinski, Kenneth. *The Psychology of Survey Response*. Cambridge: Cambridge University Press, 2000.

Tudor Walters Committee. *The Tudor Walters Report*. London: HMSO, 1918.

UKERC. *The Rebound Effect: An Assessment of the Evidence for Economy-wide Energy Savings from Improved Energy Efficiency*. 2007.

Webster, Helena. *Bourdieu for Architects*. Abingdon: Routledge, 2011.

Werczberger, Elia. 'Home ownership and rent control in Switzerland'. *Housing Studies*, 12(3) (1997): 337–53.

CHAPTER THREE

PETRA PEROLINI, MARLEEN SITCHENKO, ANTOINETTE KISLUK,
MORENA TOFFANELLO AND GENEVIEVE PARRY

Queensland College of Art, Griffith University, Australia

SMALLER LIVING: THE NEED TO OFFER BETTER HOUSING OPTIONS IN AUSTRALIAN CITIES

INTRODUCTION

The housing situation in Australia is uniquely unsustainable.

Historically, government imperatives and the impulse of resource markets strongly influenced settlement patterns in Australia. This has contributed to challenges of rapid population growth, urban sprawl, housing shortages, urban decay, increasing social segregation and the geographical, climatic, political and economic displacement of the disadvantaged.[1]

Despite Australians' international reputation for living comfortably and well in cities that are regularly judged as the "most liveable" by a range of international surveys,[2] Australia is in the midst of a housing crisis.[3]

- Housing affordability is at its all-time low,

---

1   Perolini, Petra. 'The Role Innovative Housing Models Play in the Struggle against Social Exclusion in Cities: The Brisbane Common Ground Model'. *Social Inclusion*, 3(2) (2015): 62–70.

2   Kalnins, Antra. 'Living the Australian lifestyle'. *Macquarie Globe*, last modified 19/1/2011, 2011. http://www.international.mq.edu.au/globe/2011-02/lifestyle.

3   Australian Institute of Health and Welfare. Housing Assistance in Australia 2014, edited by Australian Institute of Health and Welfare. 2014.

- Mortgage debt is amongst the highest in the world and

- Around 60 per cent of lower-income rental households are currently experiencing rental stress.

But the roots of this housing-affordability crisis lie in the changing demographic make-up of the urban population. Projections of new households and dwellings for Sydney and Melbourne from 2012 to 2022 indicate that policy makers have not grasped the scale of housing requirements for a rapidly changing demographic. For example, the nuclear family is currently challenged as 'a typical Australian home' by sole parent families, step and blended families, extended families, same-sex families, childless households and single-dwellers; and yet, detached housing still accounts for over 70 per cent of new housing.[4] We have a changing demographic but we still promote, market and build houses for the nuclear family model. Planning is out of step with the demographics.

As Australian cities struggle to meet the housing demands of a changing and increasing population, they must also get ready to accommodate significant climatic changes while maintaining their liveability and functioning as an urban system. Climate change will not only challenge the built infrastructure of cities, it will impact people's lives and livelihoods in unprecedented ways. At present, there is no coherent, adequate response to the impacts of a changing climate. Individual households, government departments, public services and industry are currently responding in an inefficient and ineffectual ad hoc manner to threats caused by extreme weather events, rain, winds, heat, fire and flooding.[5] Australian cities need to become climate defensive.

Thus, there are two threats to the liveability of Australian cities: housing affordability (caused by government policies encouraging speculative investment in housing as a commodity) and the threat of climate effects. Policy needs to be brought into alignment with both threats.

Australia needs to stop building housing at the fringes of larger cities, which is in stark contrast to the demand for single households and families wanting to engage and connect with one another, build sustainable communities and live 'smaller'. Australia needs a more versatile housing stock. This new housing model must fundamentally respond to the changes that a new climate will impose on cities in coming years. Heat islanding, fire, extreme storms, increase drought, increased intensity of rain events and rising sea levels will have an unprecedented impact on urban centres. We need to build climate defensive cities. The appropriate response needs to be preventative, adaptive, social, economic, technical and cultural.[6]

A studio project undertaken by undergraduate design students at Griffith University in

---

4   Birrell, Bob; and McCloskey, David. *The Housing Affordability Crisis in Sydney and Melbourne Report One: the Demographic Foundations.* Australian Policy Online, 2015.

5   Fry, T.; Perolini, P.; Kinnunen, N.; and Odom, W. *Metrofitting.* Griffith University, 2009.

6   Ibid.

2015 investigated a different housing model for Australian cities. The brief for this model was to fill the gap between the current development model designed to gain maximum yield for the investor and the future model where liveability, sustainability, affordability and community living are the core values. The project brief asked students to develop a concept that could catalyse an industry change. By modifying a typical 80m² two-bedroom apartment and turning it into a two-bedroom apartment, students had to explore housing models that encourage the sharing of spaces and infrastructure. The project explored rethinking the notion of dwelling in response to climate change and housing affordability.

THE HOUSING SITUATION

It is well known that the predominant form of residential dwelling in Australia has historically been detached housing. While the total detached housing stock still accounts for over 70 per cent of new housing, multi-unit dwellings (semi-detached, townhouse, unit) are playing an increasingly significant part in the new-home-building market. An incremental increase in this type of residential dwelling has led to a total market share of about 25 per cent in 2014.[7]

This shift away from the Australian Dream of a quarter-acre block for each family (originally intended to allow them to be self-sufficient in food)[8] to higher-density living is seen to be a significant part of the answer to improving housing affordability by increasing supply. It is clear, however, that it does not meet the requirements of a changing demographic or the challenges of climate change. A detailed study of the demographics shows that not only is there a drift away from the nuclear family but also the younger demographic is entering the housing market later by choosing to stay at home longer or enter the share-rental market. In addition, an increase in life expectancy and a shortage of aged care facilities encourages baby boomers to stay independent of aged care for longer. This demographic now prefers to downsize to multi-unit housing, which is low maintenance and still allows for independence.[9]

Current, developer-driven planning laws do not meet the demands and expectations of either of these demographic realities. Current planning laws favour new construction without giving appropriate consideration for the maintenance of existing building stock or for the construction of affordable housing stock. Consequently, the majority of new housing is pushed out to city fringes, where land is cheap and facilities absent: the majority of housing is based on an outdated view of what people need.

Although there is evidence that buyers are swapping the 'traditional Aussie Dream'

7   Department of Planning. *Multi Unit Housing Code*. Edited by Department of Planning. Department of Planning, 2009.

8   Kellett, Jon. 'The Australian quarter acre block: The death of a dream?' *Town Planning Review*, 2011, 263–84. doi: 10.2307/27975999.

9   Dale, Harley; and Murray, Geordan. 'The Changing Composition of Australia's New Housing Mix'. In: *Composition of Australia's Housing*. HIA Economics, 2015.

for high density apartments, the housing market is by no means reflective of today's housing needs. As a neoliberal nation, Australia has a reliance on the housing market to accommodate the population, and limited direct intervention unless forced by politics. This has produced chain effect significant policy failures.[10]

The effects of those policy failures include:

- Reduction in social housing supply

- Escalating waiting lists

- Rampant affordability problems in the major Australian capital cities

- Significant under-supply of housing relative to need/demand

- Poor quality indigenous housing

- Overcrowding.

Thus, the rapid construction of inner-city apartment blocks is not doing enough to alleviate housing shortage, housing affordability and a push for more sustainable, well-built, prized and well-sized housing that builds community by encouraging shared zones and eliminating unnecessary private space such as excess car parking.

THE EFFECTS OF CLIMATE CHANGE ON OUR CITIES

The changing climate demands new features of the built environment. Climate change and the scenarios it is likely to create will have a direct impact on the built fabric of our cities, their suburbs and rural communities. Understanding and recognising the severity of these impacts will increasingly drive the change needed in designing and building structures. Ultimately, buildings will need to do more than just provide protection against climatic conditions; buildings need to become climate defensive.[11]

An important feature of future design is a reduced ecological footprint. Currently, Australia has one of the world's largest ecological footprints per capita, consuming 6.6 global hectares per person. Australian homes are among the biggest in the world. In the past, the impact of our extravagant lifestyle has gone widely unnoticed; however, now that the effects are more pronounced we are starting to respond. The value that Australian society places on materiality and land ownership over environmental and human growth contributes to climate change on many levels. This needs to change. The *Environment Design Guide* by Mark Snow and Deo Prasad provides a framework clearly outlining the "potential effects of climate change on buildings". Figure 1 presents a partial list of predicted effects of climate change on buildings. It includes temperature rise, intense rainfall and flooding, intense hailstorms, more frequent and more intense

---

10   Beer, Andrew. Lecture: 'What Future for Evidence Based Housing Policy Under Neoliberalism? Insights from Australian Experience'. Centre for Housing Urban and Regional Planning, University of Adelaide.

11   Fry, T.; Perolini, P.; Kinnunen, N.; and Odom, W. *Metrofitting*. Griffith University, 2009.

cyclones, severe bushfires and dangerous fluctuations in humidity. Additional to the list covered in Figure 1 are sea level rises, prolonged periods of drought and firestorms. What is not explicitly made clear in the *Environment Design Guide* is the effect of climate change on the urban experience beyond the buildings themselves. Individuals, communities, businesses and the environment will feel these broader effects. Many aspects of our lifestyle beyond the built environment will be radically different.

Risk	Possible Effects
Rising temperature	Impact on external surfaces; thermal performance of building
More intense rainfall	Greater intensity of runoff; issues of structural integrity; drainage; opportunities for capturing rainfall
More frequent / intense cyclones	Greater strain on building material fixtures, claddings and fasteners; greater wind loading requirements
More frequent flooding	Sea level rise leading to coastal and inland flooding; more coastal salt spray; water damage to building contents; contamination from sewage, soil and mud; undermining of foundations
More fire events	Total or partial fire damage; smoke and water damage
More hail storms	Impact damage (mostly roofs, guttering, windows) and subsequent rain/moisture penetration
Increased humidity	Mould; condensation; decreased thermal performance of building
Decreased humidity	Higher risk of fire

Figure 1. Partial list of predicted effects of climate change on buildings[12]

There is an urgent need for adaptation strategies that target social, psychological, economic and physical processes. Many local governments have started to realise the importance of an adaptation strategy in order to redirect the actions of our community

12   Snow, Mark; and Prasad, Deo. *Environment Design Guide: Climate Change Adaptation for Building Designers: An Introduction.* Environmental, Australian Institute of Architects, New South Wales: Australian Institute of Architects, 2011.

through education. Widespread knowledge and personal responsibility of the risks causes and effects will result in community resilience and flexible decision making in the future.[13]

Implantation of such strategies in the building and infrastructure phases needs to be actioned immediately. Architects, designers and builders, planners and other professionals alike will need to recognise that buildings will need to do more than just stand against climate change. They will need to become climate defensive. In *City Futures in an Age of Changing Climate*, Fry looks at how cities can adapt and respond to the unsustainable conditions they are now facing. He is calling for cities to become climate defensive. He argues that policy makers, architects, designers and engineers are just not currently grasping the implications. Fry specifies that we need to move to designing structures that can defend us from extreme heat, cyclonic winds, rain, drought, floods and fire.

Our current model of urban construction attends to the socially constructed wants and desires of consumers in a society that values the family home as an investment, sees housing as a commodity and places no value on community. The central role of capitalism, consumerism and the nuclear family has had ontological effects on our image and design of the city. We have a fundamental inability to realise that our consumption makes us the major contributors to our ecological disruption. The narrative of economic growth demands that we believe that our lifestyle is inherently geared towards the betterment of day-to-day life. Those attempting to promote an alternative model based on community-based economics, sustainable food production and local energy supplies are portrayed as unrealistic.[14]

MORE VERSATILITY IN HOUSING OPTIONS

Australians live an enviable lifestyle. Australian cities are often perceived to be among the most liveable by a range of international studies. For example, the Economist Intelligence Unit Liveability Ranking 2010 positioned four of Australia's capital cities, including Sydney, in the top ten most liveable cities in the world.[15] However, this liveability index is subjective. In Australia, the focus has been to measure the general quality of life in a very specific area. A broader look at the impact of our urban centres reveals unchecked urban sprawl, vast consumption of resources and despoliation of the environment, while the inner-core deteriorates.

We have seen this pattern continue, despite some transformation of housing structures over the last few decades: a staggering seventy-nine per cent of Australians still live

---

13   Mitchell, John. 'Climate Change Adaptation Strategy', edited by the City of Greater Geelong. The City of Greater Geelong, 2011.

14   Department of Economic and Social Affairs. *Achieving Sustainable Development and Promoting Development Cooperation*. United Nations Publications, 2008.

15   Kalnins, Antra. 'Living the Australian lifestyle'. *Macquarie Globe*, last modified 19/1/2011, 2011. http://www.international.mq.edu.au/globe/2011-02/lifestyle.

in detached dwellings, around 12 per cent live in apartments and nine per cent live in attached dwellings such as terraces and duplexes.[16] The provision of housing, with its traditional and conventional layouts, has changed little over the last 60 years.[17] This is despite evidence of extensive change to the typical Australian family model.[18] The 'nuclear family' is almost non-existent in Australian society today.[19] The inability of the existing housing market to look beyond this expired phenomenon will be a significant roadblock in the process of innovation.[20] The ageing of the population, increased single-parent families, divorce, childless couples, migrant and same-sex families are just a sample of the types of people looking for more appropriate housing in modern Australia.[21]

For an increasing number of people, living smaller is a deliberate decision made in full cognisance of the challenges we face as a society. Selfish reasons, such as the economic benefits of saving money on heating and cooling, living a more sustainable life with reduced debt and consequently lower demands on the family income, are factors considered when contemplating downsizing. But apart from these practical and financial reasons, many reduce their environmental footprint as a conscientious choice. In some cases, mitigation of the future social impacts of climate change and the resulting environmental decay are also factors. The adoption of higher-density living is a mitigation of the future increase in environmental refugees requiring housing in cities around the world.

Green Metropolis by David Owen uses the example of New York City to show how high-density cities can actually be significantly more environmentally friendly than urban sprawl.[22] This is mainly due to lower car ownership and the impact of reduced space in limiting excessive consumption.[23] The close proximity of local destinations and the lack of public car parks mean that most residents walk or catch public transport to most places.[24] Whilst urban sprawl may make residents feel greener, it in fact increases their demands on the environment.[25] The further you get from urban hubs, the greater the distance in car travel for seemingly trivial trips.[26] Should urban

---

16   Murray, Shane. 'Housing'. *Architecture Australia*, 2007. http://architectureau.com/articles/housing-3/
17   Ibid.
18   Ibid.
19   Saggers, Sherry; and Sims, Margaret. 'Diversity: Beyond the nuclear family'. *Family: Changing Families, Changing Times*, pp.66–87. 2005.
20   Murray, 2007, op. cit.
21   Ibid.
22   Owen, David. *Green Metropolis: Why Living Smaller, Living Closer, and Driving Less are the Keys to Sustainability*. New York: Riverhead Books, 2010.
23   Ibid., 13
24   Ibid., 19
25   Ibid., 20
26   Ibid., 16

sprawl continue unchecked, all the remaining green spaces idolised by the very environmentalists condemning high-density city living will be overrun with motorways and other infrastructure necessary to support and connect the population.[27]

There is another significant advantage. Not only do high-density cities protect the environment, they also encourage better communities with more vibrancy of day-to-day life.[28] The residents of cities like New York have more access to a wider selection of activities, meaning they have more human interaction and are reducing their individual energy consumption.[29]

Australians actively need to work to promote a new residential ideal.[30] The trend to larger homes and lower occupancy seems set to continue if nothing changes.[31] The continuous over-consumption of land, energy and resources will soon result in the depletion of these resources and will result in increasing numbers of homeless people who require accommodation.[32] The time required to apply adaptive practices is in direct contrast with the speed of building new housing and is thus discouraged by today's time-poor society.[33] Design professionals, the professional group best positioned to re-educate the consumers who commission these new housing projects, are often moderated in their creative options due to the preconceived notions and economic interests of their clients, the investors in property development, real-estate agencies, finance organisations, home improvement groups, product manufacturers, homebuilders and décor retailers.[34] This broad coalition of interests constantly bombards home buyers and renovators with images of the 'ideal lifestyle', further fuelling the consumption of the unsustainable.[35] As this generation is chasing the 'Great Australian Dream' they are actually building the 'Great Australian Nightmare' for the generations to come.[36]

LIVING SMALLER PROJECT

This visual segment presents a studio project by Griffith University design students that sought to uncover a narrative of tension between our aspiration to live 'big' and an urgent need to rethink how we dwell as a response to climate change. The project, titled 'Future Living', took place from July to November 2015 and created three distinct directions:

---

27 Ibid., 39
28 Ibid., 41
29 Ibid., 41
30 Smith, N. 'Design dilemma: driving a consumption obsessed society into an unsustainable future'. First international conference on engineering, designing and developing the built envorinment for sustainable wellbeing, 2011.
31 Ibid.
32 Ibid.
33 Ibid.
34 Ibid.
35 Ibid.
36 Ibid.

1. The dream space of conceptual design
2. The material reality of housing construction, functionality and building regulations
3. And a changing world in the face of climate change.

Students were required to redesign a typical 80m² two-bedroom apartment into a pair of two-bedroom apartments. They were asked to consider aspects of spatial planning, structure, view and environmental factors to produce a dwelling oriented to future requirements.

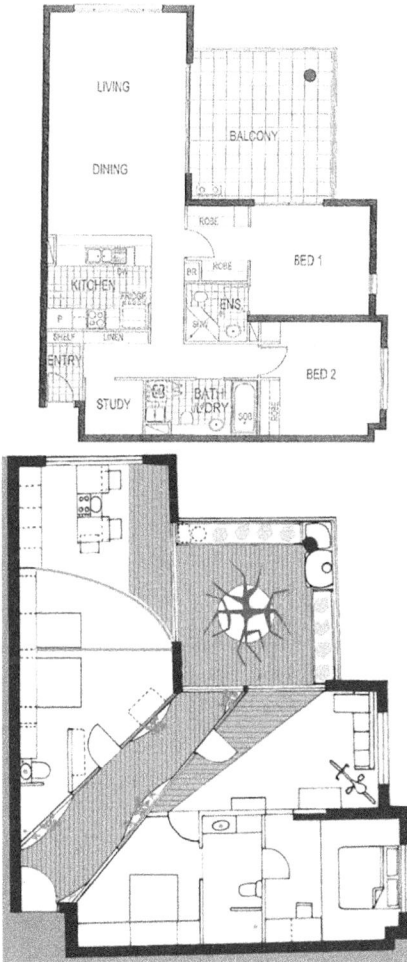

Figure 2. Left: Typical 80m² two-bedroom apartment; Right: Typical apartment redesigned into a pair of two-bedroom apartments

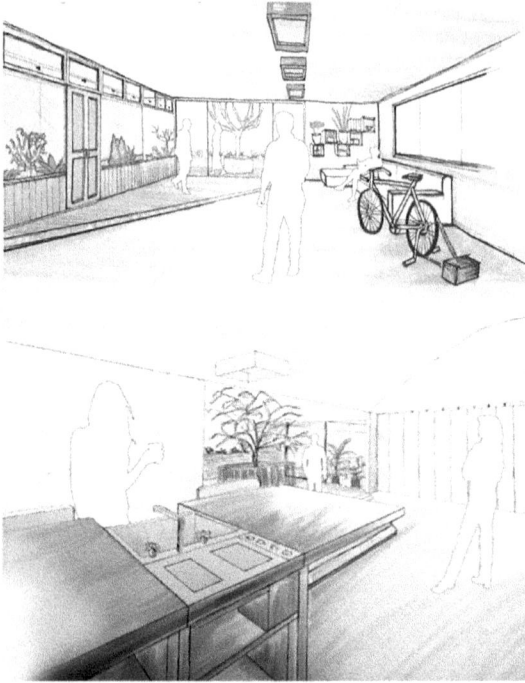

Figure 3. Above: Perspective of redesigned apartment lounge room; Below: Perspective of redesigned apartment kitchen

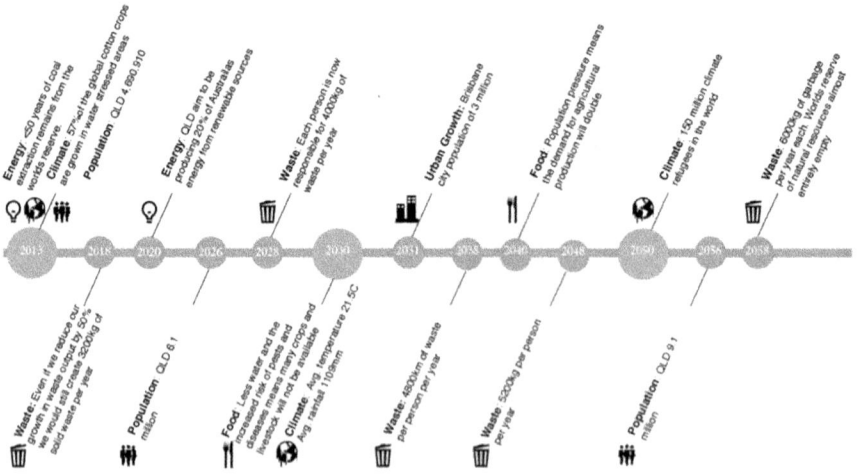

Figure 4. Timeline of future problems in Brisbane

As the world population increases and becomes concentrated in cities, the need to reduce the size of the spaces we occupy seems obvious; however, most of our existing apartments have been constructed according to a worldview developed in a time when the stresses our way of life placed on the planet were not so obvious.

Overall, the project highlighted that too many people are oblivious to the inner workings of their commodities and environments, not actually understanding the *role* and impact that those built environments and artefacts play in the context of our everyday life. These things not only influence us directly in an anthropological sense, they create global-scale ontological consequences that are drastically increasing in both size and significance.

The learning journey resulted in design outcomes that highlighted the re-conceptualisation of the idea of 'home' and the indivisible expectations that follow. The designed outcomes exhibited an aim to blur the boundaries of a typical home by designing a space designated for more than one purpose; reaffirming the idea that bigger is *not* better.

CONCLUSION

The housing crisis is a symptom of larger problems. Decades of different, but all ineffective, planning policies by Australian national and state governments have led to planned settlements, separated from the centres of activity, that become ghettos of disadvantage. In each era, planning mistakes or oversights have destroyed any possibility of the successful construction of community.

Australia has a uniquely romanticised notion of home ownership. Not only is the home ownership level one of the highest globally, at 70 per cent, housing is also seen as a tradable commodity and investment in housing a cornerstone of economic growth. This high churn of buying, selling, demolishing and rebuilding has contributed significantly to today's housing crisis and has failed to supply the right type of housing to satisfy the needs of community. People want to live in beautiful, affordable, well-built and well-sized apartments designed for real life. Many of our residential buildings are too big, unaffordable, unsustainable and placed on city fringes disconnected from centres.

Dwellings are also not designed and built to cope with a changing climate. Heat islanding, severe cyclones generating high winds and floods, fire and long periods of drought will make Australian city centres and their suburbs uncomfortable places to live. Existing buildings need to be modified and new structures need be designed differently to accommodate a changing climate and a changing demographic.

The current focus on investor specifications for maximum yield with little or no regard for the people who will live there or their impact on the environment needs challenging.

The design students of today will design the homes of tomorrow and will have to meet these challenges directly in their professional careers. By examining the challenges of building 'small' in the current environment, they are better equipped to meet these challenges and inform the design decisions of future clients and the governments, investors and financial interests that have a vested interest in continuing the current, unsustainable models that place the future liveability of our cities in such danger.

BIBLIOGRAPHY

Australian Institute of Health and Welfare. Housing Assistance in Australia 2014, edited by Australian Institute of Health and Welfare. 2014.

Beer, Andrew. Lecture: 'What Future for Evidence Based Housing Policy Under Neoliberalism? Insights from Australian Experience'. Centre for Housing Urban and Regional Planning, University of Adelaide.

Birrell, Bob; and McCloskey, David. The Housing Affordability Crisis in Sydney and Melbourne Report One: the Demographic Foundations. Australian Policy Online, 2015.

Dale, Harley; and Murray, Geordan. 'The Changing Composition of Australia's New Housing Mix'. In: Composition of Australia's Housing. HIA Economics, 2015.

Department of Economic and Social Affairs. Achieving Sustainable Development and Promoting Development Cooperation. United Nations Publications, 2008.

Department of Planning. Multi Unit Housing Code. Edited by Department of Planning. Department of Planning, 2009.

Fry, T.; Perolini, P.; Kinnunen, N.; and Odom, W. Metrofitting. Griffith University, 2009.

Kalnins, Antra. 'Living the Australian lifestyle'. Macquarie Globe, last modified 19/1/2011, 2011. http://www.international.mq.edu.au/globe/2011-02/lifestyle.

Kellett, Jon. 'The Australian quarter acre block: The death of a dream?' Town Planning Review, 2011, 263–84. doi: 10.2307/27975999.

Mitchell, John. 'Climate Change Adaptation Strategy', edited by the City of Greater Geelong. The City of Greater Geelong, 2011.

Murray, Shane. 'Housing'. Architecture Australia, 2007. http://architectureau.com/articles/housing-3/

Owen, David. Green Metropolis: Why Living Smaller, Living Closer, and Driving Less are the Keys to Sustainability. New York: Riverhead Books, 2010.

Perolini, Petra. 'The Role Innovative Housing Models Play in the Struggle against Social Exclusion in Cities: The Brisbane Common Ground Model'. Social Inclusion, 3(2) (2015): 62–70.

Saggers, Sherry; and Sims, Margaret. 'Diversity: Beyond the nuclear family'. Family: Changing Families, Changing Times, 66–87. 2005.

Smith, N. 'Design dilemma: driving a consumption obsessed society into an unsustainable future'. First international conference on engineering, designing and developing the built envorinment for sustainable wellbeing, 2011.

Snow, Mark; and Prasad, Deo. Environment Design Guide: Climate Change Adaptation for Building Designers: An Introduction. Environmental, Australian Institute of Architects, New South Wales: Australian Institute of Architects, 2011.

CHAPTER FOUR

ANNA TERNON AND DR GÉRALD LEDENT

Université Catholique De Louvain

LEARNING FROM SELF-PRODUCED HOUSING EXPERIENCES IN BRUSSELS

INTRODUCTION

LIVING IN BRUSSELS TODAY

Over the past twenty years, housing production in Brussels has become a central issue. This concern is based on three main observations.

First, the demand for housing has increased in Brussels while accessible real estate has shrunk rapidly. This lack of accessible housing affects mainly the middle and popular classes. Housing production currently amounts to approximately 4,000 housing units per year, of which less than 10 per cent are social housing.[1] Moreover, the housing demand has increased constantly. The target of the Brussels-Capital Region's Sustainable Regional Development Plan (SRPD) is to increase the public housing stock by 6,500 housing units with 60 per cent for social housing and 40 per cent for middle-class housing by 2020.[2]

Second, as a result of this first observation, there is a clear worsening of social inequalities. These inequalities are geographically distributed in a zone along the industrial canal, which connected the Port of Antwerp to the industries of Charleroi in the nineteenth century. This disadvantaged area – "*le croissant pauvre*", the so-called "poor crescent" – is characterised by its poor housing conditions (including

---

1   'Perspectives démographiques 2015–2060: population Bureau fédéral du Plan et la direction générale statisique, ménages et quotients de mortalité prospectifs', https://www.belgium.be/fr/adresses_et_sites/Urls/http_www_plan_be.

2   Plan Régional de Développement Durable, http://www.prdd.brussels/.

overcrowding, lack of privacy, poor sanitation).This situation is getting worse every year; figures indicate that the sale-price evolution has been undergoing an accelerated growth since the first decade of the twenty-first century.

Finally, the city's household structures have been evolving dramatically. The traditional nuclear family is no longer a shared standard. A great diversity of households has emerged (including isolated people, roommates, people in transit, blended families, single-person households, etc.). The traditional housing configurations do not correspond to this social diversity.

LIVING IN BRUSSELS TOMORROW?

In light of these observations, it seems necessary to find new and affordable housing configurations, production and organisation modes able to shelter a great diversity of people. Such housing solutions need to guarantee the daily quality of life of residents and enhance relations with the outside world. More generally, the purpose of these solutions is to produce more resilient responses to a fragmented territory.

This chapter examines housing projects displaying unusual, self-produced, spatial configurations, production systems and social organisations. In Brussels, citizens' movements for the right to housing are growing and the cases studied here present alternatives to the current housing production.

AN APPROACH THROUGH THE CONCEPT OF COMMONS

This chapter hypothesises that the concept of Commons can play a decisive role in integrating housing in its environment as well as in articulating a variety of ways of life. The various places of life and the journeys of people through their territories are illustrated by Jacques Lévy in his analysis of the "scales of life".[3] Commons can function as an interface between a broad diversity of life trajectories. Commons refer to the management of common goods by a group of people. Common goods can be of two kinds. On the one hand, they can be external to humankind, as is the case with natural resources. One speaks then of intangible assets. On the other hand, they are directly linked to humankind when they are built and controlled by humans. In this case, one speaks of tangible assets for objects or places. The latter definition of Commons is at stake when it comes to inhabited and urban spaces.

According to Dardot and Laval, "the central issue of Commons lies in the prospect of subtracting something from the private or the public realm, to turn it into a potential use benefiting to all those who could relate to it".[4] Therefore, in order to exist, Commons must be present at the same time in space, but also in the decision-making and the organisation of lifestyles. The stake is to enhance citizens' initiatives and collective decision-making by producing housing environments that foster the common good over individual needs.

---

3   Lévy, Jacques. *Echelles De L'habiter.* 2008.

4   Dardot, P.; and Laval, C. *Commun: Essai Sur La Révolution Au Xxie Siècle.* La Découverte, 2015.

This issue is addressed in the case of housing in Brussels. The lack of affordable housing, the resulting urban fractures and the morphology of the Brussels city block, often endowed with former industrial plots, make Brussels a fertile ground in the quest for the development of Commons.

SELF-PRODUCED HOUSING EXPERIENCES IN BRUSSELS

Three cases of self-produced housing in Brussels have been selected for this chapter. They all support collective living but on different levels and with diverse ways of functioning.

BRUTOPIA, A COLLECTIVELY BUILT HOUSING ESTATE

The first case study is a collectively built housing estate inaugurated in 2013. It is located in lower Forest, a poor neighbourhood to the South of Brussels. This collective housing project consists of 27 apartments with 53 adults, 31 children/teenagers, two cats and one dog.

Due to the lack of affordable housing in Brussels, a group of people gathered their resources. The purpose of the group was to collectively play the role of a standard developer by purchasing themselves a piece of land and constructing an apartment building.

The project has been developed within the perimeter of the 'Saint Antoine district contract'.

In Brussels, the purpose of 'district contracts' is to assist disadvantaged neighbourhoods by creating or renovating housing, rehabilitating public spaces, creating public proximity infrastructures, improving the environment and the social cohesion. In addition, for the past few years, the Saint Antoine district has undergone a new dynamic through the establishment of cultural facilities for the neighbourhood or the metropolitan region, such as the Wiels Center for Modern Art in Brussels. From the start, the inhabitants of Brutopia desired to be involved in this perspective.

To carry out their project, the inhabitants have developed a specific organisation. They have created working groups on various topics such as architecture, accounting and communitarian aspects. Within each group, a spokesperson is responsible for reporting on its work to the estate's general assemblies. This collective work continues even though the project is now completed.

The project consists of various types of space. The inhabitants' ambition was to favour the relations between their collective housing and the neighbourhood. With this objective in mind, most of the ground-floor spaces have been dedicated to neighbourhood services. There is a community supported agriculture centre, a homework school, a centre for the sick and the elderly, and a debt mediation service for the disadvantaged population. There are also three architecture offices.

In addition, the inhabitants have various community spaces to promote the group dynamic and foster relations between the different types of residents but also to limit to a certain extent the individual domestic spaces. The community spaces are a common garden, a multi-purpose hall and a common laundry. They also have a parking area with shared cars.

Yet the inhabitants value the individual realm. In this case, the surface areas of the apartments are not significantly different from those of traditional housing. Each household has an apartment, usually a duplex with a private terrace. Collective life is not necessarily present on a daily basis but takes place during formal or informal gatherings within the common spaces.

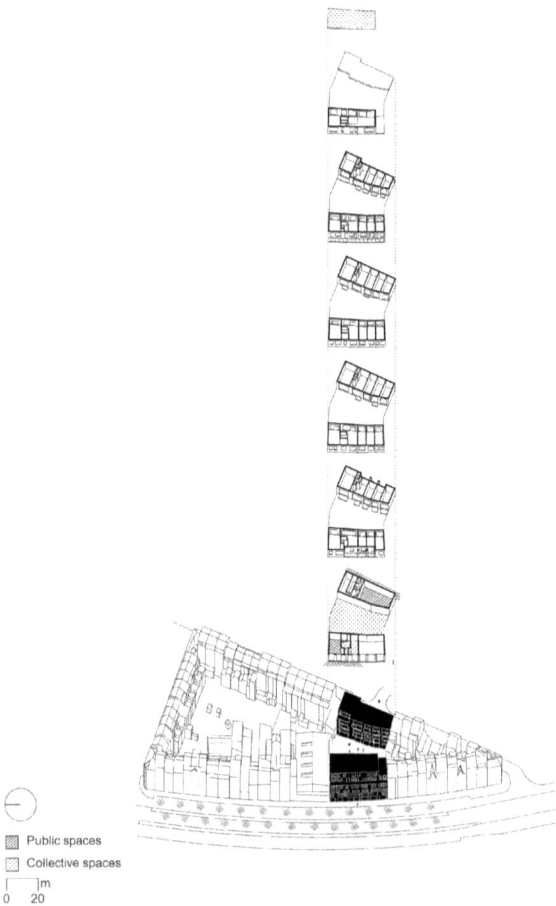

Public spaces
Collective spaces
m
0   20

Figure 1

123, A COLLECTIVE AND INCLUSIVE, YET PRECARIOUS, HOUSING PROJECT

The second case study is a squat in the centre of Brussels, known as '123'. Its story begins in May 2007 when a group of people decided to illegally occupy a building at 123 rue Royale. An agreement of temporary occupation was concluded very swiftly with the Walloon Region, the owner of the place. This agreement continued until the owner decided to renovate the building for another occupation giving the group a one-year notice period. The group was allowed to occupy the building for free and, in exchange, it permitted the owner not to pay the vacancy taxes.

The building's occupants are students, homeless persons, artists, people without papers or simply people wishing to participate in a non-classical life plan. Most of them have had difficulties finding a dwelling in a context of housing shortage or for more personal reasons, and felt the desire to live in a grouped and united housing.

In 123, there are 65 inhabitants. Depending on their personal situation, they pay a rent of 60, 90 or 120. All decisions are taken collectively during general assemblies held every Tuesday and within smaller groups meeting about specifics subjects (e.g. cultural or festive events).

Their philosophy is to open their doors to the largest possible number of people. To this end, they open a series of public spaces every week such as a bike workshop, a *table d'hôte* and a library. Those public spaces are situated on the first floor and on the ground floor of the building. All the floors are organised in almost the same way. They feature shared spaces: a kitchen, a small lounge, sanitation equipment and several specific communal spaces like a wood workshop, a painting workshop or a yoga room.

In 123, there are two kinds of residents: permanent and temporary. This status determines the size of their private space and their right to vote during the general assemblies: only the permanent inhabitants get to vote during general assemblies. They have a 35m² private space corresponding to four window-spans. If a resident decides to leave, he will always get priority coming back. This measure is taken to allow inhabitants to leave easily without being afraid of not finding anything else. Temporary inhabitants, or guests, can take part in the assemblies but do not vote. They live in guest rooms, which are smaller. The inhabitants' partners can take part in the assemblies but do not vote in the beginning. After some time, they can become permanent inhabitants and have a right to vote.

The waiting list to live in 123 exceeds 100 people. This speaks to the housing shortage in Brussels and accounts for the fight against unoccupied buildings through such initiatives.

Public spaces
Collective spaces
0 20 m

Figure 2

LA POUDRIÈRE, A SELF-MANAGED COMMUNITY

In 1958, two priests settled down in the district the 'Corner of the Devil', a disadvantaged district of the capital. Their only purpose was to provide a reassuring presence in the neighbourhood. Little by little, the priests welcomed people in need and the community built itself up. In the 1970s, the community joined the Emmaüs movement. The philosophy of this community is to experiment with an alternative to capitalism in which humans become the only priority. Its members have four founding principles: presence, friendship, hope and personal fulfilment. The notion of community is extremely important. Salaries are shared and everything is bought in common.

In the beginning, the priests were looking for activities for the people they welcomed. Their first activity was working as movers for the people of the neighbourhood. Today, their main activity is the recuperation and sale of objects of all kinds. The community also has a farming activity on the side. The sixty members of the community are living in three different geographical locations: Brussels, Pérulwez (near the border with France) and Rummen (70km from Brussels).

All decisions are discussed by the group at the general meetings held on one weekend each month and they are then legally or administratively formalised by the association council and the administrative council (five members of the community). The decisions concern the activities of the community or the buildings. The association council comprises thirteen members, ten community members and three non-members including a notary. The administrative council is composed by five members of the community. They meet once a year or whenever necessary. Besides the regular community members, some people work as volunteers. They do not participate in decision making but can be responsible for a specific activity.

The community owns an important patrimony inherited from persons close to the community. In total, the patrimony of La Poudrière is composed of sixteen buildings worth eight-million euros. The buildings are located in five different places: Brussels (the Mother House in rue de La Poudrière), Anderlecht, Vilvoorde, Pérulwez and Rumen.

The La Poudrière location occupies almost a whole urban block within which lie industrial constructions. The community interacts with the neighbourhood through the stores and their hospitality facilities. All the buildings of the block owned by the community have openings that lead to the community spaces. The community spaces occupy a large area in the centre of the block while the private spaces are at the periphery. The private spaces are divided according to the different needs of the inhabitants. For example, families have a kitchen and a dining room to allow for some family time during the weekends.

Recently, the community has been less successful than it was in the 1980s. While there were 120 members in the 1980s, there are only 60 today of which 20 inhabitants live in the La Poudrière location. The community is therefore seeking a revival and a new form of collective life. For example, they are thinking of using their assets to implement a system similar to the Community Land Trust.

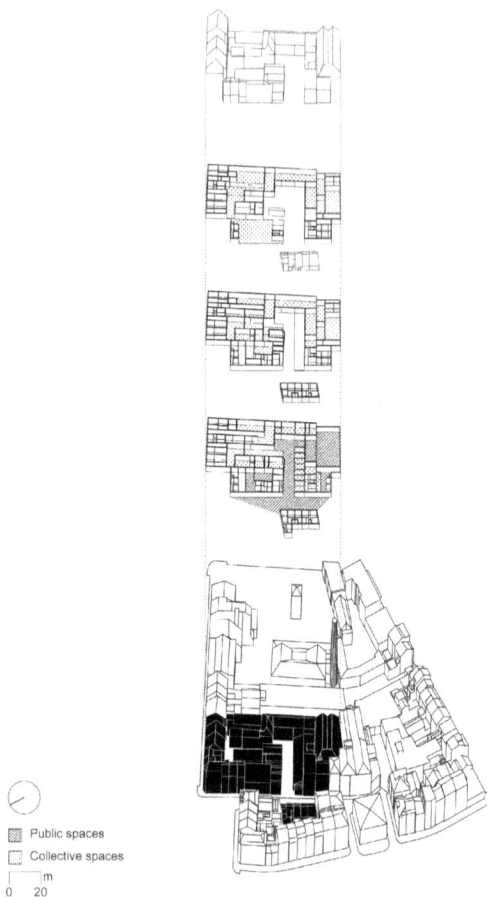

Public spaces
Collective spaces
m
0   20

Figure 3

AN ANALYTICAL FRAMEWORK

Commons play a central role in each case study. This particular model attempts to respond to the housing issues regarding their usual production modes and the changing needs of society. However, the case studies differ in terms of organisations, uses and spatiality. This essay questions which criteria favour the development of Commons as spaces for domestic as well as for urban life through a comparative analysis. The purpose of this analysis is to associate social and spatial factors in order to understand which arrangements best support the *vivre ensemble* (living together), integration in the surroundings and sustainability.

The housing experiments studied in Brussels are small but display variations in their organisation, spatial and social features. Moreover, given the current problems regarding housing affordability and the usual Brussels urban morphologies, those types of experiments are likely to multiply in the future. In this perspective, developing an analytical framework could provide a better understanding of those housing developments with respect to the contemporary issues of cities. This framework sheds light on the organisational, spatial and social features that are liable to cater to the needs of, and the changes in, society. The markers of this first analytical framework will be completed by in-depth fieldwork research.

The actual framework is organised into three dimensions.

The first dimension concerns the collective organisation, which in turn encompasses three facets.

First, to produce alternative housing from the traditional modes of production, every case study presents a different operating mode. These operating modes refer to the notion of ownership when producing or occupying the housing projects. Both La Poudrière and Brutopia produced their habitat through self-supported initiatives without any public or private funding. However, while in both cases the housing production was collective, land property is not. Indeed, the inhabitants of La Poudrière collectively own the entire estate while those of Brutopia collectively own the ground and the collective spaces but own their apartments individually. The case of 123 is different because the inhabitants are neither owners nor tenants of their dwellings but are tenants of a building belonging to the Walloon Region.

Second, the legal framework in which the projects are developed also differs from one case to the next. In all three cases, the housing projects were implemented through non-profit associations. These associations benefit from a legal personality separate from that of its members. However, the scope of these associations' action varies, being limited to housing management in the case of 123 and Brutopia while managing the entire life of the residents in the case of La Poudrière. These differences might give a hint at the capacity of the system to be long-lasting.

Finally, different governance patterns emerge in the projects. They all organise general deciding assemblies but at a pace that varies according to the development stages of the projects. In Brutopia, the inhabitants' participation was particularly important during the design process. Nowadays, the housing organisation is very similar to a traditional co-ownership scheme. However, small working groups continue to develop collective projects for the estate. At 123, general assemblies take place every week. Everyone can participate and make proposals. At La Poudrière, meetings are held every month. Everyone can participate. Yet, in this latter case, decisions are always subject to validation by the councils formed by the oldest members of the community.

The second dimension concerns spatial organisation.

First, the urban forms of the three case studies are quite similar. They are all part of a classical Brussels urban closed block. Brutopia and 123 display a similar topology since both their properties give access to a street on each side of the block. The centre of the land is treated differently, however: Brutopia offers a central garden while the entire plot is built on in the case of 123. For its part, La Poudrière occupies one half of a block with a series of connected typical Brussels houses and former warehouses.

Second, the three case studies present a different percentage of collective spaces. They do not offer the same amenities and these are distributed differently. La Poudrière has the highest percentage of collective surfaces while its number of inhabitants is the lowest. The collective spaces are for the greater part in the centre of the compound while the private spaces are spread around the periphery. The high percentage of collective spaces in Brutopia is mainly due to the area of the common garden, the remainder being devoted to the multifunctional room, the circulation spaces and the laundry on the ground floor. Collective surfaces in 123 occupy an important share of the building compared with the private spaces (which are 35m² on average). They are distributed all over the building.

Eventually, each case study presents a mix of urban activities but the situation and the management of these activities are different. The external functions in Brutopia are not managed by the inhabitants. They are rented spaces on the ground floor. The activities carried out at 123 have no lucrative purpose. They are voluntary activities and gather together residents and external volunteers. The activities of La Poudrière are mainly carried out by the inhabitants with the help of some volunteers. They constitute for the greater part their main activity and allow the needs of the community to be partially met.

The last dimension concerns the social and cultural aspects of the projects.

First, various relations between the inhabitants can be observed within the estates. The relationships in Brutopia are very similar to those of traditional housing models whereas La Poudrière proposes a completely different model. In the first case, community moments occur occasionally during festivities. In the second, all daily activities are collective (eating, cooking, working, etc.). At 123, communal kitchens on each floor are shared by a series of residents. But all residents can also use the larger collective kitchen at all times. Inhabitants choose to eat together or separately.

Second, in all three cases, the relations with the surrounding neighbourhoods are established mainly through a combination of functions. Differences can be noted however in the management of the activities held for the neighbourhood. While at 123 and La Poudrière those activities are managed by the inhabitants themselves, this is not the case in Brutopia. In the various floors of the building and several times a week, various activities proposed by 123 create bonds with the neighbourhood and the city. Moreover, most of the meals are made with food recovered from various supermarkets in the city. La Poudrière has established a strong relationship with the neighbourhood through its moving activities and its stores. Eventually, Brutopia's relations with the neighbourhood are established primarily through the centre for elderly people.

Third, farther relations, outside the city, only occur in the case of La Poudrière. Indeed, exchanges take place between the three places of life of the community. Food products cultivated in the countryside locations help to feed the Brussels community.

CONCLUSION

The diversity of housing production systems presented in these case studies could be a clue as to how to create better access to housing. However, limitations exist in each of them. Despite the contract concluded with the owner of the building, the housing future of the inhabitants of 123 is uncertain. Indeed, the contract of precarious occupancy offers only a temporary solution. For its part, the system of La Poudrière does not specify the possibility of leaving the estate after several years, thus engendering a rather peculiar lifestyle. The production system of Brutopia allows the collective purchase of private apartments at a lower cost but this does not avoid speculation upon their resale.

Although shared, group and community housing are becoming increasingly common, their legal frame still lacks a clear definition. This shortfall of effective laws to frame these new housing practices causes a series of inconveniences (loss of lone-resident status, administrative issues regarding registration, etc.). There is no specific legal regime nor a specific definition for shared housing.

Worse still, with the coming into force of a law against squatters in October 2017 it will become harder to occupy buildings the way that 123 does. Indeed, before this law, in order to obtain a contract of precarious occupation, the most effective solution was to compulsorily occupy an empty building and then, once recorded, to conclude such a contract with its owner. Today, with the new law, illegal settlers can be expelled much more easily.

In view of the evolution of the composition of households, there is an urgent need to think about a legal framework allowing the development of new forms of housing.

The central issue that stands out from an analysis of governance systems is the challenge of maintaining the inhabitants' investment in the decision-making processes and of preserving democratic and horizontal governance. In the oldest case, La Poudrière, all important decisions must be validated by the councils made up of the eldest members of the community. Yet their perceptions do not always correspond to those of the new generations, which aspire to a different organisation. The collective organisation of Brutopia was particularly important during the conception of the project but this organisation is no longer relevant in the day-to-day management of the estate. In 123, the difficulties of its horizontal governance lie chiefly in gathering all the inhabitants at the weekly meetings as well as in handling internal conflicts.

A research hypothesis would be to estimate the ideal number of inhabitants to ensure horizontal and sustainable governance.

In connection with this issue, the availability of spaces within the city of Brussels for this kind of project is at stake. This analysis shows that the case studies are integrated in existing blocks and do not easily fit into the fabric of the city. When producing larger housing projects, the issue of available space is crucial. How could such alternative projects compete with traditional private housing developments? This question might partly be answered through the projects' densities. Indeed, by producing more collective spaces and fewer individual spaces, the projects prove to be altogether more compact and hence more economically advantageous.

Moreover, a comparison of collective and individual spaces shows that the size and the use of Commons are proportional to the level of communitarianism. The inhabitants of La Poudrière have a high percentage of communal surfaces at their disposal. In return, their individual spaces are reduced. Likewise, this level of communitarianism seems to influence the diversity of uses and the connections to their surroundings. In 123 and in La Poudrière, the inhabitants themselves organise the diversity of the uses in the building as activities or services for the neighbourhood. It is also in these cases that the greatest share of disadvantaged people and variations in inhabitants' profiles are catered for. 123 presents a large opening towards the neighbourhood through its various activities. La Poudrière also welcomes a large number of disadvantaged people such as migrants or former prisoners.

From a social and cultural point of view, the overall trend tends to confirm that Commons generate initiatives on behalf of the inhabitants. The initial investment to create mutual places and services is usually compensated by the solidarity and mutual assistance generated by the Commons. As noted in the cases of 123 and La Poudrière, communal activities also facilitate the reintegration of people into society. Finally, La Poudrière displays an example of an open lifestyle and exchanges between the spaces in the countryside and the city.

Analysis of these three self-produced projects displays a reduction of the individual sphere in favour of common spaces. In addition to creating a genuine community life within the projects, those common spaces create an interface with the neighbourhood through the implementation of activities and services by the inhabitants. Spatially, this is translated by a permeability and a continuity of the common and urban spaces.

These housing projects demonstrate an ability to welcome heterogeneous sociocultural profiles, to stimulate urban space and to reconsider the traditional limits of the private sphere. These properties of these self-produced spatial and social forms of dwelling advocate their interesting role to face the housing crisis in Brussels.

	«Brutopia»	«123»	«La Poudrière»
COLLECTIVE ORGANISATION			
Production system			
Legal frame			
Modes of governance			
SPATIAL ORGANISATION			
Urban form			
Collective spaces			
Function diversity			
SOCIAL AND CULTURAL ORGANISATION			
Internal relation			
Neighbouring relation			
Farther relation			

Figure 4

REFERENCES

BOOKS

Ananian, P. *La Production Résidentielle Comme Levier De La Régénération Urbaine À Bruxelles*. Presses universitaires de Louvain, 2010.

Cohen, Maurizio; and Plissart, Marie-Françoise. *A Bruxelles, Près De Chez Nous: L'architecture Dans Les Contrats De Quartier*. [in fre] Bruxelles: Région de Bruxelles-Capitale, 2007.

Dardot, P.; and Laval, C. *Commun: Essai Sur La Révolution Au Xxie Siècle*. La Découverte, 2015.

Lévy, Jacques. *Echelles De L'habiter*. 2008.

Poudrière, Communauté de la. *Chants D'espoir, Champ D'espérance*. Communauté de la Poudrière, 1995.

ELECTRONIC ARTICLES

Bernard, Nicolas; and Andersen, Robert. 'Politiques Du Logement En Région Bruxelloise'. 2016: 608.

Bernard, Nicolas; and Lemaire, Valérie. 'L'habitat Groupé Dit Solidiare Sous L'angle Juridique: Allocations Sociales, Logement Et Labellisation', no. 2013 (3) (2013): 88.

Dessouroux, Christian; Bensliman, Rachida; Bernard, Nicolas; De Laet, Sarah; Demonty, François; Marissal, Pierre; and Surkyn, Johan. 'Le Logement À Bruxelles: Diagnostic Et Enjeux'. *Brussels Studies* (2016). http://journals.openedition.org/brussels/1346.

Smet, Aurelie de. 'Le Rôle De L'usage Temporaire Dans Le (Re)Développement Urbain: Exemples Bruxellois' (2013). http://journals.openedition.org/brussels/1195.

WEB PAGES

123. http://www.123rueroyale.be/.

Brutopia. https://utopiabrussels.wordpress.com/the-project/.

Bureau fédéral du Plan et la direction générale statisique, Perspectives démographiques 2015–2060: population, ménages et quotients de mortalité prospectifs. https://www.belgium.be/fr/adresses_et_sites/Urls/http_www_plan_be.

Durable, Plan Régional de Développement. http://www.prdd.brussels/.

Poudrière, La. https://www.lapoudriere.be/#Blog_.U/b0l.

JOURNAL ARTICLES

Neuwels, Julie. 'L'architecture (Durable) Comme Technologie De Gouvernement: Apports Et Détournements De La Sociologie De L'action Publique'. *CLARA Architecture/Recherche* (2015-04-15 2015): 63-72%N 3.

CHAPTER FIVE

ISARA KHANJANASTHITI AND LYNNE ARMITAGE

Bond University

THE RISE AND RISE OF MICRO APARTMENTS AND HIGH-RISE APARTMENTS IN AUSTRALIAN CAPITAL CITIES: A CRITICAL DESIGN REVIEW

INTRODUCTION

Detached housing is currently the dominant dwelling structure among households in Australian capital cities. However, apartments also play a very substantial role in housing in these cities as approximately 13 per cent of all capital city households were living in flats, units or apartments between 2009 and 2010.[1] In recent years, micro apartments and high-rise apartments have increasingly emerged among apartment projects in Australian capital cities. Micro apartments are becoming increasingly common due to the country's housing affordability crisis, which is relatively more severe in the capital cities. There has been an upward trend in Australia's median house price, which is currently nearly seven times the annual median household income.[2] Furthermore, two Australian capital cities, namely Sydney and Melbourne, are ranked among the ten "Least Affordable Major Metropolitan Markets" globally.[3]

---

1 Australian Bureau of Statistics. *2012 Year Book Australia*. Canberra: Australian Bureau of Statistics, 2013. Accessed 13 January 2017, https://goo.gl/3UadyC, 362.

2 Cox, Wendell; and Pavletich, Hugh. *13th Annual Demographia International Housing Affordability Survey: 2017*. Illinois: Demographia, 2015. Accessed February 16, 2017, http://goo.gl/ylW46, 17.

3 Ibid., 14

On the other hand, more and more high-rise apartments are being established in the centres of the capital cities due to the high demand and preference of overseas investors.[4] In light of these recent developments, the purpose of this chapter is to critically review micro apartments and high-rise apartments in terms of their design issues and outlook. The chapter also provides recommendations for addressing the principal issues identified.

APARTMENTS IN AUSTRALIAN CAPITAL CITIES

An apartment is "a residential unit in a multi-unit building"[5] with "three or more residential units where at least one unit [is] on top of the other."[6] It has no private grounds and shares "a common entrance foyer or stairwell."[7] Internally, an apartment is self-contained with "kitchen and bathroom and toilet facilities, under the exclusive possession of the occupier."[8] It is serviced by lift access whereas a flat can typically be accessed only by stairs.[9]

With eight different states and territories, the Commonwealth of Australia contains eight capital cities, namely Sydney, Melbourne, Brisbane, Adelaide, Perth, Hobart, Darwin and Canberra. The dominant dwelling structure in the capital cities is detached housing with the proportion of households living in such dwellings ranging between 61 per cent and 84 per cent across the cities between 2009 and 2010. However, apartments also play an important role in housing the population in these cities particularly in Sydney and Hobart where approximately one-fifth of all population were living in flats, units or apartments between 2009 and 2010.[10] Meanwhile, the majority of approvals for new dwellings in Sydney and Melbourne between 2008 and 2015 were for apartments.[11]

---

4   Buxton, Michael; Goodman, Robin; and Moloney, Susie. *Planning Melbourne.* Melbourne: CSIRO Publishing, 2016, 59.

5   Department of the Environment, Community and Local Government. *Sustainable Urban Housing: Design Standards for New Apartments Guidelines for Planning Authorities.* Dublin: Department of the Environment, Community and Local Government, 2015. Accessed 15 January 2017, https://goo.gl/NKNNrm, 1.

6   Kulu, Hill. *Fertility differences by housing type: an effect of housing conditions or of selective moves?* Rostock: Max Planck Institute for Demographic Research, 2007. Accessed 13 January 2017, https://goo.gl/moNyB3, 7.

7   '4102.0 – Australian Social Trends, 2006'. Australian Bureau of Statistics. Accessed 13 January 2017, https://goo.gl/KSTQQJ.

8   Victorian Government. *Residential Tenancies Act 1997.* Melbourne: Victorian Government, 1997. Accessed 13 January 2017, https://goo.gl/mexTcK, 9.

9   Jenny Brown. 'Flat out telling a unit from an apartment?' accessed 15 January 2017, https://goo.gl/rlpnfU.

10   Australian Bureau of Statistics, *2012 Year Book,* 362.

11   Birrell, Bob; and McClosekey, David. *The housing affordability crisis in Sydney and Melbourne Report One: The demographic foundations.* Sydney: *Sydney Morning Herald,* 2015. Accessed 15 January 2017, https://goo.gl/2YtqMu, 19.

Furthermore, apartments are projected to increase dramatically as a proportion of all housing stock in Brisbane over the next few decades.[12]

In recent years, apartments have become a major contributor to the construction of new dwellings in Australia. For instance, more than one-third of all residential building approvals in 2015 were related to apartments. Furthermore, recent apartment construction has been concentrated in three of the eight capital cities, namely Sydney, Melbourne and Brisbane.[13]

Several factors have contributed to the increase in apartment construction activities. There is progressively limited land supply due to the rapidly growing population in the capital cities, which has led to higher prices for blocks of land and detached dwellings. Meanwhile, apartments are relatively more affordable than detached dwellings due to their more intensive use of land.[14] Between 2012 and 2022, driven by the increasing need for affordable housing and the limited land supply in Sydney and Melbourne, approximately 124,000 and 78,000 additional apartments are needed in these cities, respectively.[15]

The average household commuting distance ranges from 11.5 to 15 kilometres across the Australian capital cities.[16] In this regard, an increasing number of households in these cities now desire to live in proximity to key employment centres and amenities for convenience and reduced travel times. As most new apartments are built in inner-city areas or close to key transport infrastructure, they are able to address this particular preference.[17] In contrast, empty blocks of land for detached houses are predominantly located in remote suburbs. In 2010, for example, the majority of building approvals for detached housing in the capital cities were provided for dwellings located in greenfield areas considered to be part of the urban sprawl settlement pattern.[18]

12   Urbis. *Urbis Brisbane Apartment Insights 04 Qtr 2013*. Brisbane: Urbis, 2014. Accessed 13 January 2017.

13   Shoorey, Michael. *The Growth of Apartment Construction in Australia*. Sydney: Reserve Bank of Australia, 2016. Accessed 13 January 2017, https://goo.gl/ucGZgo, 19.

14   Ibid., 21

15   Birrell and McClosekey, op. cit., 19

16   Williams, Catharina. *Australia's commuting distance: cities and regions*. Canberra: Bureau of Infrastructure, Transport and Regional Economics, 2015. Accessed 15 January 2017, https://goo.gl/QEΛDHM, 9.

17   Shoorey, op. cit., 21

18   Phillips, Ben. *The Great Australian Dream – Just a Dream? AMP.NATSEM Income and Wealth Report*, Canberra: University of Canberra, 2011. Accessed 15 January 2017, https://goo.gl/ehwF2B, 16.

MICRO APARTMENTS

WHAT ARE MICRO APARTMENTS?

In recent years, developers have increasingly provided 'micro apartments', or apartments with limited space, to increase the density of their development projects.[19] By doing so, these apartments can be sold at a lower price, thereby increasing their affordability to the public. Additionally, in a market where price continues to increase per square metre, "apartment sizes have [become] smaller to maintain [the same price point as previously]".[20]

The 'micro' home trend has been a global phenomenon particularly in such cities as New York and Hong Kong since architect Sarah Susanka first published her book, *The Not So Big House*, in 1998. A micro home is smaller, more organised and more energy efficient than a standard home. The Global Financial Crisis, which had significant impacts on both property owners and investors alike, further increased the popularity of micro homes due to their relative affordability.[21] In Australia, micro apartments are becoming increasingly popular among both developers and residents alike due to the housing affordability crisis that the capital cities are experiencing.

HOUSING AFFORDABILITY CRISIS IN AUSTRALIAN CAPITAL CITIES

The historical settlement pattern of Australian cities has led to metropolitan primacy where the capital city of each state is several times larger than the second largest city in the state.[22] For instance, Sydney, the capital city of the state of New South Wales, comprises approximately 4.4 million people in 2011 whereas the population figure of state's second largest city, Newcastle, is around 300,000.[23] With larger population centres providing a broader range of services and employment opportunities, such metropolitan regions function as magnets for population settlement, leading to rapidly

19 Brook, Benedict. 'Fears moves to set minimum size for apartments could leave city centres only for the rich'. *News*, 27 March 2016, https://goo.gl/BeSorz.

20 Higgins, David. 'What gives to keep that price point? High-density residential developments'. *Pacific Rim Property Research Journal*, 21 (2015): 44. Accessed 20 January 2017, doi:10.1080/14445921.2015.1026133.

21 Investor Genius. 'Micro-Apartments Are a Growing Trend in Australia. When They Look Like These, It's Not Hard to See Why!' Investor Genius. Accessed 20 January 2017, https://goo.gl/Lek74t.

22 Department of Infrastructure and Regional Development, *The Evolution of Australian Towns*. Canberra: Bureau of Infrastructure, Transport and Regional Economics, 2014. Accessed 20 January 2017, https://goo.gl/9hu2Nr, 88.

23 'Census of Population and Housing'. Australian Bureau of Statistics. Accessed 15 January 2017, https://goo.gl/1deDN8.

increasing housing demand in the capital cities.[24] Furthermore, the average household size has been declining due to fewer children in each family, later marriages and increased incidence of separation and divorce.[25]

On the supply side of housing, significant time lags exist for the supply of new housing stock to be provided in response to the increasing demand. This is due to several factors associated with various stages of housing construction. Firstly, there is limited availability of suitable sites in key locations, particularly in the capital cities where urban containment policies have been implemented. Secondly, once a site is obtained by a developer for dwelling construction, the complexity and length of the planning process to achieve a development approval can be extensive depending on the local council's planning scheme. Thirdly, the process of preparing undeveloped land for housing development can be costly. Lastly, the time required to build new dwellings can be significant.[26]

Due to the demand and supply factors discussed above, the capital cities have experienced housing affordability issues in recent years. Sydney and Melbourne, for example, are ranked as the second and fourth "Least Affordable Major Metropolitan Markets" around the world, with a median multiple figure of 12.2 and 9.5, respectively.[27] The median multiple figure is obtained by dividing median house price by gross annual median household income, and a median multiple figure of at least 5.1 indicates a "Severely Unaffordable" housing market.[28] Housing stress, a situation in which a household spends more than 30 per cent of its after-tax income on housing-related expenses, is also a common issue across the capital cities. For example, more than 28 per cent of households in Sydney experienced housing stress in 2011 whereas Perth's proportion of households in housing stress was 23 per cent during the same period.[29]

MICRO APARTMENTS IN AUSTRALIA

Micro apartments are becoming increasingly common across the Australian capital cities, particularly in Melbourne and Sydney where housing affordability issues are of greatest concern. For instance, from 2008 to 2010, the median size of a new one-

---

24 Australian Government, *Our Cities: The Challenge of Change*. Canberra: Department of Infrastructure and Regional Development, 2010. Accessed 15 January 2017, https://goo.gl/8UfFPy, 76.

25 O'Neill, Phillip. *Housing Affordability Literature Review and Affordable Housing Program Audit*. Sydney: University of Western Sydney, 2008. Accessed 16 February 2017, https://goo.gl/61ppKR, 9–10.

26 Hsieh, Wing; Norman, David; and Orsmond, David. *Supply-Side Issues in the Housing Sector*. Sydney: Reserve Bank of Australia, 2012. Accessed 15 January 2017, http://goo.gl/7wOfcY, 13.

27 Cox and Pavletich, op. cit., 14

28 Ibid., 1

29 Phillips, op. cit., 7

bedroom apartment in inner Melbourne dropped from 52 to 44 square metres.[30] Moreover, 40 per cent of apartments built in inner Melbourne between 2006 and 2013 have less than 50 square metres of floor area.[31] However, micro apartments in Melbourne are as small as 15 square metres, as shown in Figure 1 below.

Figure 1. An example of micro apartments in Melbourne[32]

DESIGN ISSUES OF MICRO APARTMENTS

Due to the absence of clear, minimum standards in the past, many of the recently built micro apartments are associated with low quality.[33] In this regard, the majority of them lack sufficient space for such amenities as kitchen and dining tables.[34] Windows are often few or non-existent in newer micro apartments, thus limiting the amount of natural lighting in these apartments.[35] Figure 2 illustrates other common design issues in micro apartments.

30 Martel, Andrew; Whitzman, Carolyn; Fincher, Ruth; Lawther, Peter; Woodcock, Ian; and Tucker, Danita. *Getting to Yes: Overcoming barriers to affordable family friendly housing in inner Melbourne.* Melbourne: University of Melbourne, 2013. Accessed 15 January 2017, https://goo.gl/2P1m2T, 30.

31 City of Melbourne. *Future Living: A discussion paper identifying issues and options for housing our community.* Melbourne: City of Melbourne, 2013. Accessed 25 January 2017, https://goo.gl/eCIMYW.

32 Investor Genius, op. cit.

33 ABC News, '"Dog box" apartments targeted in new Victorian design rules'. *ABC News,* 17 December 2016, https://goo.gl/x9rslc.

34 Ramirez-Lovering, Diego. *The space of dwelling: an investigation into the potential for spatial flexibility to improve volume housing in Australia.* Melbourne: Monash University, 2013. Accessed 20 January 2017, https://goo.gl/ESvawG, 33.

35 Brook, op. cit.

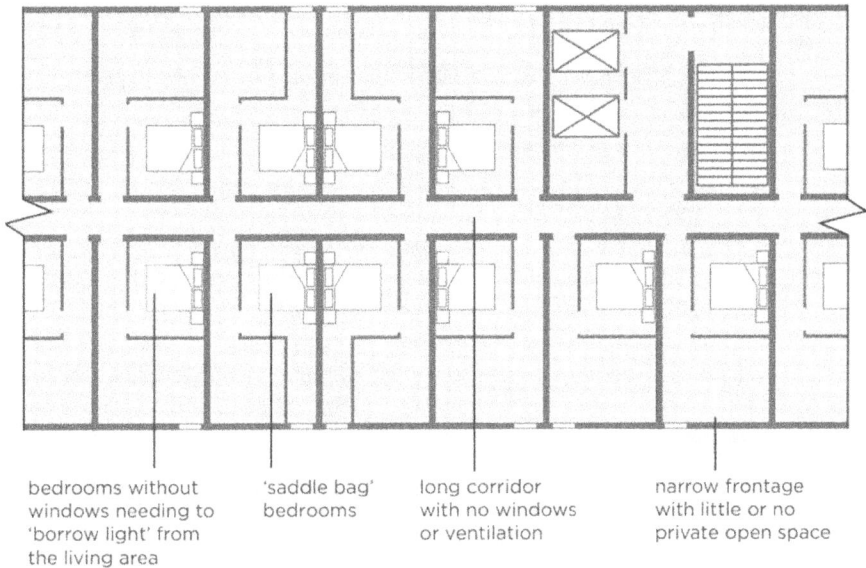

bedrooms without windows needing to 'borrow light' from the living area

'saddle bag' bedrooms

long corridor with no windows or ventilation

narrow frontage with little or no private open space

Figure 2. Design issues in recently built micro apartments[36]

Bedrooms in micro apartments frequently have no direct sunlight and need to rely on "borrowed" sunlight from the living room's single window.[37,38] Alternatively, a small hallway may be used to provide natural light to the bedroom, which is occasionally referred to as a "saddle bag" or "battle axe" bedroom.[39] The shared corridor on each floor, meanwhile, is often long and narrow with no windows or ventilation. The frontage of these apartments is usually narrow with limited or no balcony space. The latter part of this chapter will further discuss design implications of the narrow apartment format. As a result of these design issues, several of the recently built micro apartments have been associated with such pejorative terms as "shoe boxes"[40] and "dog boxes".[41]

---

36 City of Melbourne, op. cit., 70

37 Ibid., 70

38 Brook, op. cit.

39 City of Melbourne, op. cit., 68.

40 Chua, Geraldine. 'Survey shows Australian apartment dwellers don't want to live in shoe boxes'. Accessed 17 January 2017, https://goo.gl/GShhkT.

41 ABC News, op. cit.

HIGH-RISE APARTMENTS

INVESTOR-DRIVEN DOMINANCE OF HIGH-RISE APARTMENTS IN CITY CENTRES

The number of high-rise apartments has grown rapidly in recent years, particularly in the inner parts of the capital cities. For instance, the majority of apartment approvals between 2008 and 2015 in Sydney were related to high-rise apartment projects.[42] Meanwhile, with more than 100 high-rise apartment towers approved in recent years around inner Melbourne, Melbourne is now one of the top international locations for high-rise development.[43] The majority of new high-rise apartment construction in the capital cities, particularly Sydney and Melbourne, has been driven by the influx of foreign investment. There is a general preference among foreign investors for high-rise apartments, which has contributed to the significantly increasing number of such developments in recent years. The level of foreign investment in the residential property sector has historically been high due to "liberal foreign investment rules, a facilitative building code and lack of height controls, and an investor desire for diversified foreign property portfolios."[44] Furthermore, land prices have recently skyrocketed in the inner parts of capital cities, prompting developers to increase the heights of their apartment towers to recover more costs.[45]

DESIGN ISSUES OF HIGH-RISE APARTMENTS

Kerry Clare, an award-winning architect based in Sydney, has criticised several of the recently built high-rise apartments as being energy intensive and creating negative externalities for their surroundings.[46] Internally, high-rise apartments are "the most inefficient users of energy",[47] consuming 30 per cent more energy than detached dwellings.[48] Higher altitudes are associated with greater variance in ambient temperature. The extensive use of glass curtain wall systems for high-rise apartment towers also results in higher internal temperature in the warmer seasons. Given these temperature conditions, high-rise apartments consistently require air-conditioning and heating to maintain occupants' comfort. Furthermore, wind velocities are stronger at higher altitudes, which render windows unopenable above certain heights, thereby increasing the necessity for mechanical air conditioning. Extensive common areas such as car parks, foyers, lifts, plant and equipment, in addition to the lack of individual

42   Birrell and McClosekey, op. cit., 19

43   Buxton, Goodman and Moloney, op. cit., 1

44   Ibid., 59

45   Ibid., 68

46   Lucas, Clay. 'High-rise apartments are bad to live in and bad for society, says respected architect'. *The Age*, 29 August 2016, https://goo.gl/L7NTkn.

47   Buxton, Goodman and Moloney, op. cit., 2

48   Blundell, Lynne. 'Apartment blocks the missing link in sustainability'. Accessed 20 January 2017, https://goo.gl/WvrXIF.

meters, also contribute to the intensive energy consumption of high-rise apartment towers.[49] Externally, these developments create large shadows and wind tunnels, which reduce the amenity and quality of life for their surrounding residents.[50]

Clare also warned that high-rise apartments can diminish residents' involvement in public spaces at street level due to the significantly reduced number of chance encounters between people, which are more easily promoted by low-rise dwellings.[51,52] In this regard, high-rise towers can lead to "physical, social and psychological" separations in the community according to Taz Loomans, a San Francisco-based architect.[53]

A high-rise apartment typically only has one external wall. Given this constraint, several developers have increased the density of their development projects by building long, narrow apartments. Figure 3, which shows a floor plan of a high-rise apartment built in 2013 with 75 square metres internal space, illustrates an example of such apartments.

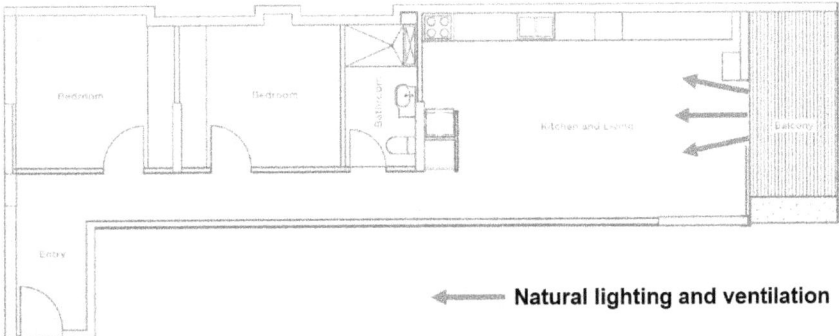

◄••••••••• Natural lighting and ventilation

Figure 3 An example of a high-rise apartment built in 2013[54]

As shown in Figure 3, due to the long corridor format, such a design suffers from limited natural ventilation and lighting from the living room's window. Meanwhile, the bedrooms and bathroom are windowless and receive no natural light due to being located adjacent to another apartment. On average, only 15 per cent of a 4-metre wide, 12-metre deep apartment have direct access to natural air and light.[55]

It should be noted that micro apartments and high-rise apartments are not mutually exclusive in Australia. In recent years, there has been an increasing number of micro

49   Buxton, Goodman and Moloney, op. cit., 72
50   Lucas, op. cit.
51   Ibid.
52   Buxton, Goodman and Moloney, op. cit., 73
53   Lucas, op. cit.
54   Martel et al., op. cit., 31
55   Ibid., 30

apartments in high-rise towers across the capital cities. This trend is particularly evident in Melbourne where several sites have enabled the development of such apartments with relatively affordable prices for most investors.[56] Poorly designed micro apartments in a high-rise tower would be associated with the design issues of not only micro apartments but also high-rise apartments.

OUTLOOK AND RECOMMENDATIONS

THE NEED FOR BETTER DESIGN STANDARDS

Poorly designed apartments can have negative health impacts on residents.[57] Due to inadequate building codes, an increasingly common design issue impacting health among new apartments in Australia is noise impact between apartments.[58] As several of the recently built apartments in Australia have been criticised for being poorly designed in the absence of design standards, the overall health of apartment residents in the capital cities may be adversely affected.

According to Craig Yelland, architect and director of Plus Architecture, micro apartments can still be highly liveable with clever design and use of spaces. To this end, innovative storage solutions such as multiple cupboards and bed storage can be adopted.[59] Furthermore, a recently conducted online survey has revealed that being able to entertain guests at home with sufficient living and kitchen spaces is an important factor for both apartment residents and detached house inhabitants.[60] Therefore, the space of the living room, where residents spend the most time, should be maximised in micro apartments.

To ensure that micro apartments built in the future are more liveable, planning and building regulations should enforce better design standards on all future apartment projects. To this end, strengthened design standards have recently been introduced by government authorities to address some of the major design issues associated with micro apartments and high-rise apartments. For example, the Victorian Government is implementing *Better Apartments Design Standards* in March 2017. This statutory document outlines several design criteria to improve sustainability and liveability of new apartments in Victoria. Some of the key design criteria include:

- Minimum ceiling heights of 2.7 metres

- Minimum sizes for living room and bedroom, and

---

56 'Dormitory city: Melbourne's brittle highrise apartment boom'. The Conversation. Accessed 20 January 2017, https://goo.gl/WiOBMq.

57 Marmot, Michael. *Fair Society, Healthy Lives: A Strategic Review of Health Inequalities in England Post 2010*. London: UCL Institute of Health Equity, 2010. Accessed 20 January 2018, https://goo.gl/9HcjT.

58 Buxton, Goodman and Moloney, op. cit., 72

59 Brook, op. cit.

60 Chua, op. cit.

- Design standards to ensure new apartments have adequate space for a bed and a fridge.[61]

However, no minimum apartment size has been set in the guideline. As discussed previously, micro apartments could still be liveable with appropriate design whilst at the same time offering relatively higher affordability. Therefore, the lack of minimum apartment size in the guideline may encourage "flexibility and innovation" by developers to provide apartments which are both affordable and liveable.[62]

Meanwhile, the state government of New South Wales has recently introduced *Apartment Design Guide*, a statutory design guideline for apartment developers. The document specifies key design criteria to ensure new apartments can achieve design principles outlined in the state's State Environmental Planning Policy No 65: Design Quality of Residential Flat Development (SEPP 65). In contrast to the Victorian Government's guideline, however, this document specifies minimum internal areas for the different types of apartments, which are displayed in Table 1.

Apartment Type	Minimum Internal Area (square metres)
Studio	35
One bedroom	50
Two bedroom	70
Three bedroom	90

Table 1. Minimum internal areas of different apartment types in New South Wales under the SEPP 65 Policy[63]

According to Yelland, such restrictions on minimum internal area could immediately increase the price of apartments by up to AUD$150,000,[64] thereby significantly reducing the level of affordability of these dwellings. To ensure a balance of affordability and liveability, further investigation should be conducted to examine the relative impacts of various design attributes and internal area of micro apartments on the liveability of their residents.

Design standards can also be used to address some of the major design issues

61   The State of Victoria Department of Environment, Land, Water & Planning. *Better Apartments Design Standards*. Melbourne: Victorian Government, 2016. Accessed 20 January 2017, https://goo.gl/1YEXKO, 9–40.
62   ABC News, op. cit.
63   NSW Department of Planning and Environment. *Apartment Design Guide: Tools for improving the design of residential apartment development*. Sydney: NSW Department of Planning and Environment, 2015. Accessed 20 January 2017, https://goo.gl/OYnNlc, 89.
64   Smith, Michael. 'Victoria's Push for Better Apartments (Part 2)'. Accessed 20 January 2017, https://goo.gl/T7UME1.

associated with high-rise apartments. For example, as discussed previously, many recently built high-rise apartments are long and narrow in format, leading to severely limited natural lighting and ventilation. In light of this issue, *Better Apartments Design Standards* specifies that every habitable room in an apartment should contain a window with a minimum width of 1.2 metres.

PROMOTION OF SUSTAINABLE APARTMENTS

As discussed previously, high-rise apartments are energy intensive in nature. Thus, in the current context of rising energy prices, living costs and temperature,[65] they are not a sustainable form of dwelling. In this regard, more sustainable apartments should be promoted in future projects. According to a developer, however, there is a "niche market which is prepared to pay for any additional sustainability products beyond minimum [regulatory] requirements."[66] However, for most prospective purchasers, the incorporation of sustainability features generates unwanted additional cost as their principal considerations revolve around the price and location of the apartment.[67] Consequently, most new and proposed apartments in Australia currently lack sustainability features.

Design standards should encourage the use of passive sustainability features, which do not add significant cost to apartment projects, such as thick walls and landscaping elements. Individual meters for all utilities should also be made compulsory to allow apartment occupiers to better track and reduce their energy, water and gas consumption. Furthermore, active sustainability elements such as rainwater tanks and photovoltaic panels, which can offer long-term savings to apartment residents, are potential solutions. These features should gradually be required for future apartment projects as they become more affordable and efficient over time. In addition, public education on the long-term cost benefits of active sustainability features could be initiated to promote awareness and increase the number of potential buyers in the currently niche market for sustainable apartments. Increasing public interest in sustainable apartments can stimulate developers to incorporate additional sustainability features to their projects. Furthermore, when newer technologies such as building-integrated photovoltaic solar windows are more fully developed and affordable, they should be made mandatory for all future apartment projects, particularly high-rise towers that are already predominantly covered by glass curtain walling.

ALTERNATIVE URBAN CONSOLIDATION STRATEGIES

Since 2000, Australian capital cities have adopted urban consolidation policies to increase population density in metropolitan areas and reduce the extent of urban

---

65   Buxton, Goodman and Moloney, op. cit., 2
66   Higgins, op. cit., 44
67   Ibid., 44

sprawl.[68,69] Such a policy context and the cities' continued reliance on a "relatively unregulated market-based provision of housing" have resulted in an urban form largely characterised by high-rise apartments in inner suburbs and poor quality micro apartments.[70] Micro apartments and high-rise apartments can stimulate higher residential density than conventional, low-rise apartments and detached dwellings, thus contributing to urban consolidation. However, apartment living in Australia has historically been a "transitory phase" for many residents prior to moving to a lower-density, larger dwelling, including a house in the suburbs or outside the city as their family size grows.[71] If the proportion of apartments in the supply of new dwellings continues to increase, the availability of other dwelling types may become limited in the future. As apartment residents, the majority of whom are young singles or couples,[72] begin their transition into larger dwellings, there may be limited family-friendly housing options available to them in the future. To investigate this prospect further, future research could examine the degree of transience in the occupation of apartments. Similarly, design solutions could be investigated to promote the adaptability of apartments for family occupation, which could extend the period of occupancy.

Furthermore, since mid-2016, several Australian banks have restricted their lending to foreign home buyers in response to growing concerns about fraud and money laundering from overseas. The restrictions vary between banks and range from reduced maximum loan-to-value ratios to total bans on lending to foreign investors.[73] Given the rapid increase in off-the-plan apartment transactions across the capital cities in recent years, such restrictions could result in foreign buyers defaulting on new apartments due to be completed over the next two years, leaving developers bankrupt.[74] As discussed previously, foreign investors are the principal buyers of high-rise apartments. Therefore, the average length of time a new high-rise apartment remains unsold on the market may increase significantly due to the increased difficulty of obtaining finance for foreign investors.

Thus, even though enforcing better design standards can help improve the liveability of apartments, they are not long-term dwelling choices for many residents and, in the current context, are overly dependent on overseas investment. Given these facts and

---

68   Malenic, Dejan; and Han, Sun Sheng. 'Urban Consolidation in Melbourne: a Case Study of the Monash Employment Cluster'. Paper presented at the State of Australian Cities Conference, Gold Coast, Australia, 9–11 December 2015, https://goo.gl/AGzvdY, 1.

69   'Density, sprawl, growth: how Australian cities have changed in the last 30 years'. The Conversation. Accessed 20 January 2017, https://goo.gl/30EZyF.

70   Buxton, Goodman and Moloney, op. cit., 82

71   Ibid., 61

72   'Dormitory city', The Conversation.

73   Bennet, Micheal; and Murdoch, Scott. 'APRA "spurred lending crackdown"'. *Australian*, 12 July 2017, https://goo.gl/Ze3itD.

74   Uren, David. 'Units boom to trigger defaults and price falls, warns RBA'. *Australian*, 15 October 2016, https://goo.gl/2XdpeJ.

the significant energy costs associated with high-rise apartments, relying primarily on micro apartments and high-rise apartments is not a sustainable, long-term solution for achieving the cities' urban consolidation objectives. High-rise apartments are not necessary to achieve high population density as some of the densest cities with the highest level of amenities predominantly comprise low- and medium-rise settlements.[75] The City of Paris, illustrated in Figure 4, is a prime example of a low-rise, high-quality urban form with more than 20,000 inhabitants per square kilometre, approximately three times the density of Singapore.[76]

Figure 4. Low-rise, high-density urban form in the City of Paris[77]

Therefore, urban consolidation could alternatively be achieved for the Australian capital cities through a mix of different types of dwellings that can respond to the different and ever-changing needs of residents. Further study into an appropriate mix of these dwellings could be initiated to inform strategic plans and land-use regulations for the cities. In addition, more flexible housing arrangements such as share housing could be encouraged and future research could investigate the most appropriate form of dwellings and design strategies for share housing.

75   Buxton, Goodman, and Moloney, op. cit., 73
76   Lennard, Suzanne H. Crowhurst. 'The High-density Liveability Question'. Accessed 10 February 2017, https://goo.gl/SsNHxH.
77   Ibid.

CONCLUSION

Driven by a relatively unregulated market and urban consolidation policies, apartments now play a substantial role in housing the population in Australian capital cities. To make their product more affordable, developers have increasingly been providing micro apartments in the cities in recent years. Meanwhile, the influx of overseas investment has fuelled the extensive development of high-rise apartments in the inner parts of the capital cities. However, a number of recent apartment projects exhibit several design issues related to noise, limited natural lighting and ventilation, and lack of essential amenities. Furthermore, high-rise apartments are associated with social separation, reduced quality of life for surrounding residents and intensive energy needs.

Based on the findings above, this chapter has provided not only the outlook for micro apartments and high-rise apartments but also three key recommendations. These include enforcement of better design standards, promotion of sustainable apartments in future development projects and alternative urban consolidation strategies through flexible housing arrangements and a mix of different dwelling types. Lastly, micro apartments, high-rise apartments and the reliance on apartments for urban consolidation are not exclusive to Australian cities. Thus, the findings in this chapter would be applicable to any city around the world with a similar context.

BIBLIOGRAPHY

ABC News. '"Dog box" apartments targeted in new Victorian design rules'. *ABC News*, 17 December 2016, https://goo.gl/x9rslc.

Australian Bureau of Statistics. '4102.0 – Australian Social Trends, 2006'. Accessed 13 January 2017, https://goo.gl/KSTQQJ.

Australian Bureau of Statistics. 'Census of Population and Housing'. Accessed 15 January 2017, https://goo.gl/1deDN8.

Australian Bureau of Statistics. *2012 Year Book Australia.* Canberra: Australian Bureau of Statistics. Accessed 13 January 2017, https://goo.gl/3UadyC.

Australian Government. *Our Cities: The Challenge of Change.* Canberra: Department of Infrastructure and Regional Development. Accessed 15 January 2017, https://goo.gl/8UfFPy.

Bennet, Michael; and Murdoch, Scott. 'APRA "spurred lending crackdown"'. *Australian*, 12 July 2016. https://goo.gl/Ze3itD.

Birrell, Bob; and McClosekey, David. *The Housing Affordability Crisis in Sydney and Melbourne Report One: The Demographic Foundations.* Sydney: *Sydney Morning Herald.* Accessed 15 January 2017, https://goo.gl/2YtqMu.

Blundell, Lynne. 'Apartment blocks the missing link in sustainability'. Accessed 20 January 2017, https://goo.gl/WvrXlF.

Brook, Benedict. 'Fears moves to set minimum size for apartments could leave city centres only for the rich'. *News*, 27 March 2016. https://goo.gl/BeSorz.

Brown, Jenny. 'Flat out telling a unit from an apartment?' Accessed 15 January 2017, https://goo.gl/rlpnfU.

Buxton, Michael; Goodman, Robin; and Moloney, Susie. *Planning Melbourne*. Melbourne: CSIRO Publishing, 2016.

Chua, Geraldine. 'Survey shows Australian apartment dwellers don't want to live in shoe boxes'. Accessed 17 January 2017, https://goo.gl/GShhkT.

City of Melbourne. *Future Living: A Discussion Paper Identifying Issues and Options for Housing Our Community*. Melbourne: City of Melbourne. Accessed 25 January 2017, https://goo.gl/eCIMYW.

Cox, Wendell; and Pavletich, Hugh. *13th Annual Demographia International Housing Affordability Survey: 2016*. Illinois: Demographia. Accessed 16 February 2017, http://goo.gl/yIW46.

Department of Infrastructure and Regional Development. *The Evolution of Australian Towns*. Canberra: Bureau of Infrastructure, Transport and Regional Economics. Accessed 20 January 2017, https://goo.gl/9hu2Nr.

Department of the Environment, Community and Local Government. *Sustainable Urban Housing: Design Standards for New Apartments Guidelines for Planning Authorities*. Dublin: Department of the Environment, Community and Local Government. Accessed 15 January 2017, https://goo.gl/NKNNrm.

Higgins, David. 'What gives to keep that price point? High-density residential developments'. *Pacific Rim Property Research Journal*, 21 (2015): 37–49. Accessed 20 January 2017. doi:10.1080/14445921.2015.1026133.

Hsieh, Wing; Norman, David; and Orsmond, David. *Supply-Side Issues in the Housing Sector*. Sydney: Reserve Bank of Australia. Accessed 15 January 2017, http://goo.gl/7w0fcY.

Investor Genius. 'Micro-Apartments Are a Growing Trend in Australia. When They Look Like These, It's Not Hard to See Why!' Accessed 20 January 2017, https://goo.gl/Lek74t.

Kulu, Hill. *Fertility Differences by Housing Type: An Effect of Housing Conditions or of Selective Moves?* Rostock: Max Planck Institute for Demographic Research. Accessed 13 January 2017, https://goo.gl/moNyB3.

Lennard, Suzanne H. Crowhurst. 'The High-Density Liveability Question'. Accessed 10 February 2017. https://goo.gl/SsNHxH.

Lucas, Clay. 'High-rise apartments are bad to live in and bad for society, says respected architect'. *The Age*, 29 August 2016. https://goo.gl/L7NTkn.

Malenic, Dejan; and Han, Sun Sheng. 'Urban Consolidation in Melbourne: A Case Study of the Monash Employment Cluster'. Paper presented at the State of Australian Cities Conference, Gold Coast, Australia, 9–11 December 2015, https://goo.gl/AGzvdY, 1.

Marmot, Michael. *Fair Society, Healthy Lives: A Strategic Review of Health Inequalities in England Post 2010*. London: UCL Institute of Health Equity. Accessed 20 January 2018, https://goo.gl/9HcjT.

Martel, Carolyn Whitzman; Fincher, Ruth; Lawther, Peter; Woodcock, Ian; and Tucker, Danita. *Getting to Yes: Overcoming barriers to affordable family friendly housing in inner Melbourne*. Melbourne: The University of Melbourne. Accessed 15 January 2017, https://goo.gl/2P1m2T.

NSW Department of Planning and Environment. *Apartment Design Guide: Tools for improving the design of residential apartment development*. Sydney: NSW Department of

Planning and Environment. Accessed 20 January 2017 https://goo.gl/OYnNlc.

O'Neill, Phillip. *Housing Affordability Literature Review and Affordable Housing Program Audit.* Sydney: University of Western Sydney. Accessed 16 February 2017, https://goo.gl/61ppKR.

Phillips, Ben. *The Great Australian Dream – Just a Dream? AMP.NATSEM Income and Wealth Report.* Canberra: University of Canberra. Accessed 15 January 2017, https://goo.gl/ehwF2B.

Ramirez-Lovering, Diego. *The space of dwelling: an investigation into the potential for spatial flexibility to improve volume housing in Australia.* Melbourne: Monash University. Accessed 20 January 2017, https://goo.gl/ESvawG.

Shoorey, Michael. *The Growth of Apartment Construction in Australia.* Sydney: Reserve Bank of Australia. Accessed 13 January 2017, https://goo.gl/ucGZgo.

Smith, Michael. 'Victoria's Push for Better Apartments (Part 2)'. Accessed 20 January 2017, https://goo.gl/T7UME1.

The Conversation. 'Density, sprawl, growth: how Australian cities have changed in the last 30 years'. Accessed 20 January 2017, https://goo.gl/30EZyF.

The Conversation. 'Dormitory city: Melbourne's brittle highrise apartment boom'. Accessed 20 January 2017, https://goo.gl/WiOBMq.

The State of Victoria Department of Environment, Land, Water & Planning. *Better Apartments Design Standards.* Melbourne: Victorian Government. Accessed 20 January 2017, https://goo.gl/1YEXKO.

Urbis. *Urbis Brisbane Apartment Insights 04 Qtr 2013.* Brisbane: Urbis. Accessed 13 January 2017.

Uren, David. 'Units boom to trigger defaults and price falls, warns RBA'. *Australian*, 15 October 2016. https://goo.gl/2XdpeJ.

Victorian Government. *Residential Tenancies Act 1997.* Melbourne: Victorian Government. Accessed 13 January 2017, https://goo.gl/mexTcK.

Williams, Catharina. *Australia's Commuting Distance: Cities and Regions.* Canberra: Bureau of Infrastructure, Transport and Regional Economics. Accessed 15 January 2017, https://goo.gl/QEADHM.

CHAPTER SIX

FRANCESCO ROSSINI

The Chinese University of Hong Kong, Hong Kong

HOUSING NEEDS AND URBAN REGENERATION: A CHALLENGING TASK FOR THE FUTURE OF HONG KONG

INTRODUCTION

In recent years, Hong Kong has experienced frequent and rapid changes to its urban structure. With several buildings constructed during the 1960s and 1970s, different parts of the city have begun, or are in the process of embarking on, a comprehensive urban renewal strategy to improve the quality of the urban environment. According to the Long-Term Housing Strategy (LTHS), to meet the housing and other development needs of the community, the government must adopt a series of policies to increase land supply in the short, medium and long term. Short-term measures focus on optimising the use of developed land as far as is practicable, including the developed districts in existing urban areas and new towns.

In Hong Kong, one of the most densely populated areas on the planet, the pressure for land has reached extremes conditions. The cityscape is characterised by a massive concentration of residential towers; indeed, if we consider all buildings taller than 100 metres, Hong Kong has more skyscrapers than New York. Despite the vast sea of high-rise buildings, figures report that Hong Kong residents live in apartments averaging approximately 45 square metres, half the size of a typical apartment in Japan and almost 60 per cent smaller than an apartment in France. In fact, the built-up areas account for only 24 per cent of the territory while the remaining areas comprise an impressive mix of tropical landscape, natural reserves, mountains, islands and country parks. This contrast between artifice and nature is tangible in many areas of the city and the interconnection between the urban fabric and the landscape creates a distinct feature of Hong Kong.

The aspects that have led to the city's evolution can be understood by analysing the different events that have transformed its structure, as we will see later. As mentioned above, the city has developed a vertical model of mixed-use functions, concentrated in towers that are interconnected by different modes of public transport. These combine two compatible yet seemingly opposed systems; that of integration and segregation.[1]

Figure 1. The cityscape of Hong Kong. Image: Francesco Rossini

---

1   Lau and Coorey, 'Hong Kong: MILU and How It Is Perceived'.

According to the long-term land planning report 'Hong Kong 2030+: Towards a Planning Vision and Strategy Transcending 2030' issued by the government, Hong Kong will need one-million flats to be built by 2046 to accommodate household growth and families displaced by redevelopment projects.[2] The social demand for decent housing represents a great challenge for the future of Hong Kong, however; the government has to step up urban regeneration efforts and policies to rejuvenate the extensive old urban fabric, promoting housing programmes with the aim of reducing social inequality.

In addition, another important factor in the renewal of old urban areas is to control and preserve the public character of the new developments. One of the stated missions of the Hong Kong government and public institutions is that of serving the public interest, but strong pressure from the private sector often directly influences the decision-making processes that affect the urban regeneration of the city. Indeed, Hong Kong represents a phenomenologically unique three-dimensional model of high density, where the high cost of land has driven profitable business for the private sector.[3] This chapter will provide an overview of the relationship between housing provision and urban regeneration in Hong Kong by exploring the changes in the urban structure of the old areas of the city.

VERTICAL DENSITY

With a population of seven-million people packed into an urbanised area of 273 square km, Hong Kong is among the most densely populated cities in the world.[4] The concentration of uses, the density of the population, the complexity of the urban form and the verticality are all urban qualities that define the character of the city.[5]

In Hong Kong, the lack of available land for development is what has created the intensity of use, and the vertical layering of different functions leads to the creation of overlapping flows of movement, generating several unconventional urban spaces. This vertical density provides an efficient solution to meet the demand for rapid urbanisation, allowing vast numbers of people to inhabit a small portion of territory. The main transformations that have interested the urban structure of Hong Kong in the last two decades are the new developments created around the public transport network, essentially the Mass Transit Railway (MTR), which is the most popular transport option in Hong Kong; and the urban regeneration of old areas to meet current and future housing needs.

2 Government of Hong Kong (GovHK), 'Hong Kong 2030+: Towards a Planning Vision and Strategy Transcending 2030'.
3 Rossini, 'Nuevos Espacios Colectivos de La Ciudad Vertical Contemporánea: El Caso de Hong Kong', 3.
4 Government of Hong Kong (GovHK), 'Hong Kong: The Facts'.
5 Shelton, Karakiewicz and Kvan, The Making of Hong Kong, 5.

Land administration in Hong Kong plays a key role in the city's economy, and government revenues largely depend on the transfer of land-use rights. At the same time, the Hong Kong government has adopted a high land-price policy, resulting in the highest urban densities on earth.[6]

Although in theory it is the government who controls the land, in practice the private sector has free reign in land development through leasehold agreements. The link between development capital and the planning function has played a fundamental role in the physical and economic growth of the territory. The city's characteristic vertical density has even been documented in the impressive works of the German photographer Michael Wolf. The reportage, entitled 'Architecture of Density', shows the obsessive repetition of the residential blocks that shape large swaths of the territory of Hong Kong. Wolf's images of density bring to life the statistics, which reveal an average density of 6,690 people per square km and a peak density in Kwun Tong district of 57,250 people per square km.[7]

THE EVOLUTION TOWARDS VERTICAL GROWTH

This unique cityscape of Hong Kong is the result of the volumetric expansion of the city over the last forty years (Figure 1). The tragic fire that broke out in the Shek Kip Mei squatter settlement on Christmas Day, 1953, established an important point in the evolution of the city. After the fire, governor Alexander Grantham launched a public housing program introducing a new Building Ordinance that replaced the previous one, which dated back to 1935. The new Ordinance changed the height limit of residential buildings, allowing for a more intensive use of the land. As a consequence, a massive housing plan with multi-storey buildings was launched, which also led to greater participation of the private sector in housing development. In this sense, it can be argued that the new ordinance of 1955 was, for Hong Kong, the beginning of the era of high-rise buildings.

During this transformation, old buildings were redeveloped into modern commercial complexes and the regeneration process often erased important features of the city's history. In March 2009, the Antiquities Advisory Board (AAB) announced the results of their assessment of 1,444 historic buildings and, to date, eighty-five more historic buildings have been added and accorded Grade 1, Grade 2 or Grade 3 status. Of the 1,444 buildings assessed, only 114 were declared monuments and highlighted for preservation.[8] The government could thus demolish the remaining buildings, those without a preservation order, despite the fact that they had been awarded the status of Grade 1 Historical Buildings.

Due to the intense pressure for urban redevelopment, the demolition of old buildings makes it possible to change the urban morphology of the city substantially. Clusters

6   Cuthbert, 'The Right to the City', 298.
7   Government of Hong Kong (GovHK), 'Hong Kong: The Facts'.
8   Antiquities and Monuments Office, 'Assessment of 1,444 Historic Buildings'.

of residential and office towers over 40 storeys tall (and typically above a commercial podium) frequently replace dilapidated settlements. At the same time, an integrative development approach has been gaining popularity and the vertical system has become more synergistic.[9]

These changes in the urban structure have transformed the symbiotic relationship between buildings and streets, which, until the post-World War II period, were characterised primarily by the shop-tenement house. Unfortunately, at present only a few reminders of this type of structure remain in the centre of Hong Kong. This typical Chinese architecture was thought out to offer a variety of services creating intense street activity.[10] Over the years, the typology of podium and towers has evolved to swelling dimensions, ultimately losing its urban scale. Mega-buildings with accompanying infrastructure have cropped up to form self-sufficient urban islands generally indifferent to the context.

According to Tieben,[11] it is remarkable that the strong typological changes in the 1970s and '80s, from shop-tenement houses to residential towers, did not impact the public–private interface. More substantial changes were felt only with large-scale urban renewal projects, first carried out by the Land Development Corporation in the 1990s and then by the Urban Renewal Authority (URA) after its establishment in 2001. Urban renewal was not satisfactory in the early years prior to the establishment of the Land Development Corporation (LDC); however, compared to LDC, which was focused mainly on redevelopment, the role of the URA has been expanded to include rehabilitation and preservation.

URBAN REDEVELOPMENT IN HONG KONG

The comprehensive strategic study 'Hong Kong 2030+: Towards a Planning Vision and Strategy Transcending 2030' dedicated a section to the rejuvenation of dilapidated urban areas, addressing key actions to facilitate redevelopment, rehabilitation, revitalisation and preservation initiatives while respecting the unique characteristics of individual neighbourhoods.[12]

This aspect represents a central objective to address and reinforce the urban renewal policy of the Hong Kong government. In the period prior to World War II, urban renewal was primarily focused on improving hygienic and safety conditions in overcrowded urban settlements. Later, during the post-war period and prior to the establishment of the LDC, urban renewal was primarily left up to the private sector. The basic working model of the LCD was the public–private partnership (PPP), set up in 1984, which

9   Lau and Zhang, 'Genesis of a Vertical City in Hong Kong'.
10   Shelton, Karakiewicz and Kvan, The Making of Hong Kong, 55.
11   Tieben, 'Public/Private Interfaces in Hong Kong: Observations in the Sai Ying Pun District', 37.
12   Government of Hong Kong (GovHK), 'Hong Kong 2030+: Towards a Planning Vision and Strategy Transcending 2030', 33.

aimed to realise urban redevelopment through joint ventures with private developers.[13] The overarching policy of this PPP was that urban renewal was to focus on a "people-centred approach", although the contents of the strategy show that it was, on the contrary, a "project-centred" approach (Figure 2).

Nowadays in many areas, such as in Sham Shui Po, in northern Kowloon, old constructions are being demolished to make space for new residential towers, which are transforming the urban structure of the district. In the last two decades, housing prices have more than quadrupled, making Hong Kong the world's least-affordable major city in which to buy a home. According to Mee Kam Ng,[14] many of the projects carried out by LDC have changed the socio-economic conditions of the areas affected by the urban renewal process. Many shops and small activities that gave character to the old urban districts were forced to close because compensation was insufficient to continue business in the same place. In most cases, tenants in old buildings are reluctant to move out of their district due to the difficulty of finding a job in the new towns, in addition to the transportation costs incurred to travel to the city.

This gentrification process is one of the consequences of the transformation: in many areas of the city, the urban renewal process is slowly changing the social composition and the economic conditions of the neighbourhoods. Traditional stores and other businesses are disappearing due to pressure brought on by the new development, effectively forcing lower-income families to relocate.

Figure 2. The urban renewal process in the Central district. Photo: Francesco Rossini

---

13   Law et al., 'The Achievements and Challenges of Urban Renewal in Hong Kong', 7.

14   Ng, 'Property-Led Urban Renewal in Hong Kong', 142.

The households displaced by the redevelopment of old buildings surely encounter greater hardships in adapting to a new environment. As such, they will be more likely to exhibit dissatisfaction, especially if the relocation is a forced one.[15] To counter the problems of land scarcity, the URA was established under the Urban Renewal Authority Ordinance (URAO) in May 2001 to replace the LDC as the statutory body designed to undertake, encourage, promote and facilitate the regeneration of the older urban areas of Hong Kong. Of great importance is the fact that the URA is charged with carrying out urban renewal in locations that the private sector finds unprofitable, in essence adopting a "people first, district-based and public participatory" approach to urban renewal. However, as Yeung Wing-chi noted in a *Hong Kong Economic Journal* article, their adherence to these tenets has drawn strong criticism from the public.[16]

While Hong Kong is facing the problematic redevelopment of old districts, the URA has been criticised for placing financial interests above the needs of communities. As a statutory body, and thus separate from private developers, the URA has the responsibility to preserve the characteristics of local culture as far as is practicable. This aspect seems to be the most hotly debated because it is nearly inevitable that the transformation process of urban renewal will affect the traditional flavour of a given area. One possible solution to mitigate this effect could be for the URA to identify local characteristics and evaluate those that should be retained, engaging residents early in the regeneration process. This would help avoid costly confrontations and delays, and ensure that the benefits of the regeneration process meet local aspirations and needs.

WAN CHAI DISTRICT

Wan Chai is one of the earliest settlements in Hong Kong, with a rich cultural heritage and traditions. According to Building Department statistics, it falls in the top-five districts with the oldest urban structures, containing 490 buildings that are fifty years old or more. Wan Chai can be considered an extension of the CBD of Hong Kong and over the years it has been transformed from a residential area to a major centre of a wide array of activities, playing a central role in the economy and the social life of the city. Surprisingly, the data from the Census and Statistics Department of Hong Kong show that despite a density of 15,477 people per square km, Wan Chai is not among the densest sectors of the urban area. The district has been identified by the URA as one of the nine target areas where there is an urgent need to improve the conditions of the urban structure by removing dilapidated buildings and preserving buildings of heritage value.

One project aroused much controversy due to opposition from local businesses and residents. This was the redevelopment project of Lee Tung Street, which began in 2007. The project, carried out by the Urban Renewal Authority, completely changed

---

15 Li and Song, 'Redevelopment, Displacement, Housing Conditions, and Residential Satisfaction'.

16 Yeung, 'Why the URA Should Dissolve Itself Now'.

the old character of this part of Wan Chai, also known as 'Wedding Card Street'. The area affected by the project measures 8,236 square metres, with a total of 52 buildings demolished. This old settlement was replaced by a complex of three residential towers of 39 floors above a commercial street made up of a series of low-rise buildings. The idea behind the plan was to recreate the façade and the atmosphere of the old tenements. However, on the whole it has been considered a complete failure. Not a trace remains of the character of old Wan Chai, which was well-known for its concentration of small businesses involved in the printing of traditional Chinese wedding invitation cards. The soaring rent prices, accessible only to luxury brands and corporate businesses, has effectively driven out the old stores originally located on Lee Tung Street. Following the completion of the project, the total floor area more than doubled to 77,348 square metres, increasing the plot ratio from 4.5 to 9.4.

As an additional effort to promote and conserve the traditional character of heritage buildings, the Development Bureau established the Old Wan Chai Revitalization Initiatives Special Committee (OWRISC). The OWRISC comprises Wan Chai District Council members, professionals and historians, and the Urban Renewal Authority acts as the secretariat. In recent years, OWRISC has implemented and initiated various urban renewal projects, the most relevant of which include Tai Yuen Street, Wan Chai Heritage Trail and the revitalisation of the Star Street District.

THE URBAN REGENERATION OF STAR STREET

The Star Street project began under the OWRI, a private–public partnership between Swire Properties and the Hong Kong government that was carried out between March 2009 and November 2012. The partnership proposed to rejuvenate the southwest end of Wan Chai, also known as 'Old Wan Chai', and add value to its historical and cultural heritage. As of April 2013, Swire properties stated on its website that the aim of the project was to generate a more modern and accessible environment that, in principle, would address the needs of the community whilst preserving the district's cultural legacy.

The development of Star Street started out in the late 1980s, shortly following the Sino-British Joint Declaration that established the return of the former British colony under the umbrella of the People's Republic of China. Despite uncertainties about Hong Kong's future, Swire properties bid in government land auctions – a strategic site in the Admiralty – in order to garner building rights to develop the exclusive Pacific Place project, a mixed-use commercial complex with offices and hotels.

The project was carried out in three phases: the first in 1988, the second in 1991 and the third in 2004. The operation was quite ambitious given that the developer's goal was to extend the atmosphere of the central financial district eastward, in an attempt to increase the commercial value of the area (Figure 3). The third phase, Three Pacific Place, was just at the edge of an old area of Wan Chai district. The area was developed in the 1900s and although none of the original terraced Edwardian-style buildings survive, the street layout does maintain the traditional Hong Kong urban planning characteristic.

Figure 3. Buildings in Star Street Precinct. Photo: Francesco Rossini

From the perspective of the developer, the site was just a clutter of dilapidated tenements and steep, narrow lanes, which negatively impacted the commercial value of the recently built properties. The main objective of this development was essentially to transform this old, slowly declining area into a stylish district with restaurants, cafes, shops and galleries. However, it is important to note that the land was not even up for sale. The thinly veiled intent of gentrifying the neighbourhood was, from the get-go, the primary goal that was being pursued.

As clearly explained in an article that appeared in the first issue of *Swire News* published in 2009, at that time the LDC was given powers of compulsory acquisition, but Swire decided to initiate negotiations with the owners on a free-market basis.[17] Under the name Alpha, a new company not associated with Swire and created in order to keep the purchases low-key and reduce costs, the developer forged ahead to acquire all 354 properties within the area. This process took almost ten years, and thereafter two residential towers – StarCrest 1 and 2 – were built, followed by the Pacific Place office complex, completed in 1999 and in 2004 respectively.

Figure 4. Dominion Square designed by the Oval Partnership in Star Street Precinct. Photo: Francesco Rossini

At first glance, the StarCrest complex appears to be a typical residential tower development; however, a quite unique product in terms of internal space was ultimately created. The intention was to increase the average size of the apartments to provide more comfortable living conditions for residents. Interestingly enough, by the time the apartments were ready for sale at the price of HK$7,000 per sq. ft, this was almost

17   Swire Properties Limited, 'Wan Chai: Evolution of a District'.

HK$3,000 above the average price per sq. ft in the area. Today, 15 years later, the same apartment can be sold for HK$30,000 per sq. ft.[18] Furthermore, a 280-metre underpass was built to connect the area to the Admiralty MTR station. The final step of this process was the renovation of the old buildings and the surrounding lanes of Star Street. This district was one of the oldest settlements in Hong Kong under a 999-year unrestricted lease.

In the early days of the colony, leases were signed for terms of 75, 99 or 999 years, subsequently standardised in the urban areas of Hong Kong Island and Kowloon to a term of 75 years with the right to renew for an additional 75 years, or 50 years up to 30 June 2047.[19] So as not to lose the advantages of this tenure, Swire worked with the government to maintain the structure of existing street patterns, which meant that the leases did not have to be surrendered and reissued. The project, completed in 2012, was carried out by the international architecture firm the Oval Partnership and focused mainly on the revitalisation of public spaces (Figure 4).

A public consultation was initiated during the renovation process and citizens were invited to share their views and comments. This engagement helped to better understand the needs and wishes of the local community and the general public in shaping the design development of the project. As one might expect, the impact of renewal significantly changed the socio-economic profile as well as the physical layout of the area. The developer, under a PPP with the government, achieved the ambitious goal of elevating property values, gentrifying the neighbourhood and transforming a working-class residential enclave into a completely new district with a glamorous ambience.

CONCLUSION

Hong Kong is facing a serious problem of aging buildings and, given the extreme pressure for land in the city, it is necessary to formulate an urban renewal strategy that is able to protect the public interest whilst improving the overall living environment. One of the objectives described in 'Hong Kong 2030+' – to implement preservation initiatives while at the same time respecting neighbourhood characteristics – has not been reflected by the recent history of the urban renewal of Hong Kong. Furthermore, the document doesn't explain how this objective could be realistically achieved.

The idea of preservation of neighbourhood atmosphere was one of the key points of the URA. As highlighted by Elaine Yau in a *South China Morning Post* article, this organisation has often been criticised for putting financial interests first and ignoring the needs of low-income residents living in the area.[20] According to Law and colleagues, it is necessary that the role of the URA in redevelopment, rehabilitation and preservation be reviewed and

---

18   Ibid.
19   Choi, 'ISE07/16-17'.
20   Yau, 'Residents Fight Back against Hong Kong's Urban Renewal Projects'.

that any changes be clearly in the Urban Renewal Strategy.[21] This strategy is a complex subject because there are countless factors to be taken into consideration in terms of a comprehensive review of the existing policies. These include the legislation related to land and buildings, the coordination between different government departments, and other related issues including compensation policy, community engagement, gentrification and the conflict between private and public interests.

The pressure on space and high real-estate prices, especially in central areas, affects all aspects of urban life. Urban regeneration projects are increasingly adding ever-higher buildings, which as a result compound the population density in these areas. The city's vertical approach to property development, and consequently a rise in the number of people per square mile, as well as the urban redevelopment of Lee Tung Street, has doubled the total floor area of existing buildings. This may produce unwanted effects such as increasing street-level congestion and overcrowding public transport systems as well as other public facilities. In old areas, this situation is exacerbated by the low provision of public open space and the consistently excessive height and width of buildings, designed to take up every square foot of available land in order to maximise economic returns.[22] In addition to concerns regarding the quality of urban spaces, shop owners who used to operate on Lee Tung Street have blasted the URA for not making any effort to preserve the atmosphere of the street. The promise to reintegrate the existing shops through preferential rents has failed and most of the spaces have been taken by luxury brands, pushing small businesses out.

Again, one of the stated approaches of the URA is to put people first; however, they should clarify who exactly these beneficiaries are. Under the current redevelopment modus operandi, the majority of residents living in dilapidated buildings are not able to enjoy the improved environment of the redeveloped site due to gentrification.[23] On the other hand, although the regeneration of Star Street is not a URA project, it is helpful to understand the government approach to the preservation of the old districts of Hong Kong. To realise the transformation of the area, the developer had to persuade all the owners to sell their property.[24] Thus, the district was totally stripped of its contents or, rather, the contents were substituted with something more akin to the idea of creating a new, trendy atmosphere in hopes of increasing the commercial value of the area.

Under a 999-year unrestricted lease, Star Street was one of the oldest settlements in Hong Kong. The area has been completely renewed, while simultaneously retaining this privileged lease from the early days of the colonial period. Substantial changes of the buildings and urban structure would necessarily lead a renegotiation of the contract between the developer and the government. As a result, the area has preserved almost the same physical aspect but with new uses.

---

21   Law et al., 'The Achievements and Challenges of Urban Renewal in Hong Kong'.
22   Kilburn and Loh, 'The Costs and Benefits of High-Density Urban Living', 30.
23   Law et al., 'The Achievements and Challenges of Urban Renewal in Hong Kong'.
24   Swire Properties Limited, 'Wan Chai: Evolution of a District'.

At first sight the result is pleasant – good quality public spaces, distinctive urban furniture, charming cafés, design shops and stylish restaurants – but sadly, no trace is left of the local atmosphere. To reiterate, the concern is not about the results of redevelopment, but rather about the scope and the power given to the private sector in guiding the development of the city. In accordance with the Long-Term Housing Strategy (LTHS), Hong Kong has been suffering an imbalance in supply and demand for both public and private housing. The property market has been rising above what many citizens can afford.

The Census and Statistics Department expects that Hong Kong's population will soar to 8.22 million in 2043. This new estimated population is catalysing policy initiatives to increase housing and land supply, in accordance with the framework established under the Long-Term Housing Strategy. The government is adopting an incremental approach to expand the capacity of new existing towns that already have links with the transport system and offer other essential public facilities and infrastructure. This is needed, seeing that in addition to future previsions of housing demand there will also be relocation of households displaced by the redevelopment of old buildings in both the public and the private sectors. Urban renewal and housing supply are two significant aspects that are transforming the structure of the densely developed urban areas. Analysing these case studies, it is clear how government policy is causing gentrification and intensification of old areas, while simultaneously pushing for the creation of new towns to accommodate future population growth and displacement.

As we have seen, the urban renewal process in Hong Kong is quite controversial, and considerable economic interests are exerting pressure on the development of these urban spaces. It is in the public's best interest that the URA lead a more sustainable Urban Renewal Strategy in order to safeguard the greater good. The case of Star Street, Lee Tung Street and, more generally, all LDC and URA redevelopment projects that have been carried out over recent years should serve to encourage comprehensive reflection on the future of urban renewal in Hong Kong.

BIBLIOGRAPHY

Antiquities and Monuments Office. 'Assessment of 1,444 Historic Buildings'. Antiquities and Monuments office Leisure and Cultural Services Department, June 2017. http://www.amo.gov.hk/en/built2.php#.

Choi, Angela. 'Land Tenure System in Hong Kong'. Legislative Council of the Hong Kong Special Administrative Region of the Peoplee2017. http://www.amo.8 December 2016. https://www.legco.gov.hk/research-publications/english/essentials-1617ise07-land-tenure-system-in-hong-kong.htm.

Cuthbert, Ai. 'The Right to the City'. Cities, 12(5) (October 1995)· 293yv.hk/research-publications/english2751(95)00073-U.

Government of Hong Kong (GovHK). 'Hong Kong 2030+: Towards a Planning Vision and Strategy Transcending 2030'. Hong Kong: Development Bureau and Planning Department, October 2016. http://www.hk2030plus.hk/document/2030+Booklet_Eng.pdf.

_____. 'Hong Kong: The Facts'. Information Services Department, Hong Kong Special Administrative Region Government, April 2015. https://www.gov.hk/en/about/abouthk/factsheets/docs/population.pdf.

Kilburn, Mike; and Loh, Christine K.W. 'The Costs and Benefits of High-Density Urban Living'. Hong Kong: LSE Cities, 2011. https://lsecities.net/media/objects/articles/the-costs-and-benefits-of-high-density-urban-living/en-gb/.

Lau, Stephen S.Y.; and Coorey, S.B.A. 'Hong Kong: MILU and How It Is Perceived'. In *MILU: Multifunctional Intensive Land Useecities.net/media/objects/articles/the-costs-and-benefits-of-high-density-urban-I*, edited by Huibert A. Haccoive Land UDeelstra, Arun Jain, Volkmar Pamer, Karolina Krosnicka and Rob de Waard. Gouda: The Habiforum Foundation, 2007.

Lau, Stephen S.Y.; and Zhang, Qianning. 'Genesis of a Vertical City in Hong Kong'. *International Journal of High-Rise Buildings*, 4(2) (June 2015): 117rnal

Law, C.K.; Chui, Ernest W.T.; Wong, Y.C.; Lee, K.M.; and Ho, L.S. 'The Achievements and Challenges of Urban Renewal in Hong Kong'. Hong Kong: University of Hong Kong, March 2010.http://www.ursreview.gov.hk/eng/doc/Achievements%20n%20challenges%20in%20UR%20Final%20report%20100505.pdf.

Li, Si-Ming; and Song, Yu-Ling. 'Redevelopment, Displacement, Housing Conditions, and Residential Satisfaction: A Study of Shanghai'. *Environment and Planning A*, 41(5) (May 2009): 1,090ay,108. https://doi.org/10.1068/a4168.

Ng, Mee Kam. 'Property-Led Urban Renewal in Hong Kong: Any Place for the Community?' *Sustainable Development*, 10(3) (August 2002): 140–6. https://doi.org/10.1002/sd.189.

Rossini, Francesco. 'Nuevos Espacios Colectivos de La Ciudad Vertical Contemporential Satisfaction: A Stu'. Departament ds Colectivos de La Ciudad Vertical Contemporential Satisfaction: A Study of Shanghai505.pdf.density-urban-living/en-gb/.factsheets/docs.

Shelton, Barry; Karakiewicz, Juatyna; and Kvan, Thomas. *The Making of Hong Kong: From Vertical to Volumetric*. London: Routledge, 2010.

Swire Properties Limited. 'Wan Chai: Evolution of a District'. Cornerstone, April 2013. http://www.swireproperties.com/cornerstone/past_issues/20130304/en/spotlight.html.

Tieben, Hendrik. 'Public/Private Interfaces in Hong Kong: Observations in the Sai Ying Pun District'. In: *Intensities in Ten Cities =: Paralleltitelservations in the Serstone/past_issues*, edited by Darko Radovis =: Paralleltitelservations in the Serstone/past_issues/20130.

Yau, Elaine. 'Residents Fight Back against Hong Kongitelservatinewal Projects'. *South China Morning Post*. 11 April 2014. http://www.scmp.com/lifestyle/family-education/article/1473931/residents-fight-back-against-hong-kongs-urban-renewal.

Yeung, Wing-chi. 'Why the URA Should Dissolve Itself Now'. ejinsight, 21 April 2015. http://www.ejinsight.com/20140421-why-the-ura-should-dissolve-itself-now/.

PART TWO

CHAPTER SEVEN

KIRSTEN DAY

Department of Architectural and Industrial Design,
Swinburne University of Technology

CREATING ENDURING FUTURE HABITATS: LEARNING RESPONSES

INTRODUCTION

The theme is 'Future Habitat', which challenges students to examine the possibilities for interior architecture in 2030 and beyond, contesting 'business as usual' assumptions, and asks them to consider the implications of change (technological, societal, political, environmental) and to reconsider the role of spatial design in the twenty-first century.

These students are participating in Stream 1 (honours year) of Interior Architecture at Swinburne University of Technology, Melbourne, with a program intended to tailor their individual design and research brief, which is themed broadly around the focus on future habitation, leading to the production of a design response. Their work over two semesters brings together many skills developed over previous years of creative research and investigation.

This theme links conceptually to investigations on Future Housing – building on the 2016 theme and international conference 'Future Housing: Global Cities and Regional Problems', which was held at Swinburne, hosted by the Department of Interior Architecture and Industrial Design with Architecture_Media_Politics_Society.

The challenge is to take predictive assumptions about life in the near future – which will be the mid-career of these students – and to contemplate what the consequences of change might be in terms of technology, data, limits to growth, ageing population and the densification of our cities. How will we sleep, eat, learn, work and relax? What type of spaces will we create? And how does this compare to what we might need and what we desire? What are our motives for innovation?

WHO DESIGNS THE FUTURE? THE ROLE OF INTERIOR ARCHITECTS

Although it is difficult to make accurate predictions about the future and the subsequent impact on design, students must explicitly understand not only the impact of change in terms of technology and the production of buildings, but fundamental issues such as climate change, resource overreach and the implications of 'building as commodity' – what is the balance between imagination and the reality of architecture as capital?[1] How does a change in global materials demand require us to reconsider the way we build and the lifecycles that we financially factor for? What are the implications of automation? The world of architecture and its associated professions is not fixed – we need to acknowledge the complex web in which we operate.

The realities of the twenty-first century have obliged the global community with a number of unprecedented opportunities and challenges. There are the overwhelming issues of global warming, increased world population, the reduction of agricultural land (leading to less land to grow food on) and the increasing urban population and its demand for places for people to live. What has been interesting in the students' responses to these scenarios are the number of projects that chose to address what it is to be human in the twenty-first century. These projects highlight tensions between global and local, social-cultural interactions, and notions of ideological and analytical expressions of culture.

The work published below is the product of students' 2016 and 2017 studies on these issues as part of their Capstone Year of study. Interestingly, the main area of concern for students was the response to community – the question of how to be human in a changing urban environment.

NGUYEN THIEN THUAT HOUSING: LOC TRAN

The increasing population in Ho Chi Minh City (HCMC)[2] includes many rural people seeking the opportunities of urban life, due to to socio economic disparities between the city and its periphery.[3] The pressure on urban space, the developing middle class in Vietnam and the processes of gentrification are points of contention.

As part of the gentrification process there is wholesale adoption of a universal 'Western standard/style' of development, which does not accommodate the particular and unique characteristics of Vietnamese cultural identity and community. Design propositions for city housing generally do not cater to the needs of resettled rural immigrants who moved to share in the increased availability of jobs, education and lifestyle that a city offers.

---

1   Tafuri, *Architecture and Utopia*, 170–1.

2   Previously Saigon

3   Guby and Le, 'Niveau de vie et déplacements dans les métropoles vietnamiennes : Hô Chi Minh ville et Hanoi'.

Figure 1. Loc Tran

This project examined how people use space – both formally and informally – and the provisions that can be included to facilitate this in the design proposition, within an understanding of the traditional values and human needs of the people for whom the development is intended. Renovating high-density apartments from the 1970s in the Nguyen Thien Thuat housing area of District 3 in HCMC (locally called *chung cu*), the project proposes a new housing model that allows for flexibility (and informal construction).

Most large tracts of this style of housing in HCMC are, or were, owned by the government. Due to a lack of funds, the buildings have not been maintained, resulting in a downgrading of facilities and neglect of basic services. The focus of the design was to improve community facilities and spaces allowing for social interaction while creating an improved and desirable place to live from dated infrastructure.

Included in the design are the renovation of a typical existing apartment block, the inclusion of community facilities (including healthcare, children's centre and community function spaces) and a museum.

TAN DINH MARKET (HCMC): THI VO

Figure 2. Tan Dinh Market – Thi Vo

This project was for the renovation of the existing *Tan Dinh* Market in District 1, HCMC, which is over 100 years old and is considered to be an authentic Vietnamese market. The design focused on function – improving the existing facilities with regard to sanitation, security, health and safety, and the buying and selling of produce whilst retaining the social and cultural aspects of the market.

This project examined how local and traditional characteristics of a traditional market can compete with the Western-style supermarkets that are becoming more popular in Vietnam. The research underpinning this project explored how people use the market and considered how to devise strategies to retain functions with authenticity – avoiding pressure to create a theme park or tourist attraction. The driving program is centred on a retention of local cultural values as they are represented in the built form. So how does the design proposal do this? The emphasis is on the collection and sales of food along with the socialisation that accompanies that practice in a market – but with increased attention to issues of sanitation, security, and health and safety.

The strategy is to add value to the market within an understanding of how the market came about and its history, taking into account how it is currently used, and improving the spatial qualities and wayfinding, to attract a younger generation as a contemporary shopping destination. Ultimately, the proposal aims to preserve an authentic essence of the traditional Vietnamese market. Part of the exercise is to encourage interaction, not only as a place to buy and sell, but also as a place for the production of food and an oasis for urban farming, all located in the centre of a city of around nine-million people.

SIRIUS: STEPHANIE VEAR

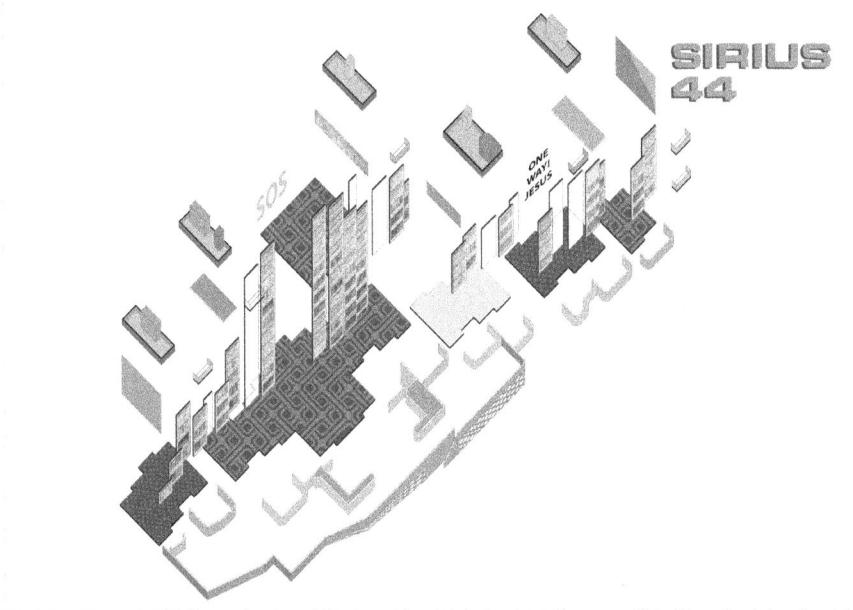

Figure 3. Axonometric of Sirius project – Steph Vear

This capstone project is focused on a green refurbishment of the Sirius building (Sydney), which is under threat as the NSW state government has decided to sell the valuable land as a site for commercial development. The original Sirius building was designed by Theo Gofers and built in 1979 after plans to redevelop The Rocks in 1960, which included the relocation of social-housing residents to other suburbs. At that time, and in response to community opposition, building unions banned works until all tenants were rehoused and those who wanted to stay were consulted so their requirements could be incorporated into Sirius. Unfortunately, the future of the building is unclear, with fears it may be sold and demolished after it was rejected from heritage listing. That matter is still to be resolved, but the building is important not so much for its Brutalist 1970s architecture as for its position as a lighthouse for social justice in central Sydney, which offered low-cost, rental housing to those in need.

This project was born out of a desire to maintain that inclusive society as well as make the most of existing building stock, and to preserve its cultural identity for 2030 and beyond. Stephanie took the political stance that government is setting a dangerous precedent: if it allows the demolition of valuable community assets to encourage commercial profiteering, the culture of our cities and of our country will be lost. She argues that "Love or hate Brutalist architecture, heritage is about much more than form and aesthetics."

The Sirius building is representative of what a community is capable of; its significance is embodied in its people and the reasoning behind its construction in the first place, so that it provides a safe central housing choice that is not for the wealthy alone. The goals for this project were to save the Sirius building, to provide housing for as much of the existing community as economically possible, and to encourage the community back to the area in order to reinstate the community facilities of the original design and to recreate the lively places that have been depicted in residents' stories of the building.

THEORY OF THE SMALL WORLD: YEN SHIN CHONG, HAWTHORN

Figure 4. Hawthorn Community Library – Yen Shin Chong

Believing that there is a story that lies behind every building, this project used Small World Theory (SWT) – sometimes referred to as 'six degrees of separation' – as design research to theoretically support the design, with the intention to mitigate the impact of the Internet on people's everyday life.

This project proposes that people share more hidden connections than they actually see, given the context of increasing population growth. SWT states that everyone can be connected to a friendship chain that creates a smaller world. Unfortunately, a real-world issue is discovered based on the findings of Small World Theory. Due to the advancement of technology, Internet and telecommunication applications are developed specifically to enhance social communication and interaction.

The initial intention is to improve people social skills and build relationships. However, the overuse of these applications tends to put people in a virtual world via compact social devices that discourage face-to-face interaction. It seems that online culture separates people. The impact on the social network will be a major concern in the future if no intervention measures are taken. Thus, the theory has to be revised and inculcated to prevent this from happening. 'Hawthorn Community Library' will be the first step to reflect SWT via the means of spatial design. This project has the potential of dissolving the distant connection between people through fostering community engagement and sustainable knowledge sharing.

Functionally, the Library accommodates different type of spaces, which include individual spaces, interactive spaces, shared spaces and digitised spaces. The majority of the spaces are designed as the communal space, yet they can be used by individuals who intend to pursue their own activities. The congregation of individual spaces is a formal representation of a sense of community and togetherness.

CONCLUSION

Cities worldwide are being subjected to overwhelming issues of the effects of global warming, increased world population and density pressures, the reduction of agricultural land to house people (leading to less land to grow food on), an increasing urban and ageing population, and the byproducts of growth – disposal of waste, a rising economic and environmental cost of energy and density that effects human health.

Designers must solve issues of innovative appropriateness of construction for this new world taking into account new issues of the appropriate materials, methods and construction, but also respecting past values, traditions and human values.

To achieve that analysis, there is a need to recognise the building as part of a network – it is the reality of that local and global interconnectivity that requires understanding, rather than considering a building simply in its place as an isolated object in the cityscape or landscape. We will need to work with an understanding that innovation should be targeted at visionary scenarios by adopting alternative futures, rather than accepting a 'business as usual' situation. Buildings, and in particular housing, need to be understood as part of a network – requiring analogical information and inventive thinking.

If architecture is accepted as being a commodity, to be traded rather than contribute to a better natural, physical and human environment, the result will produce a world of gentrification (profiting those who promote development) but at a cost to the community as a whole. An interior architect compliments the work of an architect in this exercise, showing how recycling interiors to a new purpose respects societal values and provides a better place to live.

The answers suggested by the projects shown here show a sensitivity to progress and the future that aligns with community needs and respects shared values. By retrofitting old housing stock of the city and revitalising working markets, and by adopting a gentle scale to change, these designs are formulated as a community response rather than a developer's plan. The underlying values shown here are for those who live in and use these components of the city. The return on investment is not limited to a financial scheme but one that provides added value to the city and its inhabitants.

BIBLIOGRAPHY

Guby, Patrick; and Le, Ho Phuong Linh. 'Niveau de vie et déplacements dans les métropoles vietnamiennes: Hô Chi Minh ville et Hanoi'. Cairn.info, January 2010. https://www.cairn.info/article.php?ID_ARTICLE=RTM_201_0107.

Tafuri, Manfredo. *Architecture and Utopia: Design and Capitalist Development*. 10. print. Cambridge, Mass.: MIT Press, 1996.

CHAPTER EIGHT

YENNY RAHMAYATI[1] AND RELIGIANA HENDARTI[2]

1. Centre for Design Innovation, Swinburne University of Technology

2. Binus University, Indonesia

COMMUNITY-BASED DESIGN FOR BETTER HUMANITARIAN SHELTER

INTRODUCTION

The increasing number of natural disasters has increased the demand for humanitarian products including shelter. Many designs for emergency shelter have been made, but some designs are too technical and neglect the social, economic and cultural aspects for the users which in turn creates a scenario in which those survivors are more distressed. Considering the importance of providing shelter for survivors, the Centre for Design Innovation (CDI) of Swinburne University of Technology (Australia), in collaboration with the Architecture Department at Binus University (Indonesia), embarked on a project called 'Designing temporary shelter and facilities for flood disaster, Case study: Jakarta, Indonesia'. This project focused on community-led design for suitable temporary shelter and facilities for people escaping from small- to medium-sized disasters – particularly flooding. The aim was to create a concept design for a better humanitarian shelter for a local community. The project used the case study of a flood in the eastern part of Jakarta in Indonesia.

FIELD STUDY

A series of field studies were conducted focused in Kampung Melayu, East Jakarta. This location was chosen for several reasons: it is affected by regular floods, has a strategic location near to the city centre and has an urban context that includes socio-economic, cultural and historical aspects of the urban village. The field studies consisted of meetings, site visits and interviews conducted with experts and key stakeholders. Internal meetings between Swinburne and Binus were also held to discuss the methodology, selection of locations, the expected outputs, data to be collected, list of interview questions, schedules and the themes for research.

Meanwhile, the main activities carried out during the site visits (in October 2016) were direct observation of houses, means of access, public buildings, public space, market, street/pathway, infrastructure and other facilities, taking photographs and conducting community consultations. Several in-depth interviews with key persons and potential partners were also conducted to enrich the perspectives. The results from the field studies show that there are two main aspects that influence the design of humanitarian shelter in the Jakarta context: the social cultural factors and the physical elements. The social cultural aspects encompass privacy, space, security and attention to vulnerable groups (women, children and the elderly); while for the physical elements the concern is on the thermal comfort and effect of humidity, energy supply, storage management and assembly processes.

JOINT DESIGN WORKSHOP, SHARING KNOWLEDGE AND EXHIBITION

From 13 to 15 September 2017, a joint design workshop collaboration between Swinburne and Binus was conducted in Jakarta. The title of the workshop was 'Community Based Design for Better Humanitarian Shelter'. A sharing-knowledge session was also organised during the workshop, followed by a mini exhibition and review session by the experts. This enabled the public to provide feedback and opinions on the proposed designs of the shelters and facilities produced in the workshop.

THE WORKSHOP

The joint design workshop was attended by eight students (two from Swinburne and six from Binus) and five researchers (one from Swinburne and four from Binus). The students were divided into two groups. These divisions were based on the findings from the field, which concluded that there were two possible project sites at which to establish the temporary shelter – the outdoor and indoor sites. The workshop was led and facilitated by Dr Yenny Rahmayati of Swinburne and Dr Religiana Hendarti of Binus. The other researchers from Binus were involved as the internal reviewers.

The scope of workshop included:

1. The designers' visualisation of the project

2. The design concept highlighting how it addresses the issues, requirements and any other points that the designers felt relevant to the design, including innovative design and infrastructure concepts; this included a brief statement of the following aspects: a. Innovative and work-friendly environment, b. energy-efficient design, c. safety and emergency features, and d. other design elements

3. Tentative costs of the project and choice of specifications for the proposed shelter design

4. An explaination by the designers of how the proposed structural system and/or choice of finishing materials will be managed.

Problems identified during the fieldwork were highlighted during the workshop. They were that:

1. The design is too complicated or sophisticated and so users cannot construct the shelter by themselves

2. The material is not durable and/or it does not consider the sustainability aspect (as the shelter material cannot be re-used for future regular disasters)

3. Sometimes the shelters were too heavy or needed additional construction, which is usually difficult to find in an emergency (thus creating a distribution or logistics problem)

4. The design is not suitable to local context and situations including topography, location, environmental conditions and culture/practices/habits

5. The shelters do not include provision of facilities in and around the compound such as water and sanitation, communication, safety and health facilities

6. The shelters are not specifically designed for humanitarian needs particularly on small- to medium-sized sites of disasters

7. Humanitarian agencies were not satisfied with the design of the shelters.

The workshop tried to respond to these problems through a practical approach in order to design a simple, light prototype that would respond to the local contexts and be environmentally friendly (enabling recycling and reusability). It was highlighted in the workshop that the shelters must be able to be made available in time, in sufficient quantities and on the right spot, using materials that are available locally and can be manufactured locally (specifically in Jakarta, in this context), facilitated by the right facilities – and all at an affordable or agreed-upon cost.

The three-day workshop began with a brainstorming and ideation session on the first day at which students developed their initial designs. The designs were then reviewed by the internal researchers from Swinburne and Binus. On the second day, the students revised and improved their designs based on the input and feedback of the first review session. A sharing-knowledge session was held on the same day, followed by a mini exhibition and review sessions by the invited experts and the public. On the third day, the students revised their designs based on the expert and public feedback. The final iterations were presented on the at the end of the workshop.

The outcomes were produced as technical drawings presented as posters and PowerPoint presentations. Concept models scaled at 1:50 were built to represent the final designs of the shelters. Documentation included plans, elevations, sections and perspective views.

THE SHARING-KNOWLEDGE SESSION AND EXHIBITION

Two experts from the Disaster Risk Reduction & Mitigation Foundation and Architecture Sans Frontiers International shared their experience and expertise on disaster risk reduction and mitigation, including how to manage the temporary shelters for disasters during the sharing-knowledge session. They were also involved as the external expert reviewers who reviewed the designs of the shelters proposed from the workshop. Dr Rahmayati of Swinburne gave a lecture on Humanitarian Habitat and Design during this session. Students from Swinburne (Andrew Steed and Therese McArthur) presented their design of the portable smart toilet as a complimentary facility for the shelters.

OMAH: TINY SHELTER, LESS SPACE, MORE LIFE
Andrew Steed (Swinburne), Yulianto Wijaya, Riko Yohanes, Rizaldo (Binus)

As for the outdoor shelter, the design focused on the whole aspect of the shelter including the form, material, energy source as well as space allocation to accommodate a family of up to four people. The main challenges faced by this group were the space limitations in the outdoor areas (since the shelter is particularly designed for urban villages), along with privacy and security issues due to the density of the populations and the effects of humidity.

The group came up with shelter called a Tiny Shelter or 'OMAH' which means 'a house' in local (Indonesian) language. It is a flat-pack, easy-to-assemble shelter for which the whole system comes wrapped in the roof. The shelter can accommodate a single family of up to four people for the period of one to two weeks, and can be erected in a modular system utilising available space such as roads or alleys. There are some variants of the layout available in the proposed design to accommodate the different numbers of users. The estimated total cost for one Tiny Shelter is $154.01 (USD). This shelter offers seven key significance features:

1. Low cost
2. Flexible space
3. Portable packaging system
4. Ventilation system
5. Water catchment system
6. Optional solar panel
7. Modular design.

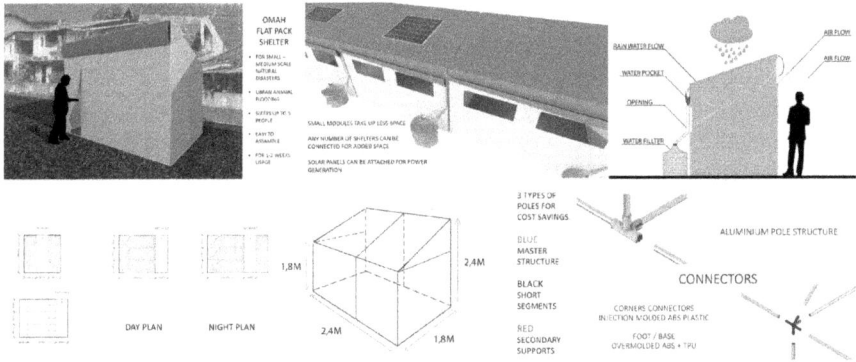

Figure 1. OMAH: Tiny Shelter, less space, more life

TARIK AND LIPAT SHELTERS (EXPANDABLE AND FOLDABLE BUNKBEDS)

Therese McArthur (Swinburne), Nafilah, Samuel Kamarudin, Pinkan Avianto (Binus)

Like the outdoor group, the indoor group also consists of four students, one from Swinburne and three from Binus. The indoor shelter focused on how to design a multifunctional modular space that could be used as a sleeping area as well as a living area, allowing the community to do other activities such as reading and studying, particularly for school-age children. The main reason for designing an indoor shelter is because, when flooding occurs, people are often forced to leave their homes and take shelter in nearby community centers such as schools or mosques. Women and children are prioritised to be accommodated in the indoor shelters. Some challenges that needed to be addressed by this group were: the space limitation, material and storage system and management. The group had to explore ideas of design for an easy-to-set-up shelter in a small pack, how to utilise the lightweight and durable materials and design a storage system for the shelter to be used during regular floods. This group came up with two types of indoor shelters in a bunked style, the Expandable Bunkbed which was called a 'Tarik Shelter' in the local (Indonesian) language and the Foldable Bunkbed which was called a 'Lipat Shelter' in the local (Indonesian) language.

EXPANDABLE BUNKBED

The expandable bunkbed was designed so that the bunks can be folded back to form couches during the day. The bunkbed takes up less space and can be easily rearranged to create more space. Each bunk needs two people and 15 minutes to set up. The containers are sturdy and can be stacked and used as a table. Other bunks which are not needed can easily be packed away to create space. Each bunk bed can safely accommodate one mother and up to three children. The rungs on the end form a sturdy ladder to climb to the top bunk. For privacy, curtains can be hung from the top side rails. During the night, the storage containers are stowed away under the bottom bunk, to keep people's belongings safe. Two bunk beds can be packed into a single storage container with five empty storage containers stacked underneath. These can be distributed by NGOs and collected for redistribution after the crisis, or owned by local community groups. The bunkbeds cost about $93 US per bunk.

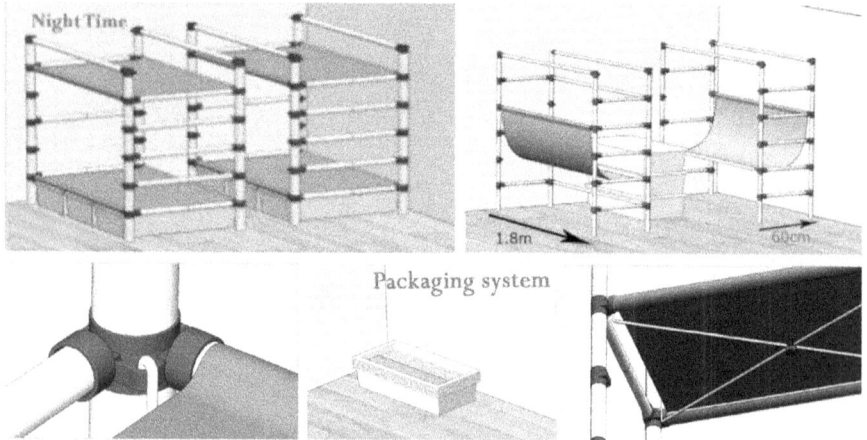

Figure 2. Tarik Shelters (Expandable Bunkbeds)

FOLDABLE BUNKBED

The foldable bunkbed was designed to be used as a bed at night and can be folded into a couch during the day to give more space. The curtain can be open, to allow users to do their activities more freely and interact with each other. Interaction between users is needed so that they can support one another during stressful times. At night, the curtain will be closed to give them privacy. A small part of the top of the curtain will have a net material to allow air to flow into the module. Each module of foldable bunkbeds can accommodate up to two adults (elderly, mothers) and six children. The elderly can use the bottom mattress, while the young children and maybe their parent will use the top mattress of the bunk bed. The stair is made from a telescopic pole, so it can be extended and shortened based on needs. Meanwhile, the mattress can be folded and made into a backpack. The total cost for this foldable bunked is around $ 120.84 (USD) per module.

Figure 3. Lipat Shelters (Foldable Bunkbeds)

SUMMARY

The designs produced at this joint design workshop have been exhibited at the Bendigo Inventor Awards 2017 held on 13 November 2017 in Bendigo, Australia, where they were reviewed by public, local and international organisations including government institutions. Swinburne has also submitted the outcomes from the workshop to the Swinburne Research Office as Non-Traditional Research Outputs (NTRO). Meanwhile, Binus is also in the process of submitting the designs of the shelters to their Research and Technology Transfer Office (RTTO) for Joint Intellectual Property Rights with Swinburne.

CHAPTER NINE

SALLY STONE, LAURA SANDERSON AND JOHN LEE

Manchester School of Architecture, Manchester UK

THE WAY WE LIVE NOW: HOW ARCHITECTURAL EDUCATION CAN SUPPORT THE URBAN DEVELOPMENT OF SMALL SETTLEMENTS

INTRODUCTION

Continuity in Architecture, a post-graduate atelier for research, practice and teaching at the Manchester School of Architecture, has been working directly with local communities to develop meaningful and productive proposals for the development of new homes that are appropriate for the changing needs of a twenty-first-century population, while also remaining sympathetic to the environment in which they are constructed.

This chapter will examine the evolution of neighbourhood planning and discuss the projects that the atelier has undertaken in recent years, before offering some thoughts for the development of future initiatives. It is split into a number of parts: part one describes the aims, aspirations and agenda of Continuity in Architecture; part two discusses the nature of a 'research through doing' project within an academic institution; part three describes the background to the research, the particular circumstances of the relationship with the neighbourhood planning committees and the projects that have been completed so far; and part four will reflect upon what has been achieved and will look to the future.

CONTINUITY IN ARCHITECTURE

Continuity in Architecture is a postgraduate atelier, which has been established at the Manchester School of Architecture for more than 20 years. The atelier runs programmes for the design of new buildings and public spaces within the existing urban environment. The emphasis is on the importance of place and the idea that the design of architecture can be influenced by the experience and analysis of particular situations. This interpretation of place can provide a contemporary layer of built meaning within the continuity of the evolving town or city.

The atelier is built upon the principals of Contextualism and agrees with Thomas Schumacher that: "Some middle ground is needed. To retreat to a hopelessly artificial past is unrealistic, but to allow a brutalising system to dominate and destroy traditional urbanism is irresponsible".[1] The text emerged as a reaction to Modernism and is now more than a generation old but given how critical the significance of heritage and the built environment is to our cultural future, it is now more relevant than ever.

Continuity in Architecture is inspired by the efforts of architects working within the existing urban fabric to produce a responsive architecture of narrative, space, intervention and detail. We aim to show that the ideas and methods we examine in the studio have real and profitable applications. The main source of our architecture is the place itself. We reflect upon the persistence, usefulness and emotional resonance of particular places and structures. We are interested in the qualities of places that have persisted and we prefer a reading of history that stresses the permanence of tradition as the subject of architecture.

Figure 1. Analysis in Bakewell using serial vision.[2]
Brull, Continuity in Architecture, 2016

---

1   Schumacher. *Contexualism: Urban Ideals and Deformations.* 1971, p.1.
2   Cullen. *The Concise Townscape.* 1961.

Tradition in architecture in this context is the embodied meaning of buildings and cities produced by centuries of lived experience. Discovery and recognition are a vital part of the design process – the architect has a duty to analyse and describe a place before it can be altered. As stated by Zucchi when discussing the work of De Carlo, "De Carlo refers more frequently to morphology than typology because, according to him, typology isolates a form from its use (and potentially from its context) whereas morphology is interested in a form only in as far as it relates to other surrounding forms and to the pattern of activities that produced them."[3]

RESEARCH THROUGH DOING

The aim of a 'research through doing' project within a school of architecture and design is to construct knowledge through the acquisition of insight and understanding. Design lies at the heart of the educational programme and, certainly within the design studio itself, it is the central locus; thus, doing within architectural and design education is the design process itself. At post-graduate level, the design process is inquisitive and analytical. Research is an activity signified by the gathering of insights about an object of research; the aim of this process is the collection of knowledge. Since design and research are inextricably linked, there is a direct relationship between knowledge production and the design process.

Design and scientific problem solving can be vastly different in that scientific understanding generally leads to a logical and concrete solution, while more artistically orientated problem solving can generally be compared with the deciphering of a riddle. Research into architecture is a hybrid subject located at the interface of connecting fields of art, science and technology; an activity defined primarily by production, of physical or virtual products. Thus, it can be argued that architecture and design are concerned with production.

Within all research, but especially research by doing, there is a fundamental difference between understanding and examining. Understanding is based upon a comparison, while examining requires a penetration of the object. That is, understanding is exercised at the surface of the object, whereas examining takes place on the inside; examining is more profound. When examining an object, place or thing, the investigator is involved with it; there is an insightful relationship between the investigator and the investigated. This implies a coming together of the theory of the design and the practice of design. This suggests that the knowledge gained from doing is less objective, and so it is more revealing. Therefore, in research by design projects, it is the design process that forms the route through which new insights, knowledge, practices or products come into being.

The inclusion of live agendas within architectural education has been increasing in popularity in recent years and this is in contrast with the tendency of the twentieth century for architectural education to be 'product' orientated, most commonly

---

3   Zucchi. *The Structure & Form of the City*. 1992, p.4.

concerning a traditional design brief to create a given building on a given site.[4] One of the key advantages of a problem-based leaning (PBL) approach is the development of employability and lifelong learning skills that begin to set the context for a lifetime of continued professional development, both formal and informal. The job of an architect requires architectural design skills alongside the ability to analyse, organise, collaborate and communicate ideas; that is, to solve problems. Within architectural education there has been an inclination to create a simulated setting that allows students to show off the full range of drafting and design skills but not necessarily the additional skills required to deal with a real-life problem. "Much design education is very remote and esoteric and even where design work has a 'real life' context there is a tendency to 'tailor' the design brief, often for valid educational reasons, in order that the creativity of the student is not limited by the reality of the context of the design problem".[5]

Continuity in Architecture is determined that students should have the opportunity to react to the live context of small settlements, while also taking into consideration the wider context and the live agenda of a small urban environment – and also meeting the wider curricular requirements of the course.

THE WAY WE LIVE NOW

It is well documented that the UK has a shortage of well-constructed and affordable housing. The situation is still deteriorating and is now commonly referred to as the 'Housing Crisis'. The Royal Town Planning Institute (RTPI) has reported upon this and explained that the cost of housing, whether in private ownership or rented, now commands a disproportionate amount of people's income. This is not actually a current trend: the cost of housing and people's earning have for some time been divorced; indeed, since 1975 real house prices have increased by 126 per cent. The RTPI supports this statement with an explanation of the current situation:

> More than three million households in the UK now spend more than a third of their income on housing... The number of 25-year-olds who own their own home has more than halved in the last 20 years (20 per cent, compared with 46 per cent two decades ago)... Average house prices are now at 7.9 times average earnings; this is particularly difficult for many young aspiring homeowners... There has been an 88 per cent fall in the amount of social housing built compared to 20 years ago... The number of homes being built which are classed as "affordable" has fallen to its lowest level for 24 years (only 32,000 new homes)... The UK is building 15 per cent fewer homes than it was in the five years before the downturn in 2008... The number of "working households" living in poverty (7.4 million people, including 2.6 million children) has reached record levels in part as a result of the housing crisis (especially in London and southern England) and high rents in the private rented sector.[6]

---

4   Bishop. *Architecture in the Community Project*. 1997, p.87.
5   Ibid.
6   Royal Town Planning Institute. *Better Planning for Housing Affordability*. 2017, p.2.

There are a number of reasons why this housing crisis has arisen, including: 1) legislation – the power for the construction of affordable housing was removed from local councils, and very rigid planning legislation put in place that makes it difficult to build within the countryside (or greenbelt); 2) nimbyism – the idea that many residents do not want the tranquillity of their current situation spoilt by the influx of a great many new residences; 3) wealth tied up within property – if house prices drop, so does the individual worth of the population; 4) land not being available in the places where the housing need is greatest; and finally 5) land banking – owners are not prepared to do anything with their land, preferring to let it accumulate value.[7]

Neighbourhood planning was part of the Localism Bill introduced in 2011 by the British government. It passes responsibility for important decisions about the development of the built environment from centralised government to the local community. This was a laudable attempt by the then-Conservative government to redistribute decision-making powers and thus speed-up the construction of new homes. The Localism Bill was very much part of the twenty-first-century movement towards the primacy of the individual and the placing of importance upon ideas of community, family and civic responsibility. One of the most significant aspects of contemporary society is the need for the individual to lay claim to the control of many aspects of the circumstances of life.

Traditional government, in which policy is formed by experts and administered by state officials, is increasingly being challenged. Top-down enforcement of regulations, rules or directives is no longer acceptable to many people who feel that the individual or small collective is much better placed to make important decisions about things that happen within their own neighbourhood. Thus, neighbourhood planning should, in theory, be a very good thing. The community is much better positioned to understand the needs and capability of their environment. Neighbourhood planning certainly enables communities to play a much stronger role in shaping the areas in which they live and work; it provides an opportunity for communities to set out a vision for how they want their community to develop in ways that meet identified local need and make sense for local people. However, there is the danger of well-meaning, but ill-informed individuals making decisions that have massive implications for the community. Town and country planning is difficult: it involves an intimate understanding of the qualities of what is already there, combined with a specific knowledge of the economic, political, social and cultural power structures of the place, and the needs and aspirations of the current population. To be truly effective as a vehicle for social change, the neighbourhood planning committee needs to have the ability to envisage an alternative future. The other problem with neighbourhood planning is the possible infiltration of the group by parties with less philanthropic and much more vested interests in developing the area.

---

7   Department for Communities and Local Government. *Fixing Our Broken Housing Market.* 2017.

Continuity in Architecture has been working on developments within small towns in northern England and Wales for a number of years. This encourages theories and ideas to be developed and tested at a small and controllable scale within the studio context. Projects have been completed in Preston, Cartmel, Grange-over-Sands, Colwyn Bay, Bollington and Bakewell. The more recent projects have begun with two simultaneous investigations: the first examined the actuality of the place, the second considered what 'home' means in the twenty-first century.

Colin Rowe and Fred Koetter describe "the city (and by our own extension, the town) as a didactic instrument"[8], that is, a place in which a desirable discourse can be formulated – and it is through these conversations that the evidence for the argument of interpretation is collected. The reading and understanding of the message of the built and the natural environment provide the basis for the discussion. We have developed a range of ways of summarising our approach, the most persistent of which is a distillation of our pedagogic method into three words: remember, reveal, construct.

The nature of the home has, over the last generation, radically changed. Many of us are no longer able to live, or even desire to live, in comfortable three-bedroom homes with small gardens and parking for two cars. Shared housing, family homes, co-housing, communal living, affordable housing, live–work units, starter homes, multi-generational living, adaptable home, homes for life, downsizing, up-scaling and homes with shared facilities are all relevant issues and pertinent to the way we live now.

This duel investigation means that all the subsequent design projects are informed by highly contemporary ideas about the modern lifestyle combined with the strong tradition of the locality. A sympathetic reading of place and culture introduces alternative views, difference, variation and change that leads to design projects that consider the surrounding vernacular traditions, the history of the site and the needs and aspirations of the future local population (much of which the local residents may not be aware of).

Over the academic year 2016–17, Continuity in Architecture has been working in the Derbyshire town of Bakewell. This is a small settlement, about 50km to the south of Manchester, set within the beautiful and highly protected Peak District National Park. The town has a higher than average elderly population, income and house price. Development of the Bakewell Neighbourhood Plan had already begun. The town was aware that it would be obliged to construct about 150 new homes within the next decade, and had established exactly where the social need for housing was; but it had not decided exactly where the housing could be constructed. This number of new homes was a somewhat controversial proposal within the extremely conservative conservation area.

---

8   Rowe and Koetter. *Collage City.* 1978.

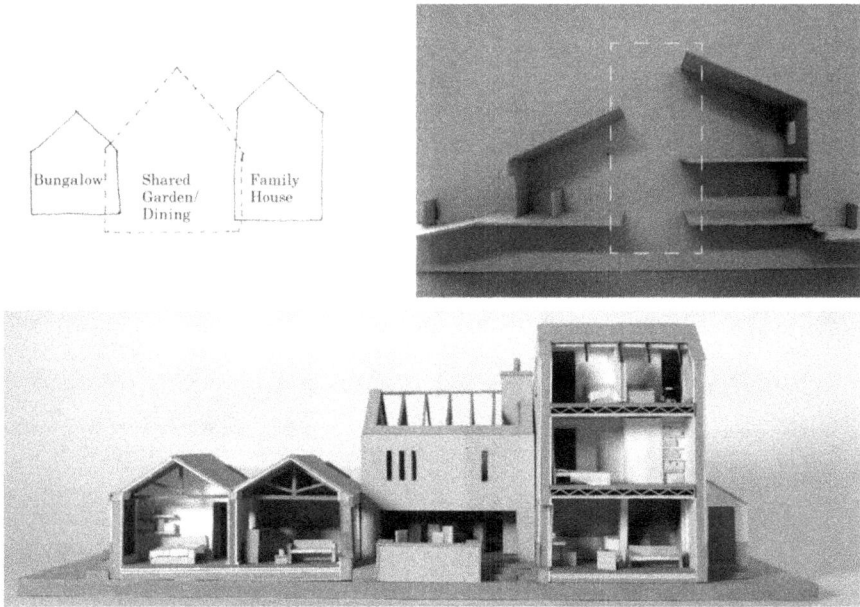

Figure 2. Project for two homes for one family with a shared dining room.
Parkinson, Continuity in Architecture, 2016

The project lasted for the whole academic year, the first semester of which focussed upon the design of a theoretical home on a small, complicated site on the edge of the town centre. This allowed the students to develop their own ideas about the manner in which the home should be occupied, combined with a particular reading of the place. This was a 'research through doing' project. The students developed some initial ideas about the physical and social context before they started to design, but these were extensively explored through the design project. The process of design encouraged reflection, which in turn highlighted further aspects that needed greater investigation. This cyclical exploratory process yielded highly productive results that formed the basis for the second semester project. Three distinct housing types emerged – live–work units, multi-generational living (Figure 2) and housing with shared facilities – and these challenged the housing types currently on offer in the town. The results were shared by the whole group, so for example, one student who was exploring live–work units would pass on their findings to another student who had maybe looked at communal living. The design proposals were deliberately radical, but not gratuitously inappropriate. The 'ideal' was for a design that completely served the needs of the contemporary society and was obviously of the twenty-first century, but also looked as if it could have always been there.

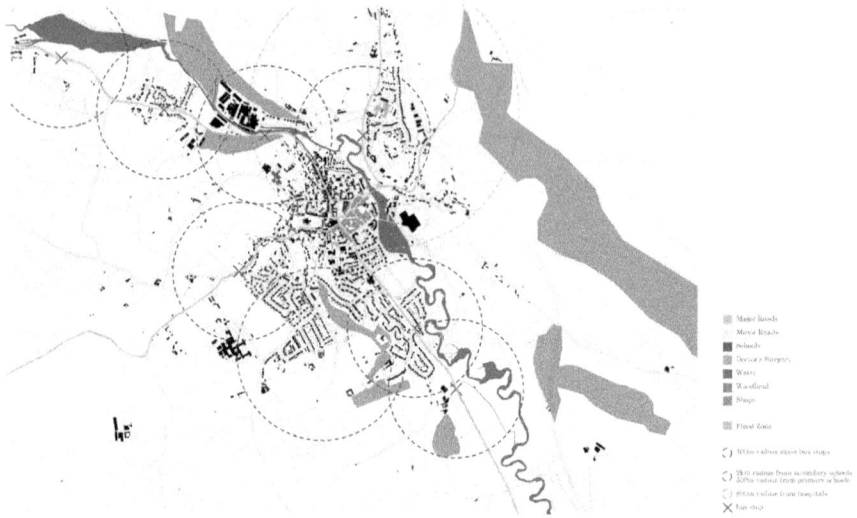

Figure 3. Analysis of potential sites in Bakewell using the BIMBY toolkit.
Continuity in Architecture, 2016

The second semester project involved working very closely with the Neighbourhood Planning Committee and the Town Council. Through a process of negotiation and using the BIMBY toolkit (Figure 3), eight sites were selected within the town that could potentially be developed. 'Beautiful in My Back Yard' (BIMBY) is a planning tool that is designed to encourage interaction between the local community and the planning authority in the selection of appropriate sites for potential development. BIMBY looks at such factors as walking distances, accessibility, bus routes, available resources and so forth. Each of the sites could potentially contain between 20 and 50 homes.

The cohort of students was then subdivided into small groups and each was allocated one of the proposed sites. The students were expected to develop contextually driven solutions based upon the earlier ideas and concerns that had been rehearsed in the first semester. They developed an organisational plan for the site, as well as determining the exact type of housing to be established upon it. All the projects included a variety of house types, thus providing affordable, market price, live–work and other types of homes for a variation upon communal living. All design solutions included a detailed examination of the exterior space, the relationship between the façade and the public space, and a meticulous investigation of the interior.

The solutions responded to the specific policies developed within the Draft Neighbourhood Plan. This was beneficial to the residents of the town, but also provided a useful and complex situation for the educational priorities of the curriculum. The three policies that the project proposals observed were as follows.

POLICY H1 (Provision of Affordable Housing) recommends "a mix of social rented, shared ownership or a mix of the two be progressed".[9] One example included four compact starter homes benefitting from shared courtyard, outdoor storage and guest house to create an affordable solution (Figure 4).

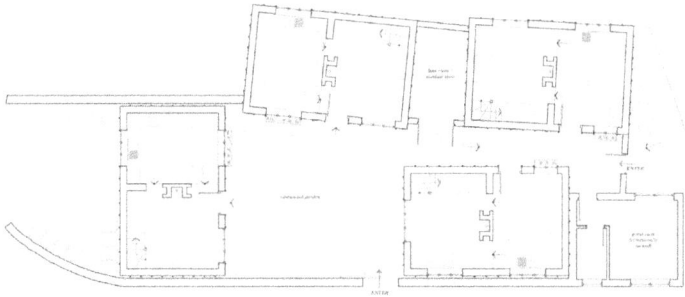

Figure 4. Four affordable houses with shared facilities.
Cooper, Continuity in Architecture, 2016

POLICY H2 (Age and Disability Related Considerations) states that developments "must meet the housing needs of the town's ageing population".[10] This was noted in a number of the student projects including one that created a community of homes that included such aspects as level-access bungalows mixed with apartments, and family homes. The social facilities were a series of shared outdoor squares, a café, allotments, a play area and a multipurpose community building (Figure 5).

POLICY H3 (Housing Mix Development) states that "all housing should be of a size in accordance with affordable housing requirements".[11] This is evidenced in a vacant building site behind the Town Hall, which has been denied planning permission to develop housing a number of times because the proposal was unsympathetically large and involved the demolition of important structures. The student scheme buffered the contentious acoustic conditions of the Town Hall with a series of live–work units, which overlooked the quieter garden to the rear.

---

9   Bakewell Partnership Neighbourhood Plan Working Group. *Bakewell Neighbourhood Plan*. 2016.
10   Ibid.
11   Ibid.

Figure 5. Mixed housing with community squares in the woodland, Bakewell.
Parkinson and Tysklind, Continuity in Architecture, 2017

The design proposals were exhibited in Bakewell Town Hall. The exhibition at the end of the first semester proved to be somewhat controversial: there were many positive comments, but there was also obvious objection to any development in the town. Surprisingly, one local resident commented: "This is too good for Bakewell". The local press reported upon the exhibition (we would have made the front page of the weekly paper if a naked intruder had not been caught on the same day the exhibition opened). By the time the second exhibition was staged, the local population had accepted the idea that development within the town was going to happen, so it was met with a much more positive reception.

REFLECTIONS

In a recent review of neighbourhood planning, Nicholas Boys Smith, the Director of 'Create Streets' quoted a senior planning inspector who expressed his frustration at the process: "Half of them are barely worth writing. They just parrot the local authority's plans".[12] Boys Smith goes on to ask: "How can we make for more effective plans? Some of the answer lies at the local level. The most powerful and effective neighbourhood plans have a very strong sense of place, of what will get built and where. The two most powerful, yet insufficiently used, tools in the Neighbourhood Planning armoury are allocating sites for development and setting out a clear and predictable Design Code for what that development should be and look like."[13]

This project takes the neighbourhood plan beyond what is normally expected by generating real proposals, through drawings and models. This allows the general public to comment on ideas that they can visualise. The projects should be viewed as an example of best practice in neighbourhood planning and disseminated further on both a local and national level.

The series of projects developed within Continuity in Architecture will lead to the establishment of the Small Settlements Research Unit. This will allow the projects to develop beyond the confines of the academic year and the architectural curriculum. To a certain extent, this has already happened: Bollington Town Council commissioned a project for traffic calming entitled 'Reclaiming the Road' (2017) which was completed in collaboration with ARCA Architects and based upon the ideas developed by the students in the academic year 2015–16.

Design is not a linear process; it is a cyclical practice that continually involves using informed research to make design decisions that in turn create the need for further investigation. Design-through-research and research-through-design practices are highly productive vehicles for student progression – and when conducted in an almost-live situation can prove to be beneficial for the students and the client. The information that was produced by the students reacted to the live conditions of the neighbourhood plan but required academic application to make it impactful. Each output was designed to challenge policy makers and propose a more place specific solution to neighbourhood planning.

---

12   Boys Smith. *Is Neighbourhood Planning flourishing or withering? And how can communities do it better?* 2016.

13   Ibid.

CHAPTER TEN

CHENG-CHUN PATRICK HWANG AND FRANCESCO ROSSINI

School of Architecture, The Chinese University of Hong Kong

DWELLING IN AN INFLUX CITY – PLACEMAKING THROUGH COLLECTIVE HOUSING

the city is like some large house, and the house is in return like some small city

Leon Battista Alberti

INTRODUCTION

Hong Kong is a city of influxes. Crisscrossing through high-speed network circulation and flows of goods and services are vast numbers of people constantly on the move. In recent years, the city has developed through the approach of tabula rasa, real-estate dominance, economic prioritisation and intrastructural efficiency with a lack of consideration for open public space. Urban transformation initiatives in the 1990s and earlier, which were designed to expand consumption, privatisation, monitoring and security, have led to a public space crisis. It is clearly necessary to reconsider the role of public spaces, especially in cities like Hong Kong where the pressure for urban development influences planning strategies. For various morphological, historical and institutional reasons, the city lacks a culture of public space. Hong Kong's open spaces have attracted research and the general conclusion is that they are far from satisfactory in terms of both their quantity and quality.[1]

Within this city of perpetual action, reaction and transaction, several questions were asked before establishing the pedagogical framework for the design studio: What role does architecture have in generating a sense of *place*, of creating a pause within

---

1   Tang and Wong. 'A Longitudinal Study of Open Space Zoning and Development in Hong Kong'.

a city that is highly transactional?[2] Is it possible to use collective housing as an agency to trigger place making through the balancing act of architectural forms and cultural/social contents? If the motivation is to make a place in a highly densified city like Hong Kong, must the premise of the design project be ambitious in scale through enormous gross floor areas or floor area ratios? Could an alternative development model be possible, allowing the propositions to fit within the existing neighbourhood rather than the prototypical blank slate approach? These are the questions posed when considering this problem to the design studio for our year-four students in the compulsory U5 studio.

LEARNING SEQUENCE

The School of Architecture at CUHK offers one of the few architectural programmes in the world that is affiliated with a faculty of social science rather than with art and design or technical institutions. What this implicitly means is that our students are keenly aware of their role as socially oriented cultural producers enabled by their disciplinary knowledge of architecture. This influence from the social sciences begins early in their education through design studios, required and elective courses in humanities, technologies and representations. Design studios are structured in a sequential manner through the six semesters of the programme. The intention is to allow better integration of studio and required courses, and to enable students to start from fundamental concepts and advance progressively to more complex issues in architectural design.

U5 STUDIO

The studio operates on the premise that the architecture of the city can contribute to place making, including well-conceived and designed collective housing. This is the first time our students are challenged with imagining not only an autonomous piece of architecture, but also a strong emphasis on its relationship to the city. As Hong Kong faces the challenge of housing shortage, particularly for those young adults starting up, what are the ways in which design and planning of architecture could help ease or alleviate this problem? Could inventive adaptation of conditions and creative arrangement of the collective housing provide a part of the solution? Behind the studio pedagogy is an attempt to use architectural design as a vehicle to contribute to alternative urban strategies and place-making in the highly densified urban environment.

The studio is organised by four main activities: Act 1, a mini architectural competition; Act 2, a public space and density study workshop; Act 3, urban investigation and preliminary design; and Act 4, the final and the longest portion, focussed on the design of a 'place of collective living' in dialogue with the existing urban fabric.

---

2   Economic exchange and monetary transaction as a form of social interaction as described by Georg Simmel in 'The Metropolis and Mental Life' (Levine, 1971).

ACT 1: MICRO-APARTMENT

Instead of arriving at architectural design during the middle and end of the semester, we begin the studio by hosting a micro-apartment design competition, which we call 'Hong Kong, NOW'.

The competition does not specify any particular site. However, students shall design the project to be situated in a site representative of the conditions in Hong Kong. The objective of this intense two-week exercise is to mobilise the students immediately at the beginning of the semester, to think and learn through the act of design and making. The small and confined, yet complex, problem allows the students to confront the grey areas of private and common space. It provides valuable learning experience to consider not only what housing is, but the limits of what it could be. The scheme calls for a creative adaptation of the residual space within the disused alleyways of Hong Kong. In addition to making scaled drawings, students are tasked with drawing their typical plan at full scale, providing them with an immediate reaction to the notion of scale.

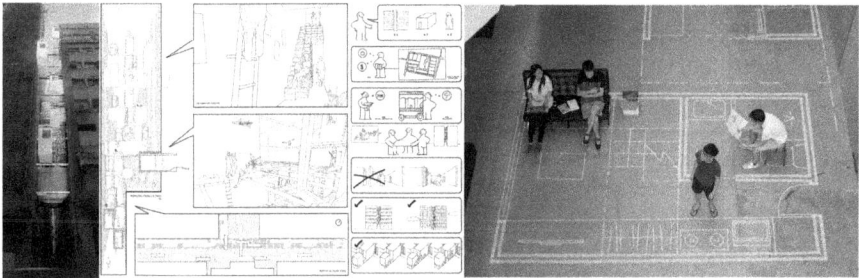

Figure 1. Micro-apartment design competition scheme entitled: MF, WF, OURS

ACT 2: DENSITY AND OPEN SPACE WORKSHOP

Densities in modern cities are controlled, in part through the mechanics of floor area ratio (FAR), a numeric assignment with extraordinary complex social and economic implications. Early architectural students rarely have the opportunity to learn and question the rationale behind the use of FAR. For Act 2, we conceived of an exercise in the form of a workshop where the students are introduced with the measure of density through the use of FAR and site coverage (COV). The objective is to explore the values in order to understand the parameters that shape the urban form of the city. From a given matrix, five different cells of FAR and COV, the students combines different parameters to experiment distinctive urban forms within an ideal site of 3600m² (60m x 60m). The exercise will be developed by a group of four-to-five students. Each group needs to produce a total of five physical models. The objective is to explore the values in order to understand the parameters that shape the urban form of the city.

ACTS 3 & 4: SITE INVESTIGATION AND ARCHITECTURAL DESIGN

Three sites are given within Kennedy Town, which is among the oldest districts in Hong Kong, each with its own unique characteristics to provide inspiration for their individual designs. Site A is the Rectangular Plot, off Forbes Street across from a mass transit station; Site B is the Park Site, next to Belcher Park and the waterfront; and Site C is the Slope Site, off Sand Street 50 metres away from a historic temple and nestled within a quiet residential neighbourhood.

Kennedy Town is a district located on the western end of Hong Kong island, a vibrant district in the midst of urban renewal and gentrification. Many of the new housing developments proposed there have an enormous FAR of between 5 and 6. Instead of following this efficiency-driven model, students were asked to work on a design in the range of 2 to 2.5 FAR and residential plus communal programmes with an accompanying open space. The dwellings can be aimed at the young and/or starter families, and may include live–work units or could be thematised according to students' research.

The objective is to highlight the notion of a 'place of collective living' in dialogue with the existing urban fabric. The emphasis is on collective living as a potential to respond and transform the larger-scale fabric in the city of Hong Kong.

PROJECT 1. LIVING IN A TEA HOUSE: MODULAR TYPOLOGY IN AN URBAN CONTEXT

WAI SUM MICHELLE HO

Situated in Kennedy Town, this project was inspired by early examples of teahouses originating in the district, which served as a communal hub for low-income workers. It proposes social housing with associated facilities integrating the 'essence' of the teahouse. The concept of the teahouse design is a reaction to the gentrification of the neighbourhood in recent years and aims to promote social exchange among the residents. The site, near Seven Terraces, was once a vivid place where residential and communal activities flourished – this atmosphere has deteriorated due to newly constructed pencil tower developments with clear and gated demarcation of boundaries.

The 'Teahouse' adopts the form as an open courtyard that leads visitors from the main street into the communal spaces within. It mediates the urban cityscape with nature, where its height assembles with the mountain at the back. Approaching the building, a swirling path leads one to wander within the landscape and finally to reach the hilly backdrop of trees. Public accessible teahouses together with some supplementary reading and cooking facilities are supplemented to facilitate communal activities.

Using systematic modular construction arranged as clusters, the proposal creates different scales and layers of public, private and in-between communal spaces with a mixture in family and studio units to foster interactions. Terraces generated as a result of the modular organisation provide private outdoor spaces for informal group activities. Semi-private tea pods provide a focal point for semi-private communal activities, and allow a visual connection with the courtyard while providing structural support to the modular clusters. The façade is made of two contrasting materials of rough stucco wall and smooth concrete surfaces. Without expressing the organisation of individual units on the façade, a sense of ambiguity is created, where individual and the community are considered inseparable in the 'teahouse' social housing community.

The project questions the common approach of vertical tower developments that emphasise individualism. It proposes an alternative approach to achieve compact living by co-habitation, while redeveloping the sense of common identity and exploring the parameters of forming a new typology of place-making. Responding to the vibrant history of the district, the project aims to reintroduce the liveliness of teahouses as a model of providing space for community and interaction to the neighbourhood in Kennedy Town.

Figure 2. Living in a Tea House by Wai Sum Michelle Ho

PROJECT 2: WITHIN | WITHOUT

ALEX KELVIN LI

The site for this project is isolated from the surrounding urban environment and Kennedy Town's narrow sidewalks, resulting in a lack of connectivity between the street blocks that in turn undermines any opportunity for neighbourhood activities. The urban condition of the area has been transforming radically during the past years. Two factors have accelerated speculation on the area: first, the construction of new high-rise residential towers; and second, the extension of the island line with the opening of the new subway station of Kennedy Town. As a response to this context, the project aims to provide communal experience through the strategy of 'without and within'. To translate this idea as an architectural response, the massing of the building is shaped to reflect the site's triangular shape. To articulate the form, the building shape gently bends inward to create a series of unique open spaces with implicit leisure programmes and private spaces connected to the pedestrian circulation. As a consequence, this project tries to mediate between the highest density possible and the spatial quality of the interior spaces.

The result of this bending also helps to create a 'frontispiece' towards the Belcher Bay Park, forming a dialectical relationship between the project and the lung (green space) of the district. The horizontal development of this building originated from the site conditions creating an urban enclave that defines a communal courtyard for both the residents and the community. Tall vegetation along the edge of the site creates an acoustic buffer zone and dramatically improves the street atmosphere and quality. The project seeks to create a place where countless events, stories and activities will culminate.

Figure 3. Within | Without: Alex Kelvin Li

PROJECT 3: INTERWOVEN

CHUN YU ERIC CHAN

Kennedy Town, backed by Mount Davis, is one of the few areas in Hong Kong that has retained traces of its rich cultural and natural history. Despite the lack of public space, residents from the area have found creative ways to make use of the streets as an extension for their communal and daily uses. Such adaptation of the street is ubiquitous in Kennedy Town. This vague definition of the public domain resembles the metaphor of 'interweaving' in fabrics. Taking this pattern of use from the streets as a concept, the project proposes to integrate the collective housing with the abundance of lush trees already existing on the site. This proximity to the natural environment makes living with nature seamlessly possible.

By interweaving the greenery with circulation and communal spaces, an indeterminate relationship is created between inside and out; manufactured and natural, wherever they are, the sense of nature and being in a community are experienced. Interwoven bands of housing units are arranged strategically to respond to the surrounding context, primarily to provide collective living conditions to the residents and to establish a close relationship to nature without neglecting the level of privacy.

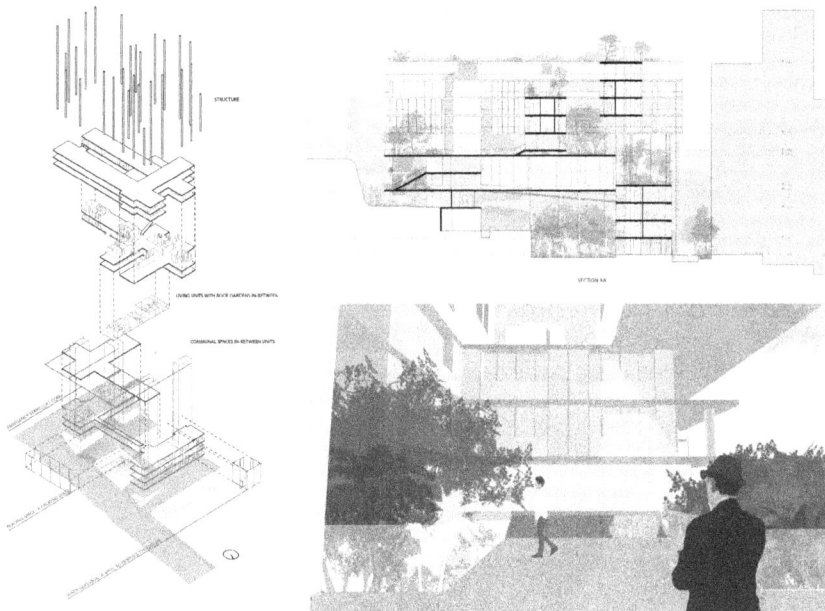

Figure 4. Interwoven by Chun Yu Eric Chan

Programmatically, the ground floor serves as public communal space with a coffee shop and garden-like space to appreciate the greenery and breeze from the southern direction. Other communal spaces include the reading and multi-purpose rooms (theatre/performance, for example) for residents. Creating an atmosphere for sharing is essential for collective living regardless of whether one is a visitor or resident: harmony of living with nature can always be felt even just passing-by. 'Interweaving' provides functional uses and sensual atmosphere with respect to the existing community and nature.

CONCLUSION

Cities are complex organisms; they are constituted by fixed and changing elements. Their main character is to grow, mutate and establish new spatial relationships within their urban structure. This adaptability of the city allows experimentation with new approaches in alternative development in the influx city. Cities represent the scenario of many human activities; there is a continuous search for balance in this almost permanent spatial condition with the mutating activities which take place there. People move around continuously and the public domain comes fluctuatingly into these spaces, often in extremely temporary ways.[3]

As described above, one of the most significant aims of the studio was to investigate the role of architecture in creating a sense of *place*. This crucial question has generated projects in which alternative urban forms and spatial conditions have given a new urbanity to buildings and spaces.

Leon Battista Alberti argued that a city's nobility was inextricably linked to the layout of its squares and streets as well as the design and magnificence of its buildings,[4] and without any doubt this symbiotic relationship between public spaces and buildings represents the essence of creating a successful architectonic organism integrated into the urban structure.

The three projects presented here addressed this question by creating collective housing with a strong relationship to its context and using place-making principles extracted from the place to meet the needs of the community. Collective places for socialising and pause have been strategically inserted not only at the ground floor but also at different levels in the buildings, creating alternate sequences of public, semi-public and private spaces. A *place* incarnates the experiences and aspirations of people. To paraphrase Yi-Fu Tuan, place is not only a fact to be explained in the broader frame of space, but it is also a reality to be clarified and understood from the perspectives of the people who have given it meaning.[5]

---

3   Hajer, M.A.; and Reijndorp, A. *In Search of New Public Domain: Analysis and Strategy.* Rotterdam: NAi Publishers, 2001.

4   Kagan. 'Urbs and Civitas in Sixteenth- and Seventeenth-Century in Spain'.

5   Tuan. *Space and Place: The Perspective of Experience.*

In this regard, the essential need for a building to be urbane is an important characteristic to increase its public presence and its relationship with the city. It is therefore the incorporation of *permeability* as an indispensable feature that makes architecture accessible and allows us to become part of it.[6]

BIBLIOGRAPHY

Hajer, M.A.; and Reijndorp, A. 'In Search of New Public Domain: Analysis and Strategy'. Rotterdam: NAi Publishers, 2001.

Kagan, Richard L. 'Urbs and Civitas in Sixteenth- and Seventeenth-Century in Spain'. In: *Envisioning the City: Six Studies in Urban Cartography*, edited by David Buisseret, 75–108. The Kenneth Nebenzahl Jr. Lectures in the History of Cartography. Chicago: University of Chicago Press, 1998.

La Urbanitat de l'arquitectura. Conferències inaugurals curs ETSAB – UPC – Conferència inaugural curs 2009–2010. Barcelona, 2009. https://upcommons.upc.edu/handle/2099.2/1236.

Levine, Donald N. (ed.). *Georg Simmel: On Individuality and Social Forms*. Chicago: University of Chicago Press, 1971.

Tang, B.S.; and Wong, S.W. 'A Longitudinal Study of Open Space Zoning and Development in Hong Kong'. *Landscape and Urban Planning*, 87(4) (2008): 258–68.

Tuan, Yi-Fu. *Space and Place: The Perspective of Experience*. Minneapolis: University of Minnesota Press, 2005.

---

6   *La Urbanitat de l'arquitectura.*

PART THREE

CHAPTER ELEVEN

CHARLOTTE JOHNSON[1], KAT AUSTEN[2], SARAH BELL[1],
AIDUAN BORRION[1], ROBERT COMBER[3] AND JUN MATSUSHITA[2]

1. UCL

2. IILAB

3. Newcastle University

CO-DESIGN AND THE DOMESTIC WEF NEXUS: A PILOT PROJECT IN A LONDON HOUSING ESTATE

INTRODUCTION

Homes are key sites of resource consumption, and how we consume water, energy and food at home is increasingly becoming the target of policies aimed at creating more sustainable cities. For example, London's new environment strategy states the ambition for the city to be zero carbon and zero waste, and to address its water scarcity.[1] Housing plays a core role in delivering these ambitions. The strategy document explains how planning targets and building regulations will contribute to these goals, but also discusses the need to use 'integrated' and 'holistic solutions' that avoid focusing on isolated issues, but address the multiple factors contributing to environmental problems.[2] This aligns with academic research into the WEF nexus, and the imperative to understand how complex water, energy and food systems interact with each other.[3] London's strategy document goes on to discuss the need to involve citizens, and to step inside homes to affect consumer behaviour and influence how people use resources and produce waste. The document discusses, for example, the need to install water and energy smart meters in homes and to encourage people to

---

1   Greater London Authority. 'London Environment Strategy: Draft for Public Consultation'.

2   Ibid., 23

3   Cairns, Wilsdon and O'Donovan. *Sustainability in Turbulent Times: Lessons from the Nexus Network for Supporting Transdisciplinary Research.*

reduce the packaging they use. These types of 'demand-side' interventions open up a growing area of research within housing studies that looks at the interaction between the design of homes and the design of infrastructure. The drive to make housing more sustainable has led to a focus on how the domestic end parts of utilities' infrastructure can be designed to bring users more reliably into the frame of resource management. However, the resident's role is typically restricted to using the equipment on their side of the meter appropriately. From shower timers to time-of-use tariffs, information and equipment are being designed to bring user interaction in line with networked utilities' distribution priorities.[4]

Engineering Comes Home takes a different approach. It uses critical social theory[5] to explore the social and material factors that affect the way that residents consume resources at home. It then uses design theory to involve residents in rethinking the way that their homes are supplied with water, energy and food. Co-design of domestic WEF infrastructure is a new area of research,[6] although it builds on the theories and practices of design for sustainability[7] and on value-sensitive design.[8] In this chapter, we outline the co-design pilot project that ran in 2016–17 in a housing estate in south-east London. The project used a co-design methodology and led to the installation of a smart rainwater harvesting tank on an estate downpipe for residents to use. This chapter starts with an overview of the design theories and practices that shaped the methodology, then provides the details of the pilot and ends with a discussion of the evaluation and reflections that were produced throughout the process by the research team and participants.

CO-DESIGN AS RESEARCH METHOD

Engineering Comes Home drew on two strands of design thinking to form the co-design methodology. The first strand focused on engagement using participatory design practices developed in the information technologies field. The second focused

---

4   For example, Strengers' *Smart Energy Technologies in Everyday Life* on smart electricity grids and Jeffrey and Gearey's 'Consumer Reactions to Water Conservation Policy Instruments' on water demand management.

5   Stirling, 'Transforming Power: Social Science and the Politics of Energy Choices' and 'Developing "Nexus Capabilities" Towards Transdisciplinary Methodologies'; Shove, 'Beyond the ABC: Climate Change Policy and Theories of Social Change'; Ingram, Shove and Watson, 'Products and Practices: Selected Concepts from Science and Technology Studies and from Social Theories of Consumption and Practice'.

6   Cairns, Wilsdon and O'Donovan, *Sustainability in Turbulent Times: Lessons from the Nexus Network for Supporting Transdisciplinary Research*; Cairns and Krzywoszynska, 'Anatomy of a Buzzword: The Emergence of "the Water–Energy–Food Nexus" in UK Natural Resource Debates'.

7   Lockton, Harrison and Stanton. 'Making the User More Efficient: Design for Sustainable Behaviour'.

8   Friedman. 'Value-Sensitive Design: A Research Agenda for Information Technology'.

on disruptive interventions using product design approaches from the sustainability design field.

PARTICIPATORY DESIGN

Participatory design has been a field of research and practice in ICT since the 1970s.[9] In its early forms it focused on improving workplace ICT systems and supporting the users of technologies to create humane and ethical workplace environments. As IT systems have expanded beyond the workplace, participatory design theorists and practitioners have moved into domestic and other settings. This field has led to specialisms such as Value-Sensitive Design, which incorporates alternative design principles based on "human well being, human dignity, justice, welfare, and human rights".[10] It has also led to more open design practices moving first to user-centred design, which observed people's practices to improve design, then to user-led design, which put users in charge of identifying the design problem, to co-design, which embraced both suppliers and users to work together in defining problem spaces and design solutions.[11] At its core, participatory design is about improving the systems that serve people and emancipating the users through engaging them in the design process.

DESIGN AND SUSTAINABILITY

If participatory design focuses primarily on human agency and social institutions supported by ICT, design for sustainability focuses primarily on the environmental impact of goods and services. Its origins lie in improving product performance to provide consumers with the same service levels while reducing the volume of resources used. Challenges such as the 'rebound effect' led design theorists to consider not only a product's performance, but also its use by people. This has led to fields such as 'design for sustainable behaviour' which encourage more sustainable consumption behaviours through product design.[12] This approach has been criticised for prioritising the individual as the locus of agency and understanding behaviour through a rational-choice paradigm based on normative assumptions that can obscure broader political questions about resource consumption.[13] Recent approaches to sustainability and design tackle some of these issues by drawing on Social Practice Theory to engage with resource using practices,[14] and Actor Network Theory to move

9   Simonsen and Robertson. *Routledge International Handbook of Participatory Design*.
10 Friedman. 'Value-Sensitive Design: A Research Agenda for Information Technology', 3.
11 McDougall. 'Co-Production, Co-Design and Co-Creation: What Is the Difference?'
12 Jelsma and Knot. 'Designing Environmentally Efficient Services: A "Script" Approach'.
13 Kuijer, 'Implications of Social Practice Theory for Sustainable Design'; Wever, van Kuijk and Boks, 'User-centred Design for Sustainable Behaviour'.
14 Kuijer. 'Implications of Social Practice Theory for Sustainable Design'.

beyond the individual as the source of agency.[15] In these two examples, both Teh and Kuijer studied social practices around resource use and then used design methods to disrupt or innovate and project possible alternative socio-material configurations and co-evolutions.

Design for sustainability as method can be speculative and allow for new possibilities to open up. It draws in the non-human world as partner and questions embedded power relations. Co-design as method widens the circle of those involved in the task and enables alternative knowledge and value systems to be part of the projection of alternative arrangements. This combined approach was followed by the Engineering Comes Home team.

THE ENGINEERING COMES HOME CO-DESIGN PROCESS

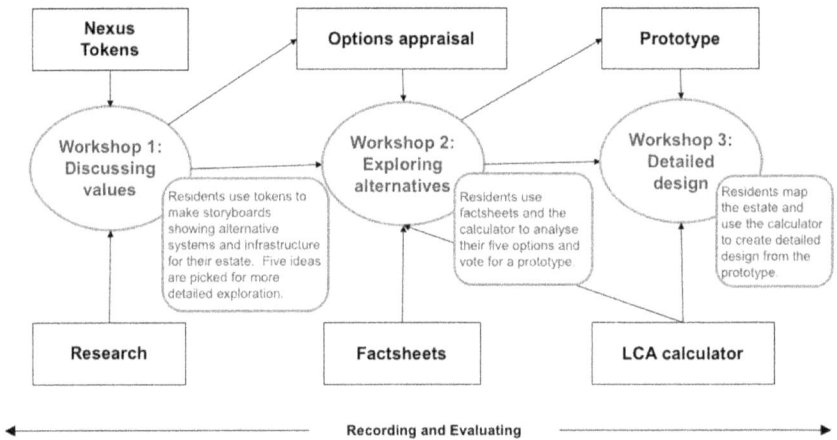

Figure 1. Co-design process for community-scale WEF infrastructure

The project put these design principles into practice in order to test whether it was possible to co-design inner-city infrastructure systems supplying water, energy and/ or food to homes. In this section we discuss the co-design process employed in our project on the Meakin Estate in Southwark.[16] This process was run along with other research activities including an initial period of qualitative research with residents to

15   Teh. 'Hydro-Urbanism: Reconfiguring the Urban Water-Cycle in the Lower Lea River Basin, London'.

16   The recruitment of the residents as partners in the process is discussed by Johnson and colleagues (Forthcoming); this paper focuses specifically on the co-design process.

understand the social context of the estate[17] and a horizon scan of technologies which could be fitted into this domestic context.[18]

The co-design process was carried out in three half-day workshops held in the estate's community hall and involved 19 residents (15% of all households). The process was run by the research team, supported by an external facilitator, videographer[19] and the local Tenants and Residents Association (TRA).

WORKSHOP ONE: DISCUSSING VALUES

The first workshop elicited values relevant to domestic WEF resource management on the estate and generated ideas for interventions that might fit these values and the material configuration of the estate. Thirteen residents participated. The first set of activities was designed to elicit values. We started with a 2-4-8 process, whereby groups of two discussed their ideas, then joined into groups of four, and then eight. At this point, each group listed all the values discussed and then presented them to the other group. This allowed us to generate a list of values reflecting all members' inputs and facilitate an open discussion about what was important to people when thinking about how they and their families consumed water, energy and food at home and on the estate.

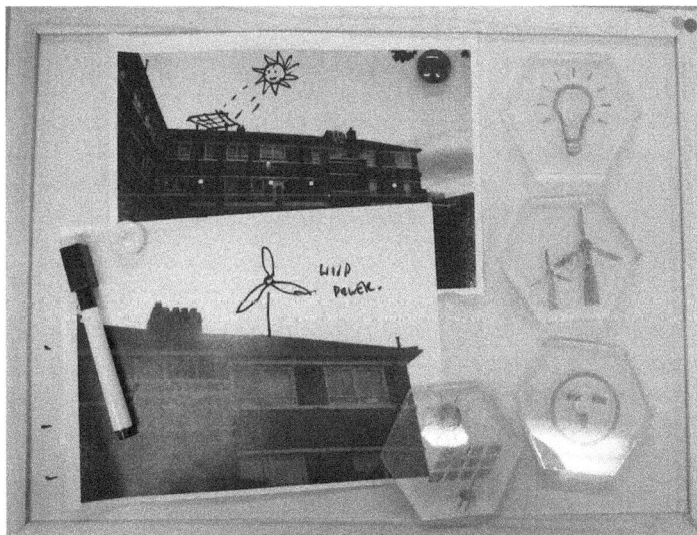

Figure 2. Electricity story

17   Johnson et al. (Forthcoming) 'Changing Resource Consumption at Home: Identifying Domestic WEF Nexus Leverage Points in London'.
18   Borrion et al. 'Development of LCA Calculator to Support Community Infrastructure Co-Design'.
19   Videos of the three workshops are available to watch at: http://www.engineering.ucl.ac.uk/engineering-exchange/video-articles/.

Figure 3. Food-growing story

We then used bespoke co-design tokens and equipment that our team had developed to facilitate discussions about complex WEF systems. The tokens had icons representing aspects of WEF systems – a toilet, a flower and a plug, for example. Participants were invited to play with these tokens and construct narratives attached to locations within the estate. We provided magnetic white boards, photos of the estate and the magnetic tokens, and participants worked in pairs or alone to construct narratives. Two of the narrative boards are shown here: one exploring possibilities for onsite generation of renewable electricity (Figure 2) and the other looking at the potential to grow food on the estate (Figure 3).

In total, participants created six narratives: food growing, electricity generation, gardens, food banks, two boards about re-using things and one with multiple narratives. As participants discussed each story, some key themes emerged. Waste came across as the most important issue for the group: reducing the volume of waste, repurposing it into something useful and improving the cleanliness of the estate's public areas. For example, Georgina[20] explained:

> my idea [is to] have a compressor that could make the bulk smaller. [At the moment,] everything on the floor and everything is blowing everywhere so those things could be avoided with proper bins.

---

20   Pseudonyms are used for all participants.

Flo commented:

> If we had… a notice board for household items, [then] we could pass it on, like a cot… someone on the estate could possibly want that cot, and we're recycling it. Plus… the money we collect from the glass, the clothes, could go into other factors for our estate, our environment, and for all of us for future generations."

A second key concern was water. Mary commented: "I think water would be the best, to be able to recycle the water and to use it in something else… Personally to me that would really help the estate". The issue transcended the local estate level as Georgina argued: "It'd also be an example to other communities as to how much water we save. It's not just for us, if we transmit to other areas, other cities in Europe, other countries". However, not everyone agreed. Neil argued against the idea: "We don't need to recycle on the estate, it's already recycled, centrally" (i.e. by Thames Water). He did not see any value in the small-scale savings offered by an estate scheme.

We had planned a narrowing strategy whereby a single issue emerged that the whole group would like to explore in detail. However, we had more participants than planned, which meant groups worked together on stories and were reluctant to narrow down the number of issues. Instead, the group identified a set of ideas that they wanted the team to explore further. These were:

- Water reuse for garden/home
- Composting for garden
- Reduction of food and material waste
- Management of material waste and/or cleanliness of the estate.

Through analysing the discussion, the team was also able to draw out a matrix of participants' values that could be used to shape the design (Table 1).

Human	Practical	Concerns	Aesthetics
Community building	Ease of use	Strangers	Pleasant to look at
Buy in from other residents	Achievable	Scale / quantity / uptake	Reduced rubbish
Wider education	Scalable		
Shared stewardship	Impact		
Care for others	Necessary		
Resilient / future			

Table 1. Residents' values for the design

The team created a shortlist of existing technologies that could fit into the estate and align with the values elicited. The five systems were: wormeries, food growing, food sharing, rainwater harvesting and waste compacting. For the second workshop, we prepared fact sheets for each of these systems and developed a bespoke LCA calculator that participants could use to gauge the fit of the technology to their community and their estate.[21]

WORKSHOP TWO: FEEDBACK ON DESIGN OPTIONS

Nine residents came to the second workshop to assess the technologies and explore how they could be implemented within the estate. We presented the five ideas, providing participants with fact sheets and showing them how to use the LCA calculator to assess different design criteria. The calculator had a scenario for each technology with adjustable input parameters such as volume of food waste, quantity and scale of technologies. These changed the volume of food that could be grown or the amount of CO_2 savings realised. Residents explored each scenario in pairs, adjusting the calculator according to their assessment of what was appropriate for the estate. These context sensitive adjustments included:

- Levels of community involvement: Clare, who'd been involved in other estate projects, decided only 50 per cent of households would participate and limited inputs to this proportion of engagement for all scenarios. By contrast, Penny decided some of the technologies could be designed to increase engagement. For the waste compactor, she put small manual compactors at each stairwell on the basis that residents would regularly see them and be encouraged to use them.

- Aesthetics and estate layout: participants used their knowledge of the estate and of different community members' use of communal space. For example, in the gardening scenarios participants anchored their designs in parts of the gardens the community would accept as food-growing areas.

- Utility of outputs: although the LCA calculator was designed to show the resulting CO_2 emissions reductions, these savings were not very meaningful to the group. Participants tailored designs according to other outputs. For example, when assessing the wormeries options, Mary looked at how much fertiliser could be produced and whether the TRA would be able to sell or exchange this amongst local gardening groups.

After participants had explored each scenario we regrouped and discussed the design options each pair had chosen. This allowed the group to share the different priorities and assessments that had informed their adjustments of the LCA calculator parameters. After the group had explored all five ideas, participants voted on a single design option to move forward with. Discussing the vote, participants raised other

---

21   See McDougall's 'Co-Production, Co-Design and Co-Creation: What Is the Difference?' for the horizon scan of existing technologies and the development of LCA calculator.

context-specific values and knowledge they felt should be factored into the group's selection. Governance was a key concern, particularly how much management any design would require. Another concern was misuse by "uninitiated outsiders". For example, waste compacting was seen as potentially dangerous if people didn't know how to use the compactor properly; likewise, food sharing was felt to be open to mismanagement. All participants had a first and second vote and rainwater harvesting won the most votes.

The vote gave the research team one idea to turn into a more detailed design. However, workshop two had also shown limits to the residents' knowledge of unknown systems. Although we worked to address this during the workshop by providing information sheets and responding to questions, the research team wanted to provide hands-on experience of a rainwater tank prior to workshop three. We sought permission to install a smart rainwater tank on a downpipe on the estate and were able to show participants a working system.[22]

WORKSHOP THREE: DETAILED DESIGN

The third workshop aimed to get residents' feedback on the prototype and create a detailed design for rainwater harvesting on the estate. The research team created a bespoke rainwater harvesting module for the LCA calculator that let residents explore design details such as tank size, number and location, rooftop area to be used to catch rain, position of outflows and whether or not to pressurise and pump water. Seven residents joined for the third workshop to experiment with the detailed design.

The workshop started with an overview of rainwater harvesting covering technical and operational details as well as its role within the broader picture of London's water governance and infrastructure. We then split participants into groups and walked round the estate mapping existing drainage infrastructure and potential uses for stored rainwater. Figure 4 shows one of the maps created by the participants. The residents have marked the downpipes that are free from household wastewater and identified points where water could be used. The walkaround was an opportunity for residents to engage fully with the socio-material context of their estate and how a rainwater harvesting system might be integrated into this context. For example, we discussed who would use the water. Participants felt it would be useful for the shared gardens, residents' own gardens, for cleaners to clean common areas and for residents to wash their cars. We discussed tank positioning. Upper walkways meant there could be a

---

22   Installing the tank exposed some of the difficulties of implementing neighbourhood-scale WEF infrastructure. At the Meakin there were a number of different departments involved in the installation and use of the water. The tank would have to be located in the garden of the housing management board (Leathermarket JMB), connected to a downpipe managed by a different department and the water was to be used by the TRA for their planters. The groups had different interests and levels of scepticism towards the tank and its usefulness. Nonetheless we managed to get all parties to agree to the installation.

---

pressurised supply without the need for a pump, but raised questions about how the pipework would look. Participants also discussed access and safety concerns. All these details were then used by the participants to come up with detailed designs. They worked in pairs using the LCA calculator to gauge different technical modifications. We regrouped and reviewed the designs, discussing additional factors such as implementation and maintenance. Workshop three ended with a reflection on the project overall and an evaluation survey.

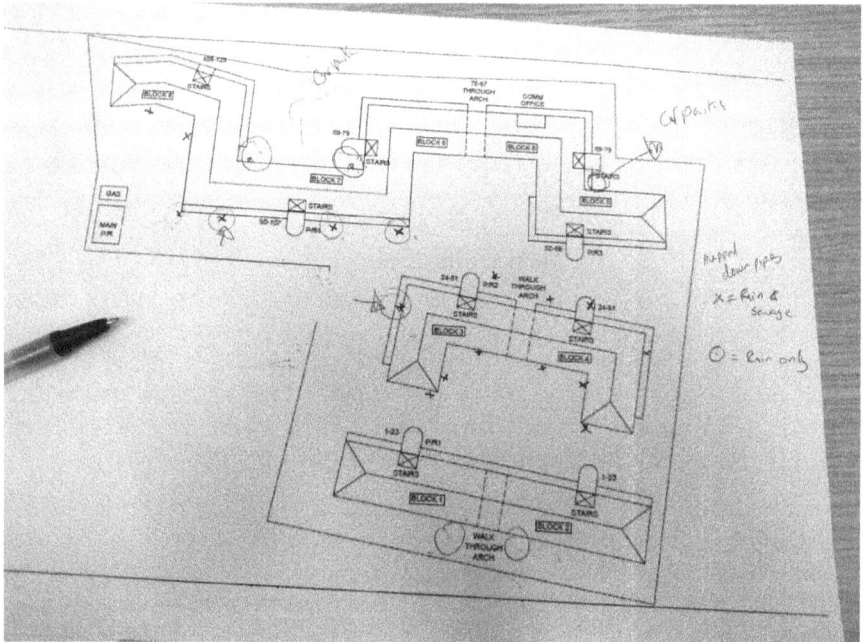

Figure 4. Mapping rainwater infrastructure for detailed design

REFLECTIONS AND EVALUATIONS

The objective for the Engineering Comes Home project was to pilot the co-design process. Therefore, we invited evaluation and feedback from the participants, but also had an on-going process of evaluation and reflection amongst the team.

PARTICIPANT EVALUATION

Participants were encouraged to provide feedback on the process. This was managed through formal mechanisms such as seeking group consensus on next steps, but informal feedback was also captured. For example, Justin commented at the end of the first workshop "Nice to see so many people interested. I want to make the estate better and I'm pleased to see that there are other people here interested too". This helped us gauge motivations for participation that we formally tested with an evaluation questionnaire at the end of workshop three. This asked how confident people felt in being able to contribute to the activities and whether they felt their ideas had been listened to, and gave some free spaces for comments that some people used to discuss their motivations for participating. The nine questionnaires we received were overwhelmingly positive, but did show some variation. Seven of the nine strongly agreed with the statement that "the ideas came mostly from the community", but only four strongly agreed with the statement that "I've helped influence the outcome of the project". This may indicate people supported other ideas that did not get selected. It may also be a result of our inclusive process for participation, as we allowed new residents in at every stage. This meant some people participated at later stages who'd not helped establish the value-based criteria or of assess the range of alternative ideas.

In the free comments we got further insights. Four respondents specifically cited coming together as a community as a benefit of the project. Two stated they had learnt through the project. These themes – infrastructure literacy, participation and community context – were also ones that were picked up by the research team's self-reflective evaluation.

RESEARCH TEAM EVALUATION

The team's reflections were captured through observational notes on the workshops and written pieces on the process. Four themes are clear and reflect those mentioned above by the participants.

TECHNOLOGICAL LITERACY

Participants having little prior knowledge of the shortlisted technology options was an important learning outcome. We struggled over the question of how much to 'educate' participants. An engineer in the team commented: "what's the balance between participants coming up with ideas and being educated with alternative ideas, at a co-design workshop?" We needed to gauge how far to challenge participants' assumptions about existing or potential systems, aware that we would then shape the outcome of the process. We also found it hard for people to engage deeply in the design of an object or a system as an abstract concept. However, by the third workshop we had a working prototype for people to use and the team felt that by the end of the workshop we had managed to raise levels of technical literacy about urban drainage and water management.

DESIGN THINKING

Throughout the workshops, the participants tended to focus on established design solutions and the practicalities of implementing these within their estate. As one of the design team said "there was a definite jumping in with pre-formed solutions" that limited the 'problem space', the process of generating new questions based on personal experiences and values. We felt that overall the process was closer to user-led design than co-design. In other words we had successfully led participants through the "process of describing and solving problems for themselves"[23] but had not managed to get to the stage where the participants were helping the designers to understand a problem/solution they'd identified through their own experience.

PARTICIPATION

All 123 households in the estate received a written invitation to the project followed up with a visit to their home for a face-to-face invitation. Through this recruitment strategy and our decision to allow newcomers at every stage of the project, we were able to get 15 per cent of the estate's households involved in at least one of our activities. Our approach meant that we had some difficulties with continuity: previously dismissed ideas were revisited by people who'd not been part of the initial screening steps, for example. Nonetheless, as the Principal Investigator pointed out, "we managed to have enough participants throughout to test the methods and to get some meaningful data for research. It would have been better to have a more consistent cohort and even more people participating, but it is impressive that people have been willing and interested to engage so far." Our approach also meant we were able to engage with people motivated by very diverse reasons, including those interested in improving their local environmental quality as well as those more interested in community-building activities.

INSTITUTIONAL CONTEXT

The institutional context also shaped the process. We worked with the estate's governing body (Leathermarket JMB) and the TRA. Both were supportive and helped us recruit participants. The management board adopted a hands-off approach; in contrast, the TRA had more at stake and therefore took more control of the process, steering it to align with existing initiatives or previous agreements within the community. The PI reflected that "this has placed some constraints on the 'design thinking', closing down options early in the ideation process". The social researcher also reflected that later workshops "felt like TRA meetings", meaning those used to this governance structure were more vocal in expressing their opinions and proposals, while participants who weren't TRA regulars were less vocal. Nonetheless, the surveys from participants showed people found it easy to contribute to the discussions. And, as the PI pointed out, working within an institutional context is "an important part of the design lifecycle, [and involves] understanding local capabilities and constraints. In adapting the process in the future to enable deeper engagement in the co-design process, we might think about how we can capture this more productively, to acknowledge local context, knowledge and risks, whilst still keeping design possibilities open."

---

23   McDougall. 'Co-Production, Co-Design and Co-Creation: What Is the Difference?'

CONCLUSION

Engineering Comes Home demonstrated that residents were willing and able to play a meaningful role in rethinking how their housing estate could be supplied with water, energy and food. We started the co-design workshops completely open to any form of WEF nexus intervention that could be placed in the home or the estate. We ended with a rainwater tank providing water for the TRA's flower beds. This specific design solution evolved from the participants' values of managing waste and pioneering water stewardship.

The co-design process was iterative and responsive to the context. Through it we have found:

- A willingness to engage in the co-design process

- That people are motivated by the idea of saving WEF resources beyond rational choice models

- That we could generate a set of shared values to create a design brief

- It was possible to build technical literacy amongst participants.

The pilot has allowed us to explore the interaction between housing, reduced resource consumption and increased urban sustainability. As discussed in the introduction, housing is assigned a key role in enabling cities to deliver on their sustainability targets. Much research focuses on building new high-performing housing to meet these targets, while retrofitting existing housing is seen as harder to achieve, particularly in cases such as the Meakin, where the housing is inhabited by residents with a mix of tenures. Here we have shown how a group of social tenants, private tenants and owner occupiers are motivated to work together to improve their housing estate and to rethink how WEF resources can be supplied and consumed in their neighbourhood. The pilot has allowed us to test the process and create a set of co-design method statements that are freely available for others to build on.[24] This first case study provides an encouraging example of how residents can be included in the technical work of creating less resource intense, more liveable cities.

BIBLIOGRAPHY

Borrion, A.; Matsushita, J.; Austen, K.; Johnson, C.; and Bell, S. 'Development of LCA Calculator to Support Community Infrastructure Co-Design'. *Journal of Life Cycle Assesment*, n.d.

Cairns, Rose; and Krzywoszynska, Anna. 'Anatomy of a Buzzword: The Emergence of "the Water–Energy–Food Nexus" in UK Natural Resource Debates'. *Environmental Science and Policy*, 64 (2016): 164–70. https://doi.org/10.1016/j.envsci.2016.07.007.

Cairns, Rose; Wilsdon, James; and O'Donovan, Cian. *Sustainability in Turbulent Times: Lessons from the Nexus Network for Supporting Transdisciplinary Research*, 2017.

---

24   The full methodology and tools are available at: https://ech.iilab.org.

Friedman, Batya. 'Value-Sensitive Design: A Research Agenda for Information Technology'. *Value-Sensitive Design Workshop*. Seattle, 1999.

Greater London Authority. 'London Environment Strategy: Draft for Public Consultation'. London, 2017.

Ingram, Jack; Shove, Elizabeth; and Watson, Matthew. 'Products and Practices: Selected Concepts from Science and Technology Studies and from Social Theories of Consumption and Practice'. *Design Issues*, 23(2) (2007): 3–16. https://doi.org/10.1162/desi.2007.23.2.3.

Jeffrey, P.; and Gearey, M. 'Consumer Reactions to Water Conservation Policy Instruments'. In: *Water Demand Management*, edited by David Butler and Fayyaz Ali Memon, 302–29. London: IWA Publishing, 2006.

Jelsma, Japp; and Knot, Marjolijn. 'Designing Environmentally Efficient Services: A "Script" Approach'. *Journal of Sustainable Product Design*, 2(3–4) (2002): 119–30.

Johnson, Charlotte; Bell, Sarah; Borrion, Aiduan; and Comber, Robert. 'Changing Resource Consumption at Home: Identifying Domestic WEF Nexus Leverage Points in London'. Forthcoming.

Kuijer, Lenneke. 'Implications of Social Practice Theory for Sustainable Design'. Delft University of Technology, 2014.

Lockton, Daniel; Harrison, David; and Stanton, Neville A. 'Making the User More Efficient: Design for Sustainable Behaviour'. *International Journal of Sustainable Engineering*, 1(1) (2008): 3–8. https://doi.org/10.1080/19397030802131068.

McDougall, Sean. 'Co-Production, Co-Design and Co-Creation: What Is the Difference?' Stakeholder Design, 2012. http://www.stakeholderdesign.com/co-production-versus-co-design-what-is-the-difference/.

Shove, Elizabeth. 'Beyond the ABC: Climate Change Policy and Theories of Social Change'. *Environment and Planning A*, 42(6) (2010): 1273–85. https://doi.org/10.1068/a42282.

Simonsen, Jesper; and Robertson, Toni, eds. *Routledge International Handbook of Participatory Design*. Routledge. Abingdon, Oxon.: Routledge, 2012. https://doi.org/10.4324/9780203108543.

Stirling, Andy. 'Developing "Nexus Capabilities": Towards Transdisciplinary Methodologies'. The Nexus Network, 2015. https://doi.org/10.13140/RG.2.1.2834.9920.

_____. 'Transforming Power: Social Science and the Politics of Energy Choices'. *Energy Research & Social Science*, March 2014: 1–13. https://doi.org/10.1016/j.erss.2014.02.001.

Strengers, Yolande. *Smart Energy Technologies in Everyday Life*. London: Palgrave Macmillan UK, 2013. https://doi.org/9780203108543.

Teh, Tse-Hui. 'Hydro-Urbanism: Reconfiguring the Urban Water-Cycle in the Lower Lea River Basin, London'. September 2011.

Wever, Renee; van Kuijk, Jasper; and Boks, Casper. 'User centred Design for Sustainable Behaviour'. *International Journal of Sustainable Engineering*, 1(1) (March 2008): 9–20. https://doi.org/10.1080/19397030802166205.

CHAPTER TWELVE

NADIA BERTOLINO AND SANDRA COSTA SANTOS

Department of Architecture and Built Environment, Northumbria University, UK

TESTING THE THEORY OF 'PLANNED COMMUNITIES': AN EXPLORATION OF THE LINK BETWEEN COMMUNITY DESIGN AND EVERYDAY LIFE THROUGH A PARTICIPATORY APPROACH

INTRODUCTION

The interdisciplinary research project 'Place and Belonging: what can we learn from Claremont Court housing scheme?' examines the case study of Claremont Court, a Modernist housing scheme in Edinburgh, built between 1958 and 1962 as part of the Scottish national housing drive. The research project relates to the critical understanding of the linkages between the spatial features of the place and the individual and collective sense of belonging. This chapter introduces a reflection on Basil Spence's idea to foster a sense of cross-class community in Claremont Court through the design of areas dedicated to communal activities and the combination of diverse housing typologies.[1] In fact, the scheme comprises 63 dwellings of six different typologies, grouped in L-shaped low-rise rectangular volumes around two landscape courtyards.

Consistent with the key principles of the post-war Scottish housing drive, this scheme was aimed at improving the living conditions of the masses, enabling at the same time the idea of a mixed development, based on new meanings of home and communal life. This was a constant aspect of Spence's design approach during his appointment as President of the RIBA (1958–60): to improve the public profile of architects and drive architecture into the wider socio-political debate, sustaining the role of the architect in an era of developer-led architecture.[2]

1   Costa Santos et al. 'Place-making theory behind Claremont Court'.
2   Long and Thomas. *Basil Spence Architect*, 19.

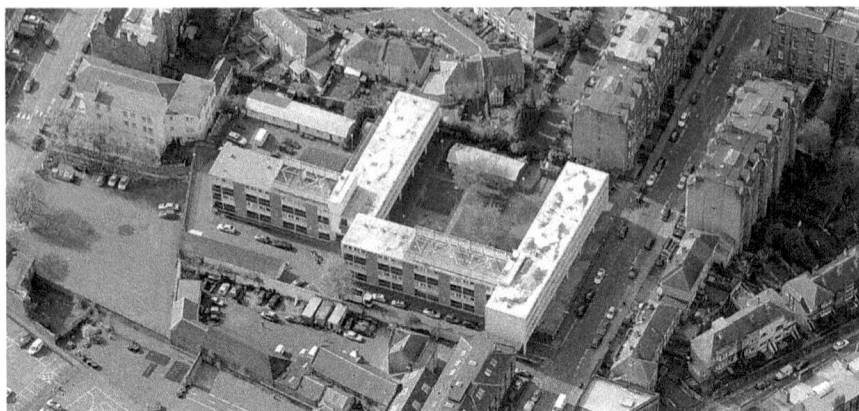

Figure 1. Claremont Court housing scheme; view of the two L-shaped volumes around the landscape courtyards

The original social approach contributes in making Claremont Court a relevant case study within the broader framework of Modernist housing in UK. Although Spence did not make explicit his theoretical agenda, the spatiality of Claremont Court may suggest connections with the avant-gardist theory of a planned community, developed by Team X as an alternative to the socially alienating developments proposed by orthodox Modernism. According to Team X, spatial hierarchy was essential for social life to function and to foster a sense of community. This principle was translated into specific architectural features, such as grouped medium-rise blocks, joined by open decks for pedestrians or organised around communal courtyards.[3]

This chapter first contextualises the Claremont Court project as an advocacy of the idea of planned communities. In the following section, the link between architectural features and community behaviours is introduced, taking Coleman's study on postwar mass housing in Britain as the starting point. Finally, the authors discuss the outputs of a participatory workshop, through which the effectiveness of Spence's attempt in relation to current spatial practices has been assessed.

THE DESIGN OF A 'CROSS-CLASS' COMMUNITY IN CLAREMONT COURT

Inspired by traditional patterns of socialisation and the thesis of the link between spatial arrangement and social behaviour in planned communities, Claremont Court is considered here as a relevant case study to analyse and interpret how architectural spaces in post-war mass-housing design have enabled or fostered the process of cross-class community formation.

---

3   Smithson. *Team 10 Primer*, 36.

Glendinning points out that the post-war estates designed by Spence[4] were structured upon the principles of fostering 'community' through the planning of self-contained neighbourhoods, spaciously laid out to maximise sunlight and open air, with low-rise blocks of flats and cottages, frequently in parallel rows or around cul-de-sacs.[5] In fact, the Claremont Court development is set up with the six blocks facing the two internal courtyards, closing up on East Claremont Street and creating a more private secondary road for car access along the northern side. This ensured a clear division between pedestrian, bike and car access points; provided the scheme with an inner mobility system and parking provision; and gave the communal areas the character of enclosed spaces for the community. Thus, building on the CIAM guidelines, Claremont Court dwellings were provided with open space, sunlight and integrated social facilities responding to the need to improve the quality of life in residential areas.[6]

Raising the living standard of the masses and promoting the creation of inclusive communities were ideas put into practice by Spence in the post-war period, consistent with his public commitment as RIBA president. In doing so, he tried to translate into architectural language the Modernist ideal of designing houses 'for all'.[7] This involved a radical rethinking of the type of users the units were for, as suggested for the very first time on the occasion of the cutting-edge exhibition Britain Can Make It in 1946 and later the Ideal Home Exhibition, 1949. In fact, Claremont Court contains thirteen housing types, such as two-bedroom flats and maisonettes, cottages for the elderly as well as one-bedroom dwelling units,[8] offering a home of one's own to new family types (such as married couples with no children and single people, including increasing numbers of working women).

According to Spence, a sense of community and belonging could be created through casual encounters in the stairs and drying areas, informal chats on the balconies and by sharing common facilities. Consistently with the Smithsons' theories at the time, vertical living was seen as a cause of lack of social contact among neighbours, while generously sized public areas, with open decks, and triple-height crossings were considered able to "invite one to linger and pass the time of day".[9] Similarly, Basil Spence paid attention to the design of stairwells (mainly at the junctions across

4   Such as Sunbury Urban Districts near London (1947), Beechwood Avenue (1947–52) and two in southern Scotland: Bannerfield in Selkirk and Summerfield in Dunbar (1945).

5   Miles Glendinning. 'Hanging Gardens of the Gorbals: Hutchesontown 'C', flawed masterpiece of mass housing?' In: Campbell, Glendinning and Thomas. Basil Spence Buildings and Projects.

6   Alan Powers The Modern Movement in Britain, 32–8.

7   Hubert-Jan Henket. 'Modernity, Modernism and the Modern Movement'. In: Henket and Heynen. Back from Utopia: The Challenge of the Modern Movement, 10.

8   According to the guidelines released by the Scottish Housing Committee of the time.

9   Smithson and Smithson. Ordinariness and Light. Urban theories 1952–1960 and their application in a building project 1963–1970, 54.

different blocks) and open decks. According to these premises, the spacious landing at the junction of blocks I and II would allow members of the two families to engage in conversation when coming in and out or using the refuse chute. Also, the generous stairwell allowed easy visual contact with adjacent floors.

Four main design actions have been identified in Claremont Court through which Spence aimed to encourage a sense of community and catalyse social interaction:[10]

- Typological variety, suggesting that units were designed to house different users and family groups;

- Vertical and horizontal distribution across the different blocks, with attention to the design of stairwells (mainly at the junctions across different blocks) covered walkways and open decks to increase the opportunities for interaction between neighbours;

- Unit interior layouts, so that all the balconies (and in particular those serving the living room) face the courtyards and eventually facilitate communications between neighbours;

- Provision of communal areas such as the two enclosed landscape courtyards and the drying area on the roof of blocks II and IV.

ARCHITECTURAL DESIGN AND SOCIAL BEHAVIOUR IN POST-WAR HOUSING ESTATES

Building on Newman's theory of 'defensible space' (1972), Alice Coleman conducted a comprehensive study in 1985 to assess how spatial arrangement could affect the quality of life and influence social behaviours in Modernist housing schemes. According to Newman, 'anonymity' is one of the three principles explaining how antisocial behaviours are made difficult to prevent and most likely to happen. It is defined as an "impersonal character of areas where a community structure has failed to develop and people know few other residents, even by sight".[11] The lack of interaction between residents also makes it difficult for them to establish relationships and co-operate as they're not sure whether they can rely on one another. Drawing on these premises, Utopia on Trial reports an extensive set of data referring to over 4,000 residential blocks to demonstrate how specific architectural design features (such as corridors, types of entrance and number of storeys) have a direct impact on the residents' perception of safety and overall comfort in those residential areas.[12] Even more recent works, such as Gehl's *Life Between Buildings*, endorse the view that communities grow spontaneously when

---

10   Costa Santos et al. 'Place-making theory behind Claremont Court'.
11   Newman. *Defensible Space*, 27–8.
12   Coleman. *Utopia on Trial: Vision and Reality in Planned Housing*. London: Hilary Shipman, 1985.

opportunities for casual social interaction are offered within communal areas of housing developments.[13]

Coleman agrees with Newman, stating that community structures and behaviours are affected by the layout and spatial arrangement of the housing development. Coleman lists "design variables and design values"[14] divided into four main categories:

- Size variables (dwellings per block, dwellings per entrance, storeys per block, storeys per dwelling);

- Circulation variables (overhead walkways, interconnecting exits, vertical routes, corridor type);

- Entrance characteristics (entrance position, entrance type, blocks raised above stilts, blocks raised above garages);

- Features of the ground (spatial organisation, blocks in the site, access points, play areas).

Based on Coleman's classification of these design variables that typically describe the communal areas in post-war housing tenements, a photo survey has been conducted in Claremont Court focussing on: (1) types of entrance and relation with the street; (2) covered walkways and stairwells; and (3) landscape courtyards. The survey of these design variables in Claremont Court's communal areas confirmed that they are typical of some post-war Modern housing estates in Britain.

Although an initial stage of the investigation relating to communal areas was structured on Coleman's design variables, in a later stage we developed an original cross-disciplinary methodological approach to integrate the data describing the physical space with the community's perception of those areas. In fact, as Coleman noticed, a large number of participants interestingly "voiced criticism of the common parts of the block without specifying precisely which" during the interviews.[15] Similarly, throughout the first and second round of interviews with the research participants, we collected a number of complaints in relation to the quality and maintenance of the shared spaces in Claremont Court, with interviewees reporting uncomfortable feelings attached to these. For example, Nicolas and David, a young couple in their thirties who recently moved to the court, highlighted the gap between the outdoor areas, perceived as unsafe, and the familiar, safe interior. With particular reference to the open-deck access, for them this type of access "has maybe a stigma to it".[16]

---

13   Jahn Gehl, *Life Between Buildings: Using Public Space*. Washington: Island Press, 2011.

14   Coleman, *Utopia on Trial: Vision and Reality in Planned Housing*, 34.

15   Ibid., 33

16   Costa Santos and Bertolino. 'Claremont Court Housing Scheme: a post-occupancy evaluation of Modernist dwellings supporting current spatial practices'.

Figure 2. Claremont Court: types of entrance and relation with the street. Images: Nadia Bertolino (2016)

Figure 3. Claremont Court: covered walkways and stairwells. Image: Nadia Bertolino (2016)

INVESTIGATING COMMUNITY AND SENSE OF BELONGING THROUGH A PARTICIPATORY APPROACH

The variety of research strategies that we have applied to the case study respond to the understanding of place as a physical and socio-cultural reality.[17] According to the theoretical framework underpinning the project, we consider places as "repositories and contexts within which interpersonal, community, and cultural relationships occur", and "it is to those social relationships, not just place qua place, to which people are attached".[18] With these premises, biographical and photo-elicitation interviews allowed us to study verbal behaviours, while the outcomes of the interactive session described in the following sections helped us understand more critically the spatial factors affecting the development of a sense of belonging to Claremont Court.

Most scholarship on place relates place attachment to place identity, which is intended as "a component of personal identity",[19] and the process through which people come to describe themselves as belonging to a particular place and adopting identifications which reflect places.[20]

In the case of Claremont Court, we assumed that a sense of attachment to a place can be of a different nature if we refer to the private space of the dwelling or to the communal areas of the development, such as the landscape courtyard and the roof terrace.

The novel methodology we developed included a session of data gathering through a participatory workshop, organised in November 2016 in partnership with Claremont Court Residents Association. Voluntary research participants were recruited through word of mouth and by circulating an email invitation among the members of the Residents Association.

The findings of this facilitator-led workshop allowed us to compare the original intention of designing a community in the 1960s with the current communal life in Claremont Court.

---

17   Bertolino and Costa Santos. 'Towards a definition of "place". Cross-disciplinary methodology for interpolating architectural and sociological data in Claremont Court, Edinburgh'.

18   Low and Altman. *Place Attachment*, 8.

19   Cross. 'Processes of Place Attachment: An Interactional Framework'.

20   See: Hernández et al., 2007; Stedman, 2002.

Figure 4. Community workshop with Claremont Court residents. Images: Nadia Bertolino (2016)

WORKSHOP METHODOLOGY

The workshop aimed at understanding the users' perceptions of the shared spaces in Claremont Court and defining a hierarchy of elements according to their criteria. During the workshop, the participants were invited to take part in two main facilitator-led activities. First, they were asked to sketch their 'mental map' of Claremont Court, where the architectural space becomes distorted according to each individual's perception of such a familiar place.

Inspired by Robinson's exercise,[21] the process of developing a cognitive image of Claremont Court served to develop the ability to gain a spatial understanding of the place and reflect on the meaning that the individuals associated to that place. The cognitive images varied from person to person and were shaped heavily by past experiences, personal perceptions and their everyday lives: "Cognitive mapping is a process of a series of psychological transformations by which an individual acquires,

---

21   Robinson. 'The varied mental maps our students have'.

stores, recalls, and decodes information about the relative locations and attributes of the phenomena in his everyday spatial environment".[22] However, when different individuals relied on some of the same features in composing their mental maps (such as oversizing the parking area or putting landscape elements at the core of their map) they intended to reinforce the importance of these features in representing the physical environment.

The second type of activities complemented the mental maps and allowed the decoding of hidden meanings attached to the representation of the place. The participants were given a simplified map of the court and asked to highlight (through icons):

A. Where the neighbours you interact with most frequently live;

B. The access you use more frequently;

C. Your path to go home and go out;

D. Your most-liked places in Claremont Court;

E. Your least-liked places in Claremont Court.

Some of them added key words to explain more effectively positive (such as open, pleasant, scenic etc.) or negative feelings (such as messy, dark, oppressive etc.) associated with the place.

The outcomes of this second stage, overlapped with the mental maps and compared with Coleman's findings, confirmed or denied some of the initial assumptions about the community perception of the place and the sense of attachment.

PERCEPTION, ATTACHMENT AND SENSE OF BELONGING: A VISUAL NARRATIVE

The outputs produced by the participants in the short time given provided an interestingly rich variety of clues for critically understanding the character of the communal areas in Claremont Court. Some of those spaces already identified as critical by Coleman have been confirmed to be associated to behavioural or perceptional stigma in Claremont Court too (such as the secondary stairwells and accesses from the side road where antisocial behaviours have been widely reported). However, in addition to these, the sketches suggest the need to analyse more deeply some original aspects of the communal areas in the court, such as the perception of the courtyard as a privatised community garden and the relevance of the landscape elements in it, or the pleasant feeling associated with the visual connection to Edinburgh city centre.

---

22   Downs and Stea. *Maps in Minds: Reflections on Cognitive Mapping*, 7.

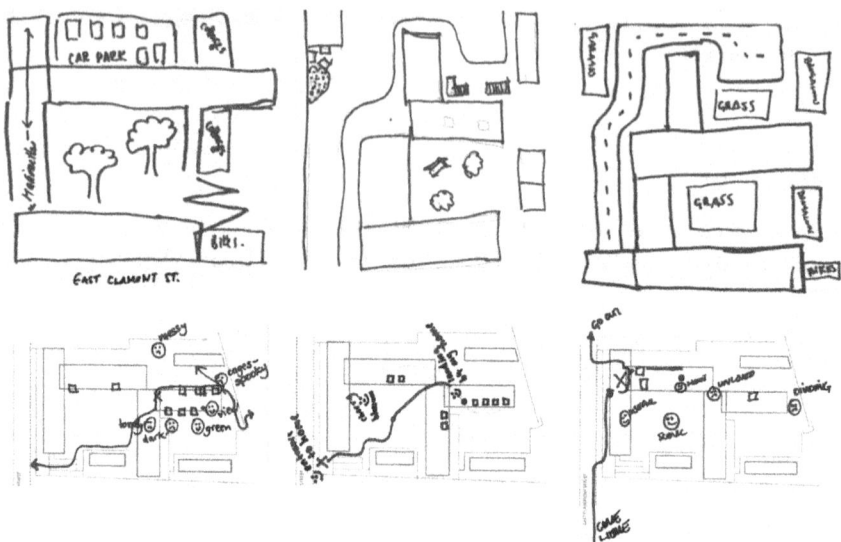

Figure 4. Samples of the sketches produced by Claremont Court residents during stage 1 (top line) and stage 2 (bottom line) of the participatory workshop in November 2016

We noticed, for example, that although the design of the landscape courtyards does not correspond to Coleman's design values, which make the residents perceive a place as "safe" (such as clear boundaries, private access from the public street etc.), in Claremont Court they have been sketched as *starting points* by most residents developing their cognitive map of the scheme. This partially suggests the effectiveness of creating an enclosed neighbourhood to create a sense of belonging; with this premise, the courtyard could be seen as the core of a potential community life.

The two landscape areas are definitely *most-liked* spaces in Claremont Court, and positive adjectives have been associated to them. However, only two out of 10 participants cross the courtyard in their everyday in/out paths, even when they come from the main road. Instead, many bypass the (intended) main access and use secondary accesses, although most residents associated bad feelings with these and reported antisocial behaviour and lack of maintenance, consistent with Coleman's observation.

CONCLUDING REMARKS AND FUTURE RESEARCH

This work contributes to the still open debate on the idea of 'planned communities' and questions,[23] in particular, whether the provision of communal areas (such as open decks or landscape courtyards) within post-war residential clusters has been able to replace and reproduce the liveliness of the street in working-class districts. Just before

---

23   Moran. 'Imagining the street in post-war Britain', 166.

the design of Claremont Court began, Young and Willmott's influential assessment of post-war housing estates had criticised their alienating loss of community and social solidarity.[24] We questioned whether Spence's intention to build up a cross-class community could be seen as a response to the growing negative view of the estates of the 1930s and 1950s as less social than other housing forms.

In particular, this chapter focused on the value of the communal areas as places able to catalyse processes of social interaction and foster a sense of belonging. To this extent, the outputs of the participatory workshop allowed us to make a critical reflection on the effectiveness of Spence's attempt in relation to current spatial practices in Claremont Court.

A future stage of this research project will put the findings of the photo-survey and the narrative originated from the community workshop in relation to the verbal behaviours included in the interviews. This will allow a comprehensive understanding of the physical and socio-cultural evidences determining a sense of belonging to the place.

BIBLIOGRAPHY

Bertolino, Nadia; and Costa Santos, Sandra. 'Towards a definition of "place". Cross-disciplinary methodology for interpolating architectural and sociological data in Claremont Court, Edinburgh'. Paper presented at A Panel on Inter and Transdisciplinary Relationships in Architecture, Athens 3–6 July 2017.

Campbell, Louis; Glendinning, Miles; and Thomas, Jane. *Basil Spence Buildings and Projects*. London: RIBA Publishing, 2012.

Coleman, Alice. *Utopia on Trial: Vision and Reality in Planned Housing*. London: Hilary Shipman, 1985.

Costa Santos, Sandra; Bertolino, Nadia; Hicks, Stephen; Lewis, Camilla; and May, Vanessa. 'Place-making theory behind Claremont Court'. Paper presented at the 19th International Conference on Architectural Theory and Construction Process, Zurich, 17–18 January 2017.

Costa Santos, Sandra; and Bertolino, Nadia. 'Claremont Court Housing Scheme: a post-occupancy evaluation of Modernist dwellings supporting current spatial practices'. Paper presented at the International Conference Arquitectonics: Mind, Land and Society, Barcelona, 1–2 June 2017.

Cross, Jennifer Eileen. 'Processes of Place Attachment: An Interactional Framework'. *Symbolic Interaction*, 38 (2015): 493–520.

Downs, Roger; and Stea, David. *Maps in Minds: Reflections on Cognitive Mapping*. New York: Harper & Row, 1977.

Gehl, Jahn. *Life Between Buildings: Using Public Space*. Washington: Island Press, 2011.

Henket, Hubert-Jan; and Heynen, Hilde. *Back from Utopia. The Challenge of the Modern Movement*. Rotterdam: 010 Publishers, 2002.

---

24   Young and Willmott. *Family and Kinship in East London*, 27.

Hernandez, Bernardo; Hidalgo, Carmen; Salazar-Laplace, Esther; and Hess, Stephany. 'Place attachment and place identity in natives and non-natives'. *Journal of Environmental Psychology*, 27 (2007): 310–19.

Long, Peter; and Thomas, Jane. *Basil Spence Architect*. Edinburgh: National Galleries of Scotland, 2007.

Low, Setha; and Altman, Irwin. *Place Attachment*. New York: Plenum Press, 1992.

Moran, Joe. 'Imagining the street in post-war Britain'. *Urban History*, 39(1) (2012): 166–86.

Newman, Oscar. *Defensible Space*. New York: Macmilan, 1972.

Powers, Alan. *The Modern Movement in Britain*. London, New York: Merrel, 2005.

Robinson, Lewis. The varied mental maps our students have. *Canadian Geographic*, 101(1) (1981): 52–7.

Smithson, Alison (ed.). *Team 10 Primer*. Cambridge: MIT Press, 1968[1962].

Smithson, Alison; and Smithson, Peter. *Ordinariness and Light. Urban theories 1952–1960 and their application in a building project 1963–1970*. London: Faber and Faber, 1970.

Stedman, Richard. 'Toward a Social Psychology of Place Predicting Behavior from Place-Based Cognitions, Attitude, and Identity'. *Environment and Behavior*, 34(5) (2002): 561–81.

Young, Michael; and Willmott, Peter. *Family and Kinship in East London*. London: Penguin Modern Classics, 2007.

CHAPTER THIRTEEN

CATJA DE HAAS

Catja De Haas Architect

THE GIANT DOLLS' HOUSE PROJECT

INTRODUCTION

The Giant Dolls' House project is an ongoing collaborative arts project that engages local communities and has raised money for the housing and homelessness charity, Shelter. The goal of the project is to make people aware of the importance of a home and community for all. It shows that all people are similarly idiosyncratic.

The Giant Dolls' House project works as follows: each participant (anyone – children, parents, grandparents and students) in the project is asked to make an individual dolls' house room of any function in an empty shoebox. The boxes are assembled onto a black canvas and linked with ramps, ropes and ladders to create a series of connected spaces that form a community of dolls' houses.

THE DOLLS' HOUSE: IMAGINATION AND MAKING

The dolls' house and miniature have proven to be ideal media to explore ideas about the home, communities and society. The project unites three elements: the dolls' house and what it represents; miniature and the imagination; the art of making.

REPRESENTATION OF THE DOLLS' HOUSE

In seventeenth-century Amsterdam, a number of women made elaborate dolls' houses. One of the surviving examples, and arguably the most elaborate, is on display at the Rijksmuseum in Amsterdam: the dolls' house of Petronella Oortman.[1] Petronella

---

1   Pijzel Dommisse. *Het Hollandse pronkpoppenhuis- Interieur en Huishouden in de 17de en 18de eeu.* [The Dutch Pronkpoppenhuis: Interior and Housekeeping in the 17th and 18th Century], 5.

Oortman spent over twenty years assembling her dolls' house. Even though it has been described as merely a wealthy women's hobby,[2] many of its contents coincided with the cultural production of the time and the dolls' house was visited by travelling scientists and royalty from abroad.[3] The dolls' house of Petronella Oortman contained around seven hundred objects, which together pictured an ideal household as a model of its society and how it was run.[4]

In the nineteenth century, the dolls' house became synonymous with the bourgeoisie and the way their habits of self-preservation turned them away from society. This image was captured in Henrik Ibsen's play A Doll's House[5], first performed in 1879. The dolls' house in the play represents a house, isolated from the real world and its developments, where the hypocritical values of the bourgeois male protagonist rule. Nora, the wife, brought up as a doll in a dolls' house, always shielded from the daily life and people outside of it, has to leave and enter the real world to become a complete person.

In 1972, the artist Miriam Schapiro, with Sherry Brody, made a dolls' house as part of Project Womanhouse in California.[6] Their dolls' house was placed in a cabinet, not unlike the cabinets of the dolls' houses of the seventeenth-century Netherlands. They used objects to alter what had become the stereotypical 'gendered space' of dolls' houses. A studio displays a female artist painting bananas and a male model. In the third instance the dolls' house and its interior challenged the established order by offering and imagining a narrative for a new reality in miniature.

MINIATURE, IMAGINATION AND MAKE BELIEVE

Miniaturisation, as it is interiorised in the dolls' house, can be explained as a romantic, nostalgic pass time: the result of a desire for a past that is no longer there. The writer Jan Willem Duyvendak sees nostalgia as a product of the imagination. In his book The Politics of Home: Belonging and Nostalgia in Europe and the United States he also sees aspiration, norms and dreams as located in the imagination.[7] In her 2010 essay, anthropologist Irene Cieraad observes that university students complete the actual home they live in with elements of their imagination.[8] Imagination is, according to the philosopher Gaston

2   Balducci. 'Revisiting Womanhouse: Welcome to the (Deconstructed) Dollhouse', 21.

3   The art historian Heidi de Mare states that an interest in the home linked painting, architecture and writing in the early seventeenth century (de Mare. Huiselijke Taferelen: de Veranderende rol van het beeld in de Gouden Eeuw [Homely Scenes: The Changing Role of the Image during the Golden Century], 620).

4   See: Pijzel Dommisse, op. cit.

5   Ibsen. 'A Doll's House'.

6   Gouma-Peterson and Nochlin. Miriam Shapiro: Shaping the Fragments of Art and Life, 71.

7   Duyvendak. The Politics of Home: Belonging and Nostalgia in Europe and the United States.

8   Cieraad. 'Homes from Home: Memories and Projections'.

Bachelard, a vital part of living in the home, an active ingredient that helps people negotiate their daily life. Through imagination only, we can change the world around us. Bachelard writes in his book *The Poetics of Space*: "The world is my imagination. The cleverer I am at miniaturising the world, the better I am at possessing it."[9]

MINIATURE, IMAGINATION AND MAKE BELIEVE

The art of making and building is an important aspect of the Giant Dolls' House project. In the seventeenth-century dolls' houses, all objects were made by professional craftsmen and the end product was a testament to their skill. Miniaturisation of everyday objects was often a requirement for admission to a professional guild.[10]

The writer Richard Sennett sees making as a social activity. In his book *Together: The Rituals, Pleasures and Politics of Cooperation*, he writes:

My hope is that understanding material craftsmanship and social cooperation can generate new ideas about how cities might become better made.[11]

He continues:

My quest is to relate how people shape personal effort, social relations and the physical environment. I emphasize skill and competency because in my view modern society is de-skilling people in the conduct of everyday life.[12]

The Giant Dolls' House project, as a community arts project, shapes imaginary miniature cities through making. The connecting ladders and ropes and ramps set it apart from purely individual doll-house-in-a-shoebox projects. The educational value of the latter has been recognised by Audrey Rule.[13] In her analysis of doll-house story themes and related authentic learning activities, she identified six themes: imagination, science fictional changes in space and time, diversity and friendship, courage and Independence, creativity, and care of belongings. These themes could provide important social–emotional and intellectual skills for success in today's diverse, challenging world.[14]

INSTALLATIONS

Since 2014 we have made several dolls' house installations and have therefore assembled over a thousand dolls' house-boxes. Each box has been different and has a different story to tell. A few of the events will be listed below.

---

9   Bachelard. *The Poetics of Space*, 150.
10   Fock et al. *Hot Nederlandse interieur in beeld, 1600–1900*.
11   Sennet, Richard. *Together: The Rituals, Pleasures and Politics of Cooperation*, x.
12   Ibid.
13   Rule. 'Dollhouse Story Themes and Authentic Learning'.
14   This conclusion was formulated in conversation with education expert Helene van Lookeren.

TESTBED01

Figure 1. The TESTBED installation. Photograph: Karem Ibrahim

The first installation was at TESTBED01 in Battersea in 2014. We raised money for Shelter and had around 140 boxes from children from local schools as well as from children from North London, Islington, students of Artescape, led by Lala Thorpe. We also held a drop-in workshop, where adults became as involved in making a dolls' house as the children.

#TRANSACTING

At the Giant Dolls' House installation #Transacting, 11 July 2015, organised by Critical Practice, on the parade ground in front of the London University of the Arts Chelsea, we explored what would happen if instead of taking the inhabitation of the boxes as the starting point, we used their trade value. Empty shoeboxes were assembled onto the canvas before the market opened. The boxes were undecorated and linked with the ramps and ladders, not unlike a newly built, architect-designed, uninhabited housing scheme. The Giant Dolls' House wouldn't expand during the day; no new boxes were added. We speculated there would be a shortage of boxes at the end of the day and almost hoped for heavily decorated boxes and a queue of disappointed buyers.

At the start of the market anyone could 'purchase' a box by donating £1 to Shelter, and then decorate it. Participants were then encouraged to sell their box on. If the owner chose not to sell, the box remained as it was. On the day, we found that most adult participants were more than willing to sell their shoebox houses after they had bought them and had added some furniture or wallpaper and no-one wanted more than one box. The only group of participants who did not want to sell their shoebox house, who in fact wanted to bring their box home after the fair, were children who had become attached to their house and had become completely absorbed in the project. The fact that the boxes were pre-assembled made no difference to them.

Figure 2. Left, #transacting; right, one of five panels in the Maestro Arts Gallery LFA2016.
Photographs: Karem Ibrahim

LFA2015

In 2015, the Giant Dolls' House was part of the London Festival of Architecture, with an installation at the headquarters of Shelter. It was a highlighted event. Children from Duncombe Primary School made the dolls' houses and Lenny George from Shelter visited the school to explain the charity's work. The installation was created in collaboration with Lala Thorpe from Artescape. For the theme of the festival – 'Work and the development of the city' – we wrote:

> The Giant Dolls' House is a work in progress that reflects the way in which communities could grow. It also highlights the need for housing as an integral part of work life. In a post-industrial society, where people can work anywhere, the home though important as a site to get away from the grind of work life, has become intrinsically linked to work and is often the site of work itself. The city after all can be compared to a large home where one can eat, sleep and work. The conglomeration of dolls' house spaces that will grow over the period it is exhibited, therefore embodies the idea of a work in progress and comments on the way individual homes and work spaces are linked to one another to form a larger community.

LFA2016

In 2016, the theme of the London Festival of Architecture was 'Home and Community' and we wrote:

> The Giant Dolls' House is a work in progress that reflects the way in which communities could grow. It highlights the need for people to have a place to call home to be an integral part of a community. The conglomeration of dolls' house spaces is a literal illustration of the idea of community and the role the home plays in it. However, not all participants may choose to make a home: last year one participant made a disco and another a playground. By letting participants be free to decide what they want to make, the installation will perhaps become a community with shared gardens, access between homes and a miniature disco, illustrated in a playful manner.

Diony Kiryos from the Bartlett made a diorama of paper. Pepper from T-SA made a study of Saint Jerome for the office, children from Saint Joseph's Primary made dolls' houses and Lenny George came to talk about Shelter again. Many of the children made their boxes at home and one of the mothers, who had helped make her child a dolls' house (bigger than was allowed), confessed: "I always wanted to be an architect." Boys from Tower House School in Barnes as well as children from the Roche Primary School in Wandsworth also made dolls' houses.

A number of the boxes came from the Red Cross Refugee Destitution Support Centre in Dalston. A collaborator on the project and volunteer at the centre, Cindy Hanegraaf, wrote the following:

> The Red Cross Refugee Destitution Centre in Dalston, East London, provides support for refugees who are in the process of applying for asylum and those who have been refused but are appealing, as well as those who have been successfully granted asylum but fall between the benefits of asylum-seekers support and finding employment.
>
> Many are homeless or are living in very short-term accommodation. Some spend the night on public transport, some in parks or on the street, some in homeless shelters.

She continues:

> there was a ready source of shoeboxes thanks to a recent donation of new shoes from a retailer. The materials for furnishing the boxes came primarily from the trash left behind from the packaging of the food parcels; red net bags from onions, cardboard boxes from tinned sardines, cellophane and photographs from food packaging. Other material came from the clothing bank and from bags of donated toys and children's art kits. At first, it was mainly the volunteers who made the boxes, sitting at tables where the centre's beneficiaries were reading or chatting or having tea. The questions came slowly: what are you doing, why are you doing this, can I make a suggestion, can I help, can I do one of my own? In most cases, the beneficiaries preferred to dictate what would go into a shoebox room, and they had very definite ideas of what a room should have.
> A window.
> A key.

A box for clothes.
A bed.

LFA2017

On 19 June 2017, the third installation for the London Festival of Architecture finished. The installation was mounted in the lobby of JW3 in Finchley. A direct mailing had gone out to supporting architecture offices and more architects participated. The project was redefined according to the new theme of the London Festival of Architecture, just as Venice in Italo Calvino's 1972 book *Invisible cities* is redefined. We are, in Calvino's words, "simply recounting some of the myriad possible forms a city [or giant dolls' house] can take".[15] For LFA 2017 we wrote:

> The theme of the London Festival of Architecture this year is 'Memory'. Not only does the dolls' house and the community it generates bring people back to a time when divisions were less prominent (see also Putman), the dolls' house is also a medium to process individual memories. Just sitting together and making things is for many adults a memory they want to pass on to the next generation and a skill that is no longer self-evident in an age of computer games, internet and mobile phones. Thereby the dolls' house can be seen as a repository of personal wishes and memories.

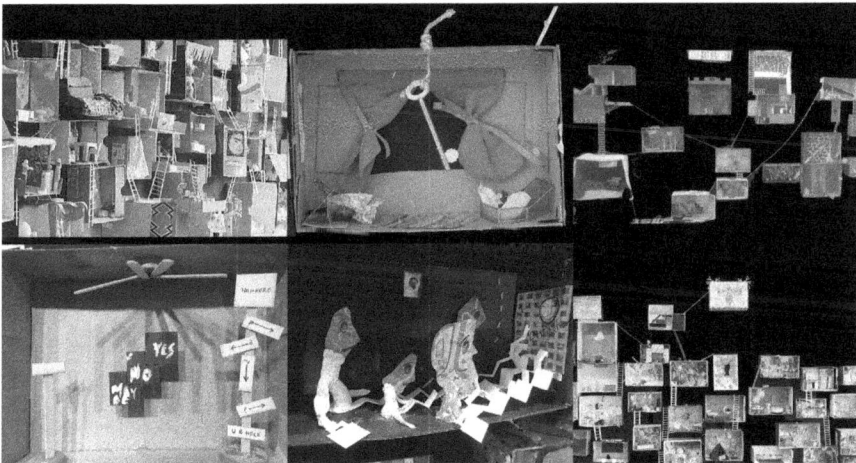

Figure 3. From the top left, clockwise: Shelter installation, photograph by Karem Ibrahim; dolls' house made by beneficiaries from the Red Cross Destitution Centre, photograph Karem Ibrahim; a Giant Dolls' House created with the BA Architecture third- and fourth-year students, University of the arts Bournemouth, who were encouraged to work in groups of three to explore connections between the boxes; installation at JW3, at the top the MAKE Dolls' House and the Homes Miller Dolls' House below, photograph by Will Jennings; box by Sylva Karakit; AUB Dubai

---

15   Calvino. *Invisible Cities*, 38.

The model shop of MAKE made a dolls' house with the theme of memory in the city, Homes Miller Architects from Glasgow sent their box by post and SPPARC, Child Graddon Lewis and Erika Suzuki contributed dolls' houses. Nursery children from Fitzjohns Primary School, children from Swiss Cottage School and Chigwell Primary School, and children from Artescape with Lala Thorpe, who collaborated on the project and ran the workshop, all made boxes.

DUBAI, AUB

In November 2016, as part of a workshop at the arts department of AUD in Dubai Art, interior design and animation students as well as their staff and their children made dolls' houses. The architecture students helped to assemble the boxes and make the links between them.

After the introductory lecture, the evening before the workshops started, an electrical engineering professor asked if he could make a box: he liked the idea of thinking with his hands and developing ideas through making, as children tend to do in the project. He worked on his box between 4 and 5 pm for three days (see Figure 3). The art students participating in the project used the idea of the dolls' house as a critique on events in their world: a Syrian arts student, Cham Al Malla, made a typical Syrian interior, with material from her home town. She covered the interior using a lid with a crack in it so that the interior was only visible through this crack. In January 2017, the project was taken to thejamjar gallery in Dubai in the AL Quoz District. Another Syrian artist, Sylva Karakit, made a shoebox about the situation in her homeland: a miniature Guernica (Figure 3).

CONCLUSION

The project uses the ideas of miniature, imagination and making to visualise communities of dolls' houses with the dolls' house considered as a medium to imagine and explore individual spaces. Linked together, these spaces form a community of sorts, with an imagery that everybody seems to recognise immediately as such and that seems to engage visitors: "I can see myself go out and borrow a carton of milk". "It looks like one big house".

Anyone can participate in the Giant Dolls' House project and participants are absolutely free to do what they want in the space of their box. There are no prizes for making 'the best' box and no boxes are excluded because of how they look. People of all walks of life and ages, between three and eighty years old, have attended our workshops or have participated in installations.

The Giant Dolls' House project is not a community participating project in the architectural sense, as we are not working towards a specific project. The Giant Dolls' House is an end product, a fund and awareness raiser, and discussion piece about issues relating to home, inclusiveness and communities. It does not solve anything, unfortunately, but we hope it makes people think. The direction of the project is changed for each installation by the people who become involved, but its principle remains the same. As the project grows, our collection of images of the installations (all dolls' houses are documented) grows. Participation therefore is on two levels: first of all, on the level of the individual giant dolls' house installation and second on the level of the collection of installations that grows as the project expands.

Figure 4. Giant Dolls' House in thejamjardubai, the result of workshops at the AUD and in the gallery. Photograph: thejamjar

BIBLIOGRAPHY

Bachelard, Gaston. *The Poetics of Space*. 1996 [1964].

Balducci, Temma. 'Revisiting Womanhouse: Welcome to the (Deconstructed) Dollhouse'. *Woman's Art Journal*, 27(2) (2006): 17–24.

Calvino, Italo. *Invisible Cities*. San Diego: Harcourt, 1978.

Cieraad, Irene. 'Homes from Home: Memories and Projections'. *Home Cultures*, 7(1) (2010): 85–102.

De Mare, Heidi. 'De verbeelding onder vuur. Het realisme-debat der Nederlandse kunsthistorici. [Image Making under Fire. The Realism Debate among Dutch Art Critics]'. *Theoretische Geschiedenis* [Theoretical History], 24(2) (1997): 13–137.

____. *Huiselijke Taferelen: de Veranderende rol van het beeld in de Gouden Eeuw* [Homely Scenes: The Changing Role of the Image during the Golden Century]. Nijmegen: Vantilt, 2012.

Duyvendak, Jan Willem. *The Politics of Home: Belonging and Nostalgia in Europe and the United States*. Basingstoke: Palgrave Macmillan, 2011.

Gouma-Peterson, Thalia. 'Miriam Schapiro: An Art of Becoming'. *American Art*, 11(1) (1997): 10–45.

Gouma-Peterson, Thalia; and Nochlin, Linda. *Miriam Shapiro: Shaping the Fragments of Art and Life*. New York: Harry N. Abrahams Inc., 1999.

Ibsen, Henrik. 'A Doll's House'. In: *A Doll's House and Other Plays*, edited by Peter Watts, pp.145–232. London: Penguin Books, 1965.

Pijzel Dommisse, Jet. *Het Hollandse pronkpoppenhuis- Interieur en Huishouden in de 17de en 18de eeuw*. [The Dutch Pronkpoppenhuis: Interior and Housekeeping in the 17th and 18th Century]. Amsterdam: Waanders uitgevers-Rijksmuseum, 2001.

Pijzel Dommisse, Jet; Fock, Willemijn; Eliens, Titus M.; Koldeweij, Eloy F. *Het Nederlandse interieur in beeld, 1600–1900*. Zwolle: Waanders Uitgevers, 2001.

Rule, Audrey. 'Dollhouse Story Themes and Authentic Learning'. *Journal of Authentic Learning*, 2(1) (2005).

Sennet, Richard. *Together: The Rituals, Pleasures and Politics of Cooperation.* New Haven, London: Yale University Press, 2012.

CHAPTER FOURTEEN

LO TIAN TIAN, MARC AUREL SCHNABEL AND TANE MOLETA

Victoria University of Wellington, New Zealand

DIGITALLY BUILT HOUSING COMMUNITIES: HOW POSSIBLE IS IT?

According to Vitruvius architecture was the combination of three virtues: *utilitas, firmitas and venustas*. He forgot *humanitas*... That, I felt, needed changing – *Lucien Kroll.*[1]

INTRODUCTION

This chapter describes a design research project that simulates a participatory design process employing technologies and gaming systems with the aim of developing a prototype and, later, a fully functioning model for technology-led participatory design. It is seen as particularly relevant to urban contexts characterised by high-rise living and a dense urban environment such as Singapore, which was used as a case context. Singapore is a context in which the urban population is increasing and high-rise density in cities is already the norm. However, it is also a context in which it is generally accepted that the social interaction between the people living in these high-rise buildings is reducing. Repeated the world over, these dense living conditions mean that even between neighbours living next to each other there is rarely much interaction and the close community bonds that once existed in smaller village and town communities

---

1   De Graaf, Reinier. 'Few architects have embraced the idea of user participation; a new movement is needed'. *Architectural Review*, 26 July 2016. Accessed Nov 2016, https://www.architectural-review.com/rethink/viewpoints/few-architects-have-embraced-the-idea-of-user-participation-a-new-movement-is-needed/10008549.article.

have declined remarkably.[2] In this context, this project seeks to explore the potential of using digital tools to facilitate collaborative design processes between communities and architects and, importantly, between the individuals of those communities. The intention in this regard is not only to develop a potential porotype system technically but to explore 'virtual collaborative design models' and facilitate the learning of lessons about community participation and the community building through design.

Although there are notable exceptions, such as Herman Hertzberger in Holland, architects have often been so focused on creating quality, functional buildings that they have neglected the importance of these issues and the profession's possible role in dealing with them. Housing is a key issue to consider in delivering healthy and attractive communities but equally important to a successful housing project are good communities. It is a key argument of this chapter that rather than assuming the designer's job in housing developments is to 'design houses', more importance should be placed on the architect's interaction with communities in the process of design and the creation of community that can result.

If we look back historically, various examples come to mind. One is Frei Otto's 'Ökohaus' – a successful attempt to bring a group of neighbours together to build their desired living space.[3] The design process itself took two years, even though it was a small project for only a few households. The outcome, however, was extraordinary with neighbours enjoying the company of each other and a genuine sense of 'community' resulting. Lucien Kroll's 'La MeMe' is also generally considered a successful example, bringing students (the occupants) together in similar ways. It was not a project without its difficulties, of course – Kroll was even fired at one stage – but the outcome is often considered a 'masterpiece' of participatory design.

There are a number of self-evident advantages in trying to build successful communities, from the health and well-being of the residents, to the resilience and security of the neighbourhood.[4] These benefits are evidenced in any number of projects we could cite. One such example from the UK is the work of Redditch Co-operative Homes, an organisation that has created 400 homes spread around the town of Redditch through a series of five neighbourhood co-operatives, each self-managed by residents. Studies suggest that the residents demonstrate higher levels of civic engagement than normal and claim higher levels of satisfaction than are typical with regard to the quality of

---

2   Numerous urban-sociological studies suggest that social interaction is needed for better quality of life and key to this is interaction with neighbours. See: 'Quality of life indicators – leisure and social interactions', Eurostat Statistics Explained, accessed May 2016, http://ec.europa.eu/eurostat/statistics-explained/index.php/Quality_of_life_indicators_-_leisure_and_social_interactions.

3   Israel, N. 'La Ciudad Viva'. Accessed June 2014, http://www.laciudadviva.org/blogs/?p=14164.

4   Barton, Huge, et al. The Routledge Handbook of Planning for Health and Well-Being: Shaping a Sustainable and Healthy Future. Routledge, 2015.

their homes and their sense of community spirit.[5] Other examples of projects with similarities and similar evidence of increased levels of satisfaction can be found across the world, with a few examples including Applemead Co-operative Homes in Canada, the Batikent project in Turkey and Deutsches Haus in Germany.

In Singapore, where this research has been carried out and is intended to be applied, the demographic makeup of residents is highly varied. In part due to this, the government Housing Development Board (HBD) stresses the importance of community building to bring about harmony and understanding among neighbours living in close proximity to each other in the high-rise apartments that dominate the housing stock. These high-rise apartments do not have a front yard, balconies are often blocked off between units to provide total privacy between living units and, often, the only communal spaces are corridors and lift lobbies. Such designs clearly limit the possibility of 'community building' through everyday social interaction and can contribute to neighbours actually being unfamiliar with each another, with a concomitant lack of bonding on any social level.[6] The design of these buildings is clearly a problem and in any search for alternative approaches this chapter suggests that a greater level of community and resident engagment is essential. However, it does not just argue for more social awareness from architects, but proposes a model for community partcipation in the design of housing that uses the *ModRule* digital platform to coordinate interaction between households. In doing so, it will suggest that the theories of John Wood are a useful and highly practical guide in developing the digital participation techniques needed.

DIGITAL TOOL FOR COMMUNITY BUILDING – *MODRULE*

ModRule is a platform intended to facilitate collaboration between architects and future end users of design projects. It is particularly useful as a tool in the preliminary stage of mass housing design, where projects are typically too large to facilitate much personal interaction between residents and designers and are premised on pre-established typological approaches.[7] Using *ModRule*, individuals set their desired parameters for the design of their living space by completing a questionnaire about the problems they identify with their current living space and solicit ideas on improving this by asking participants about their 'dream' living space. A personal or family profile is also be generated through the questionnaire that is intended to help designers correlate preferences with additional data.

---

5   Butterworth, I. 'The Relationship between the Built Environment and Wellbeing: A Literature Review'. Prepared for the Victorian Health Promotion Foundation, Melbourne, 2000.

6   Israel. 'La Ciudad Viva', op. cit.

7   Lo et al. 'ModRule: A User-Centric Mass Housing Design Platform'. In: *The Next City – New Technologies and the Future of the Built Environment*, by G. Celani, D.M. Sperling and J.M.S. Franco. Sao Paolo, 2015, 236–54.

Not only does the technology allow residents to interact (indirectly) with designers, it allows them to interact with, and learn from, each other by facilitating the sharing of preferences and ideas. Each participant can, for example, view the profile of other participants on the site with the aim of identifying good practices and better understanding the preferences and dislikes of the community.[8] While such contributions may be considered small, these small contributions to community building are key to the concept of interaction as a way of building bonds between people and, in this regard, *ModRule* can be paralleled conceptually, with John Wood's concept of micro-utopia. Rather than setting aspirational goals that are clearly out of reach, as per standard readings of utopia, Wood suggests it is more practical to take a progressive, or in Wood's words, "a tentative, temporary, pluralised or truncated"[9] perspective on utopia.

Working in small experimental steps has its advantages. The results are clearer for a start, and it becomes easier at any stage to take a step back from the process and evaluate failings or problems as they arise before moving on. This characterises the project under development and described here, the steps of which can most succinctly be broken down to the following:

1. Breaking through participants' psychological barriers

2. Providing a means for co-sharing

3. Determining the participants' needs versus desires

4. Generating the outcome for visual observation and exchange

5. Engaging the participants towards a practical outcome.

Even though the project operates through a digital platform and this is seen as its greatest asset, the first step towards creating this form of 'micro-utopia' in the design of residential settings is neither technological nor political. It is psychological.[10] Such psychological challenges in this regard involve the question of how to engage end users in the design process and how to engage them with each other. Since the target audience is, in its majority, an audience without architectural or design knowledge, alternative modes of engagement need to be found. In this project, the proposed mode of engagement is gaming.

---

8   The technical aspects and functions of *ModRule* are also explained in detail here: Lo et al. 'A Simple System for Complex Mass Housing Design Collaborations: A System Development Framework'. *Complexity & Simplicity – Proceedings of the 34th eCAADe Conference*. Oulu, 2016: 137–46.

9   Wood, John. *Design for Micro-Utopias: Making the Unthinkable Possible*. England, 2007.

10 Sanchez, Jose. 'Block'hood – Developing an Architectural Simulation Video Game'. *Real Time – Proceedings of the 33rd eCAADe Conference*. Vienna, 2015, 89–97.

Gamification has proved both to promote participation and to simplify the process of communication between various parties as it is a non-professional form of interaction and communication that is also a fun activity for users, helping to break down barriers. There are problems, however. Through the involvement of end users, the complexity of the design process is likely to increase especially in the context of mass housing. Recognition of a layperson's interest in the conceptual design stage necessitates immediate communication with the architects and opens up the problem of dovetailing the layperson's demand and maintaining the professional architect's quality control.

In *ModRule*, users experience the design platform as they would in games such as *SimCity* and *MineCraft*, which have previosuly been used in the context of architectural design discussions in non-professional contexts.[11] Such platforms allow users to venture around created virtual environments freely and to design their environments using basic skills sets, in these cases starting with a tabula rasa. *ModRule* also has similarities with *SecondLife*, in that it also allows multiple users to be virtually present in a single system/space and to communicate with each other in that space. Whilst this has obvious limitations, such as participants being confined and restricted by artificial rules and logic like operating in a gridded environment and using a limited range of building elements provided by the system (Figure 1), it does have some great advantages, namely familiarity in most cases and ease of use. Also important is that *ModRule* uses a simple system in the first instance to allow users to get familiar with a basic design participation system in a virtual environment before moving on to a more sophisticated and complex version in the full design process, as explained in detail later.[12]

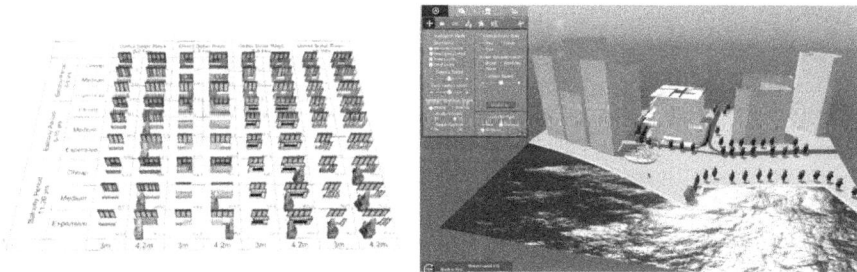

Figure 1. (left) Designated components set by architects for users to use in *ModRule*; (right) Bird's eye view of the open virtual world for multiple users to venture within

After using a basic template by way of introduction, it is proposed that the participants in this process be slowly brought to the main site to start the next stage of design. This process should involve setting up a personal profile that, compared to the simple 'avatars' typical of say *SecondLife*, involves providing more than the character's

---

11   Ibid.
12   See also: Lo et al. 'A Simple System for Complex...' op. cit.

physical features. More importantly, in terms of the actual spatial design processes that take place in this virtual environment, the architects set the system's parameters within which the participants set their spatial preferences, including things such as budget, orientation, view and daylight. These initial settings create the primary features of the 'desired way of living' for each participant to which are added more specifics. The model echoes features from games such as *Mass Effect* and *Until Dawn* – role-playing games (RPGs) that follow a particular storyline but require players to make decisions that change the course of the story, thus resulting in individual and unique endings for each participant. In these games, such decision-based tasks are 'stored' automatically in a 'black box' in the background, freeing the player to focus on the game story. Similarly, in *ModRule*, the design tasks and decisions taken are not overly highlighted in the interface so the users can focus on visualising the outcomes generated by the decisions in question.

GAMIFIED COLLABORATION

Assuming the psychological barriers to participant engagement with the virtual platform are overcome, the use of *ModRule* allows us to deal with the next of the five steps outlined earlier: co-sharing. In Wood's model, the second step to a truncated version of utopia is to "co-imagine the dream in a more shareable form" and to achieve this in the context described here, the design process has to become more complex at this stage – users having to look at one another's profiles and form 'groups' through which to build up social community while simultaneously designing their individual living spaces. Again, the references to gamification are key, with games such as *Clash of Clans* and *Mobile Strike* offering precedents for online coordination of participants. As the co-development of strategies obliges collaborative interactions, these games involve the development of an understanding of the capabilities of multiple teammates and effective online communication skills.[13] The key issue in our context is that, through a process requiring the joint development of unified behaviour, a sense of community can be formed. In this case, *ModRule* functions along the same lines, being a gamified housing-design process that initiates and requires interaction on a shared communication platform.

This stage of collaboration, as per Wood's model, is intended to create the context in which participants can, collectively, cross check needs with desires or, as it was put in the project we are describing, whether "we really want what we have dreamed of".[14] At the beginning of the process, every user specifies characteristics of themseleves, thus creating a personal profile. This allows participants to 'get to know each other' better, allows others, including residents and designers, to suggest relevant ideas and facilitates them in identifying design concepts and proposals that are suited to their

---

13   Segard, et. al. 'Open Communitition: Competitive design in a collaborative virtual environment'. In: *Open Systems: Proceedings of the 18th International Conference on Computer-Aided Architectural Design Research in Asia*. Singapore, 2013: 231–40.

14   Sanchez, op. cit.

needs by acting as a form of reference chart. Based on these profile preferences, it is expected that participants would begin to interact with each other as neighbours and thus begin to identify traits, routines, preferences and bonds that will characterise their personal 'real-world' interactions.

These personal interactions do not, however, operate in a completely free-floating design context. In *ModRule*, key parts of the building being designed collaboratively do have to be pre-set, with architects planning an outline layout premised on fixed features such as the building core, access and utility spaces. This overall planning is based on a gridded spatial substratum within which the individual preferences of the community and the individuals within it will develop their autonomy, most obviously at the level of the designed individual living spaces. With regard to the level of individual design taking place at this stage, there is an interesting cross-referencing system used in *ModRule* that again stems from the world of gamification – a checklist of targets based on the end user's stated preferences. Described as a goal-orientated measurement tool, it relates to the 'objectives' players attempt to reach in games. In the *ModRule* interface, a 'goal bar' is used to measure this and moves in response to design decisions taken by individuals and the community, as they relate to the preferences laid out by individuals at the beginning of the process (Figure 2). The simple graphic tool of the goal bar is a quick indicator to individuals as to whether the emerging design is likely to meet their needs and desires. It is not only intended to ensure that the design is suitable, but that it also acts as an indicator of whether any one individual is gaining too much in relation to another, acting as a form of restraint. Visible to all participants, it is not simply an individual reference point but a communal one.

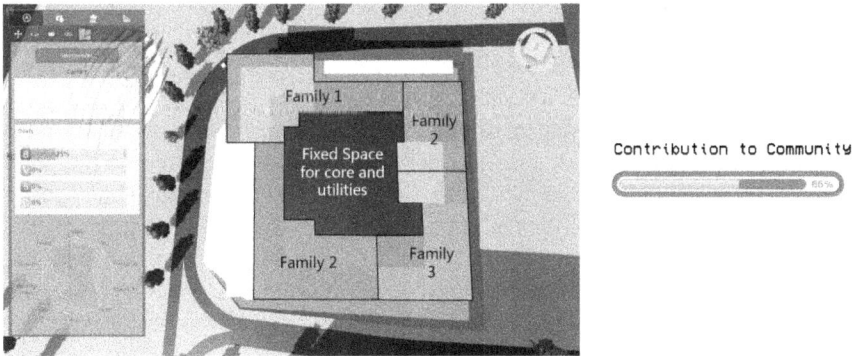

Figure 2. Screenshot of *ModRule* showing two sets of 'goal bars'

These gamification characteristics of *ModRule* also make full use of 'game logic' in encouraging end users to share information resources and design their living space together, with contributions to any one design benefiting from the input of both the individual user of a given unit/space, the community more generally and the professional architects coordinating the exercise. This occurs not only with respect to design issues but also in agreements between the community on lifestyle and mutual support. For example, if end user A offers to maintain the cleanliness of a given communal area, he or she will be identified as 'worth' more than end user B who contributes nothing to the community. In return, end user A becomes eligible to receive some form of remuneration, such as 'discount per square area' as agreed in advance and set as part of the overall system parameters by the architects. The incentive-led approach is measured on a community 'goal bar' and is intended to encourage users to support the broader community.

VIRTUAL PRODUCTION

At this stage in the process, a developed design will have emerged and we enter the phase at which it becomes necessary to 'visualise' the resulting spaces more clearly, a process that requires an exponential increase in the direct role of the architect. The intention is to 'see how much of the dream is attainable' and to do so, the recognisable architectural components of buildings such as walls, windows, doors, furniture, as well as the more specialised concepts of sun-shadowing, lighting and views will have to be discussed, visualised and assessed. To maintain high participation levels and minimise any sense of exclusion from this more technical phase of the process, it is proposed to keep this interaction between the architects and end users as simplified as possible. Referring back to gaming – or at least computing – once more, virtual reality (VR) technology is proposed that, in the gaming context, is assumed to increase the sense of participation (literally).[15]

Currently, *ModRule* operates on an online web platform with limited visualisation capability. Although VR would be the best option, the current system is incapable of effective linking with high-quality VR systems. As a result, the design process we describe here would, at this stage, switch to the *Fuzor*[16] software, which allows a fairly seamless transition to basic VR visualisations that are sufficiently advanced to give participants a reasonable four-dimensional experience of the spaces designed. Through *Fuzor*, the participants can, for example, move the architectural components and adjust the dimensions of their spaces until they feel the outcome fits their preferences and needs. It gives the end users a close-to-real sense of their designed homes and, in addition, allows them to interact with neighbours in the common spaces of the planned building (Figure 3). Having created a virtual environment in which the space is not only visualised but also experienced spatially, the final stages of the design can be carried out in virtual time and virtual space.

---

15   'What is Virtual Reality?' Virtual Reality Society, accessed May 2016, http://www.vrs.org. uk/virtual-reality/what-is-virtual-reality.html.

16   Fuzor, Kalloc Studio, accessed May 2016, https://www.kalloctech.com/.

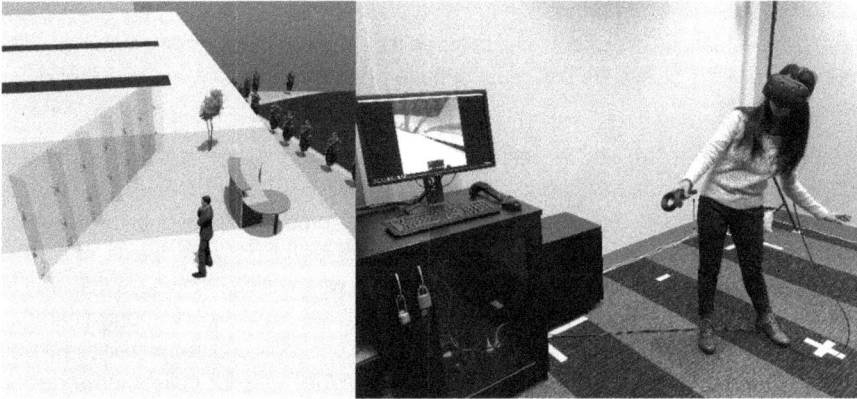

Figure 3. A user manipulates the components in a virtual environment using VR gear

Once the design process itself is complete, we then move on to the final stage of our design process model in which the individual 'micro-utopias' created through the process are finally synthesised to form a common overall architectural design. Again, at this stage, there is a significant role for the architects whose professional expertise, and the template of core spaces set at the beginning, allows them to bring together the individualised spaces of the participants into a coherent and workable whole.

CONCLUSIONS

The use of digital technologies to facilitate a collaborative design process discussed here clearly has some limitations, the most obvious of these being technical in nature. As *ModRule* is continually enhancing its features, there are still a few technical glitches that slow down any process such as this and frustrate participants. However, the project has been a great success in trialling the system and has already led the researchers behind it to draw some conclusions about the nature of participatory design that are not only fundamental to the future of digital-based participatory design, but could be of relevance to more standard 'real-world' participatory design processes. In short, the experience has shown us that three elements seem to be necessary for a community-building, user-oriented collaboration to be initiated: communication, transparency and understanding.

As housing design involves many activities that are complex for non-professionals, there are numerous skills and important pieces of knowledge users have to pick up during the design process. Constant communication between architects and users help avoid doubts and confusion that slow down the design process. In a digital methodology such as this one, there are some advantages in this regard: for example, users are able to communicate in real time with any other users or the architects and are able to annotate and archive any problems they face instantly, meaning that valuable information is less likely to be lost. In terms of transparency and effective communication, it is important that each user knows who is on the other side of any virtual conversation. This occurs naturally in a real-life setting but in this context requires personal profiles or avatars that must operate openly and, ideally, are as full of detail as possible.

Both these issues are key in ensuring an efficient level of understanding between participants and future neighbours, which is the key issue for a community to become successful later. As in 'real-life' settings, this is hard to control; indeed, in these virtual/ digital contexts, it is even more so. The personalities of the participants affect the design process and its outcomes significantly, and when using techniques that are still new – despite the use of references to gaming that are relatively commonly shared in the context of Singapore – the understanding between individual personalities is even harder to account for, clearly making the use of virtual tools for collaborative design currently problematic. In this regard, the architects play an influential role. They can underline to participants that their actions and preferences, even when 'virtual', do affect the community more broadly and that compromises are necessary to produce a fair and ultimately successful project and, more significantly perhaps, a sustainable community.

These three features of the participatory process were all laid bare in this project. Each refers us back to some of the principles laid out by Wood, whose ideas not only give us a model for a simple step-by-step approach but also give us a more inspirational agenda to consider. Wood's larger ideas were tied into the following aims for participatory design: to incorporate a unification of social, cultural, managerial and design practices; to orchestrate simultaneous ideas and processes in a shareable form, accessible to all; to be perceived as a primary source of wellbeing and fun to attract support and engagement; and to create conditions that would encourage incentive returns, promoting resilient communities.

We cannot claim at this stage that the project laid out here achieves this or will certainly do so if tried out in a none-trial setting; or that the integration of digital tools to enhance the design process in housing projects would do so either. However, the project does suggest that it is feasible to believe that participatory design is a workable and sustainable model; and that simulations such as this can help teach people to interact better in the development of mutually benefiical housing projects that, in turn, cannot help but contribute to better community understanding and, one would hope, better, more sustainable housing communities generally. If the technology advances, of course, the potential for this model to be developed into a full-blown functioning model for collaborative pre-design processes is obvious – as too, we hope, are its potential benefits.

BIBLIOGRAPHY

Avi, Friedman. *Decision Making For Flexibility in Housing.* UK: Urban Press, 2011.

Cook, Diane J.; and Das, Sajal K. *Smart Environments: Technology, Protocols and Applications.* Wiley-Interscience, 2004.

Cowan, Dave; and Marsh, Alex. 'Community, Neighbourhood, Responsibility: Contemporary Currents in Housing Studies'. *Housing Studies*, 19 (2004): 845–53.

de Lapuerta, Jose Maria. *Collective Housing: A Manual.* Barcelona: Actar, 2007.

Fassbinder, Helga; and Proveniers, Adri. *New Wave in Building: A Flexible Way of Design, Construction and Real Estate Management.* Van Gorcum, 1992.

Habraken, John. *Support – An Alternative to Mass Housing.* London: Architectural Press, 1972.

Harper, Richard. *Inside the Smart Home.* Springer, 2003.

James, Anne; and Nagasaka, Dai. 'Theoretical Connection Points Between Multimedia and Architecture'. *Journal of Asian Architecture and Building Engineering*, 10 (2011): 171–8.

Kendall, S.H.; and Teicher, J. *Residential Open Building.* Taylor & Francis, 2010.

Kroll, Lucien. 'Utopia interrupted'. *Domus.* Accessed May 2016, http://www.domusweb.it/en/architecture/2010/06/30/lucien-kroll-utopia-interrupted.html.

Landry, Charles; van Westrenen, Francien; and Venhuizen, Hans. *Hans Venhuizen: Game Urbanism: Manual for Cultural Spatial Planning.* Amsterdam: Valiz Book and Cultural Projects, 2011.

Lee, Jae Hoon; and Lee, Woo Jung. 'A Study on the Impact of Ubiquitous Street Furniture on Human Behavior Based on Media Poles Installed on Seoul primes Gangnam Boulevard'. *Journal of Asian Architecture and Building Engineering*, 12 (2013): 181–8.

Lo Tian Tian; Schnabel, Marc Aurel; and Moleta, Tane J. 'Gamification for User-Oriented Housing Design: A Theoretical Review'. *22nd International Conference of the Association for Computer-Aided Architectural Design Research in Asia (CAADRIA).* Suzhou, 2017.

MVRDV. *SpaceFighter: The Evolutionary City.* New York: Actar, 2007.

Narahara, T., and Terzidis, K. 'Multiple-constraint Genetic Algorithm In Housing Design'. *Proceedings of the 25th Conference of the Association for Computer-Aided Design in Architecture World.* 2006, 418–25.

Painter, Joe. 'The politics of the neighbour'. *Environment and Planning D: Society and Space*, 30 (2012): 515–33.

Ricquebourg, Vincent; Menga, David; Durand, David; Marhic, Bruno; Delahoche, Laurent; and Loge, Christophe. 'The Smart Home Concept : our immediate future'. *1st IEEE International Conference on E-Learning in Industrial Electronics*, 2006.

Schnabel, Marc Aurel; and Ham, Jeremy J. 'Virtual design studio within a social network'. *ITcon*, 17, special issue (eLearning 2.0: Web 2.0-based social learning in built environment) (2012), 397–415.

Serkan, Anlllr; Linner, Thomas; Suay, Halit Bener; and Bock, Thomas. 'Application of Infra-Free Motherboard (IFM) in a Decentralized Community for a Customized Real-time Processing Multidirectional Energy Supply Network'. *Journal of Asian Architecture and Building Engineering*, 8 (2009): 407–14.

Tekinbas, Katie Salen; and Zimmerman, Eric. *Rules of Play: Game Design Fundamentals.* The MIT Press, 2003.

Willis, B.R.; Hemsath, T.L.; and Hardy, S. 'A Parametric Multi-Criterion Housing Typology'. *Proceedings of the 32nd Annual Conference of the Association for Computer-Aided Design in Architecture (ACADIA).* San Francisco, 2012, 501–10.

Wood, J. *Design for Micro-Utopias: Making the Unthinkable Possible.* England, 2007.

Zichermann, Gabe; and Joselin, Linder. *The Gamificaion Revolution: How Leaders Leverage Game Mechanics to Crush the Competition.* US: Mcgraw Hill, 2013.

CHAPTER FIFTEEN

SADANU SUKKASAME

School of Architecture, Planning and Landscape, Newcastle University, UK

PARTICIPATORY HOUSING PROCESSES: A STUDY OF THE KAREN IN THAILAND

INTRODUCTION

Many indigenous Karen dwellers in the forests of the Thai Kaeng Krachan National Park (KKNP) were forcibly evicted from their village homes by armed Thai forces and national park officials in 2011.[1,2] They were relocated to new areas further from the Thai–Myanmar border where they constructed provisional dwellings. In 2014, the Thai Community Organizations Development Institute (CODI) approved funding for the Karen Housing Development Project (KHDP) in Banggloy village,[3] to which the Karen had been moved, and I was appointed to conduct the project as an architect. Currently, this project is being implemented cooperatively with workshops and meetings by encouraging the Karen people to be the core actors and to decentralise the solution-finding process, focusing on people's participation to repair and build new houses. This chapter offers insights into the change of the indigenous houses and how the Karen have managed to create and adapt their houses within the strict regulations of the National Park. Fieldwork was carried out between 2013 and 2016 to document the functional and structural changes to the new dwellings.

---

1   The Karen are the largest ethnic minority group in Thailand. See Ratanakul and Burusrat, 1995: 1.

2   The Kaeng Krachan forest was declared a national park in 1981 and is the largest national park in Thailand. See Thai National Parks, 'Kaeng Krachan National Park', https://www.thainationalparks.com/kaeng-krachan-national-park.

3   The Community Organizations Development Institute (CODI) is a public organisation under the Ministry of Social Development and Human Security, formed by a combination of the Urban Community Development Organization (UCDO) and the Rural Development Fund in 2000. See CODI, 'CODI History', http://www.codi.or.th/housing/FrontpageHistory.html.

POLITICAL CONTEXTS

In 1896, the Royal Forest Department (RFD) was established to preserve national parks and forests, and increase the area of forests in Thailand.[4] Unfortunately, the problems of deforestation are often blamed on the Karen and other hill tribes that live in the forests, causing conflict between them and conservationists and the state.[5] Between 1996 and 2011, National Park officers and the military forced the relocation of the Banggloy Karen people in the National Park away from the Thai–Myanmar border. Increasing pressure from the KKNP forced the Karen in Banggloy Village to end their cultivation–fallow cycle in the forest. Some Karen received land in allocated areas, while some households have no land to farm. The number of Karen in the new village has increased continuously from 57 households in 1996 to 129 households in 2015, while the quantity of allocated land remains stable.

In 2011, the Thai government submitted a proposal to UNESCO to inscribe the Kaeng Krachan Forest Complex (KKFC) as a Natural World Heritage Site. Most of the villagers living in the KKFC areas are concerned about this project since they received little information regarding the proposal.[6] There are no clear solutions for the evicted Karen community and they are still living in poor conditions with insufficient land for farming.

The forestry officials have blamed ethnic minorities as the "shifting cultivators", for the rapid loss of forests. This may be because the Karen are the largest ethnic minority group, thus the Karen image becomes one of "forest destroyers". Yos Santasombat, a Thai academic of anthropology and sociology, nonetheless, noted that in the past the image of the Karen was as forest guardians and conservationists.[7] While the images of the Karen within the environmental discourse portray them as "wild people" (*chao pa*) or as "tribesmen" (*chao khao*) and as "nature conservationist",[8] the use of the term 'tribesman' within official Thai discourse reflects the prevailing stereotype of a single group of highlanders and denies the rich cultural, ethnic, historical and linguistic diversity of the indigenous peoples.[9] Therefore, the indigenous communities have had to struggle to maintain their identities under the society and politics of the Thai nation.

In 2004, it was estimated that almost 10 million people were living in areas classified as reserves or conservation forests, where they experienced restriction on cultivation and residence rights.[10] One impact of this policy was a rise in the number of offences by indigenous people when cutting down trees for building houses in the protected areas surrounding their homes.[11] In August 2010, the Thai government resolution to

---

4   Tungittiplakorn, 1995

5   Delang, 2003

6   Erni and Nilsson, 2015: 280

7   Santasombat, 2004

8   Erni and Stidsen, 2003: 258

9   Erni, 2002: 272

10   Erni, 2005: 330

11   Areerat, 'About 40 Karens prosecuted for forest encroachment', http://www.prachatai.com/english/node/4450.

restore the Karen's livelihoods was an attempt on the part of the government to solve a long-standing problem faced by the Karen as a result of misunderstandings about their traditional way of life. This covered five main issues: revitalisation of ethnic identity, natural resource management, citizenship rights, culture transmission and education.[12] However, the implementation of activities is currently being discussed by the agencies involved and the situation remains unclear for implementing laws and policies protecting human rights. Therefore, the overall situation of the rights of the Karen still needs to improve.

PARTICIPATORY DESIGN APPROACH

This chapter draws on Participatory Action Research (PAR), founded by Fals Borda who combined people's wisdom to generate the theoretical guidelines for PAR.[13] This can be used to empower people by involving them in research to generate knowledge through the lived experience of the participants[14] and changing or improving a social situation.[15] Thus, participatory design is understood as a social process with various approaches and techniques. Rachael Luck defines the coordination of design as a plural phenomenon and a multi-faceted concern acting through the self-organisation practices of the participants,[16] while Hussain defines it as an empowering process.[17] Henry Sanoff, Professor Emeritus of Architecture, an authority on community participation and democratic design, points out that participatory design is a force for change in the creation and management of environments for people.[18] It can be used for grass roots, bottom-up slum upgrading and can become a strong approach for systems design to develop workable and innovative solutions through engaging multiple voices.[19,20]

In general, community participation is concerned with community-member engagement and active involvement in issues which affect people's lives and communities through engagement in interrelated factors promoting community development and social empowerment.[21] It is also related to the concept of representative and participatory democracy by involving people in the planning process under the slogan "planning is for people".[22,23]

---

12 PCPDI, 2011
13 Fals Borda, 2000
14 Lennie, 2006
15 Alston and Bowles, 1998
16 Luck, 2003
17 Hussain, 2010
18 Sanoff, 2007
19 Pimentel Walker, 2016: 65
20 Binder, Brandt and Gregory, 2008: 1
21 Talo, Mannarini and Rochira, 2014
22 Williams, 2006: 202
23 Soen, 1981: 105

Preliminary work on modes of participation was undertaken by Sherry R. Arnstein, the author of the highly influential ladder of participation. She developed the ladder of citizen participation to classify citizen participation in the United States of America and other developed countries.[24] However, she fails to acknowledge the inconsistency of criteria to distinguish forms of participation[25] – for instance, there is no difference in the level of power between placation, consultation, informing, manipulation and therapy, in which power remains in the control of the authorities. In 1996, Marisa B. Guaraldo Choguill adapted Arnstein's approach to present a revised ladder of community participation for developing countries.[26] She related community participation and self-help activity to the degree to which they receive support from external and governmental institutions.[27]

These levels of community involvement have been applied to the Karen community engagement providing a base for conciliation, partnership and empowerment based on Choguill's ladder. Empowerment represents the highest level of involvement, where the Karen would have total control over the project and the participatory approach is driven by people's needs. The mode of participation can assist in producing clarity about how the research is able to conduct and travel in an effective direction through the Participatory Housing Process (PHP).

STRUCTURE OF INTERVENTION

FRAMING THE PARTICIPATORY TASKS

The framework followed the action-planning method and sequence of workshops with integrated implementation tasks. The aim of this section is to develop an understanding of the participatory process. First and foremost, identifying beneficiaries to attend the workshops followed funding from the CODI for the 91 households that were relocated between 1996 and 2011. However, we focused on 43 households who needed to build new houses and were invited to attend both workshops. The next stage was to identify ways to bring the researcher closer, to understand how we might work better, as well as encourage the Karen to explore what would be good practice in the current circumstances. Additionally, development of initial trust was created through a working relationship by presenting them with the aim of the project, which was to help them to improve their present circumstances. Thus, the key agenda was established to manage the framework at each stage (such as the observing, reflecting, planning and implementation stages) under the specific time frame and limited resources.

PREPARATORY WORKSHOP

The initial task was meeting the Karen groups to gain a clearer picture of the current context by observing and reflecting on the place, people, activities and time. These

---

24   Arnstein, 1969
25   Yab, 1987
26   Choguill, 1996
27   Schinkel, Angela and Schröder, 2014: 18

activities became the formulating descriptions by respecting and listening to the Karen's voices. Furthermore, the observation-based practice is centred on the visual explanation as the representational subject matter to formulate an account of community situations. The informal meetings discussing the general issues also generated a preliminary picture of the cultural context in the early stage of the processes and the formal meetings reflected the wishes and actions for change of the Karen.

HOUSING DESIGN WORKSHOP 1

Following the preparatory section, the first workshop was held in December 2015 focusing on designing their own houses. To start with, I presented the outline of the programme and reviewed the land use and the KKNP's policy to open the discussion and to summarise the community's situation and opportunities. The next step was discussing the limited budget divided into three phases, totalling 91 households. The first workshop was divided into two groups: building and extending the houses. We concentrated on 14 households who will build new houses. This group divided into small groups of four-to-five members in order to manage the discussions. The workshop aimed to be an interactive learning activity to share different ideas by exploring alternative ways to solve the dwelling problems. The workshop resulted in a clear understanding of how to prepare and build the houses following their design. Following the Housing Design Workshop, 24 houses were built completely within the timeframe of eight months. However, due to constraints, especially access to materials and National Park regulations, not all action plans have been implemented; but in turn, this became a worthwhile lesson for the next workshop.

Figure 1. A building house group of Phase 2 was selected to design their houses in the Housing Design Workshop 1 at the community house in December 2015. Some households brought their children to the workshop.

HOUSING DESIGN WORKSHOP 2

This workshop was conducted in September 2016 under the ideas and strategies for better living based on what we had learnt from the implementation of the previous workshop. The discussion therefore focused particularly on housing challenges and aspirations of the community with respect to affordability, quality and construction. The key issues were how they can use the materials in the village effectively in order to save the limited budget.

Similar to the first workshop, we began by introducing the background of the project and the aim of the workshop including summarising the remaining budget. Before designing, the discussion on possible materials and cost of construction allowed them to think over building options. The process of the workshop was explained using the photos of the previous workshop. Additionally, the bamboo models were an excellent tool to help them to imagine the structure, space and form of the houses. The workshop was completed with 30 households that would start building the houses in January 2017.

Figure 2. Housing Design Workshop 2, held in September 2016, focused on saving the cost of building materials. Individuals created drawings to explain why and how they need, change and adapt their houses.

The design approach encouraged the Karen to be actively involved in the processes to ensure that the result of the building met their specific needs. Both workshops were an empowerment stage for the Karen community connecting to the adaptation of culture, tradition and economics to the real practice under the National Park regulation.

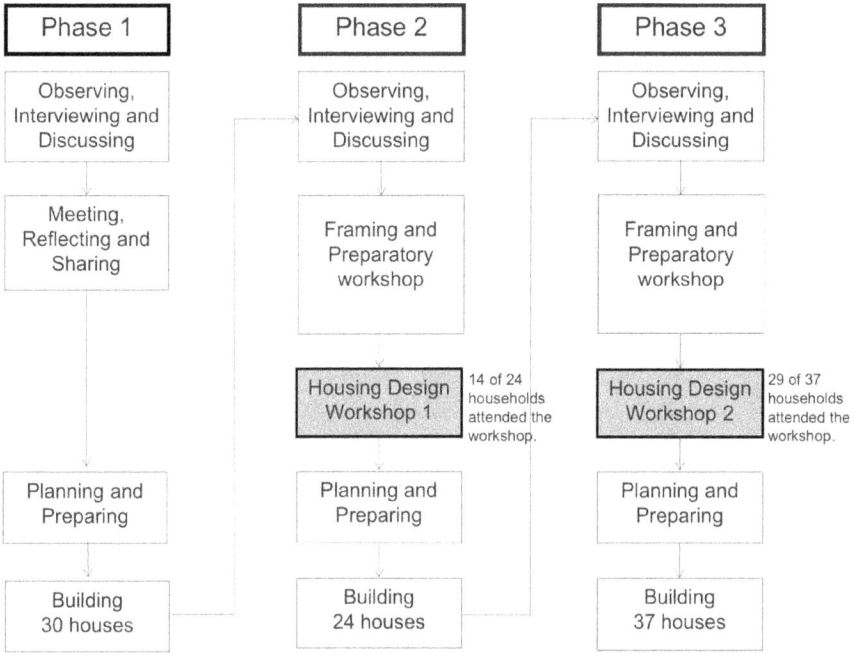

Phase 1	Phase 2	Phase 3
Observing, Interviewing and Discussing	Observing, Interviewing and Discussing	Observing, Interviewing and Discussing
Meeting, Reflecting and Sharing	Framing and Preparatory workshop	Framing and Preparatory workshop
	Housing Design Workshop 1 — 14 of 24 households attended the workshop.	Housing Design Workshop 2 — 29 of 37 households attended the workshop.
Planning and Preparing	Planning and Preparing	Planning and Preparing
Building 30 houses	Building 24 houses	Building 37 houses

Figure 3. The structure of the PHP based on the PAR approach

The role of facilitator opened up opportunities to get closer to all households. In turn, my role also effects and influences the ideas and attitudes of the community. In practice, my role is not only a researcher and facilitator but also a coordinator to connect between the Karen, CODI and KKNP to build trust and to work towards consensus between the different actors and institutions involved in the project. An architect planner role is helping the Karen to plan and design the project following the funding plan divided into two levels such as strategies planning and action planning. Through these roles I learnt how to conduct action research to encourage the Karen to get involved. So far, I found that there is no best formula for planning because it often relies on the circumstances at that moment. The most important role is therefore providing flexible and coordinate ways that enable the Karen to act and implement their ideas comfortably.

RESULT OF IMPLEMENTATION

THE CHALLENGE OF THE TRADITIONAL HOUSE

The result of implementation may be explained by the fact that the most obvious reason for building, rebuilding and extending a house was to achieve more dwelling space. These processes enabled me to identify the characteristics and describe culturally specific patterns of built form and social organisation by examining relationships in the Karen dwelling sphere. Most reasons related to their current status under the regulations, for instance, building materials, shortage of dwelling or building conditions. Thus, the Karen people seek to adapt their house to current behaviour needs and household members' activities.

To improve the lives of occupants, they often confront the limitations of the budget. Therefore, the alternative solution to increase house space is flexible planning available for extending in the future. The issue of income is also evident in the building processes affecting the house form and space, which becomes a summation of dwelling identity, social identity and personal development. Additionally, after negotiating with the KKNP in 2015, the KKNP now allow the use of precast concrete footing for the house structure. Access to industrial materials challenged the Karen's traditional design, as they currently reproduce the house space by combining the local and industrial materials leading to structural change in producing the new spaces.

The house of Supasa Chaya and Vichai Wormor in 2013

Supasa Chaya attended the Housing Design Workshop in December 2015.

They demolished the house and started building following design from the workshop.

The key structure was built.

A temporary house was built after demolishing the old house in 2016.

After roofing and completing floor structure, building materials were taken from a temporary house to the new house.

A temporary house demolished and the materials moved to build the new house.

Started building the walls and floors and living inside unfinished building.

Vichai Wormor shows the designs before and after the workshop.

The verandah was built at the last process.

Figure 4. Diagram of the transformation sequence of a Karen house. Transformation of this house between 2014 and 2016 allowed the occupants to adjust the house and express ideas to meet the needs under the national park regulation.

FEATURES OF DWELLING – REFLECTING LIFE

The traditional Karen house is built as a simple form on stilts, commonly employing bamboo floors and walls, thatch roofing and, more recently, galvanised-iron sheets and roof tiles. The available building materials and the agricultural lifestyle are the key to house form as well as socio-cultural factors. The open space beneath the house is versatile and used in different ways such as storage, living area and a place to keep livestock. Verandas are not only the transitional space but also the place for preparing food, washing, weaving and doing other works, and a place to chat with neighbours.

The invention of a new fireplace somewhat changed the nature of the dwelling and the place of the fire within. The fireplace is the heart of the Karen house[28] and is still the symbol of traditional domesticity, whereas the newly introduced brazier tends to be an item indicating contemporary life. Under such conditions, the Karen use both industrial and local materials to reproduce the form. Certain materials relate to use in a previous dwelling prior to evacuation, while some provide examples of knowledge of local technology, such as sophisticated woven bamboo walls. Contemporary features and materials are generally introduced after rebuilding and extending the house.

Currently, the Karen adapt their behaviour to fit the physical environment, particularly when they are under National Park regulations. The results of the investigation show that the Karen houses express the fact that societies share certain experience and goals under the regulation forces that can be seen in materials and social aspects which affect form.

THE PHP AS A SUSTAINABLE APPROACH

The result of this study shows that the PHP can promote the concepts of social sustainability and sustainable development to meet the need of the participants. The design process intends to achieve practical sustainable outputs. The contributory process has confirmed that the characteristics of the Karen house after attending workshops and re-housing are: firstly, simplification of house form and plan as well as modular design, which are an effective way to reduce cost and waste of materials such as joists, rafters and beams; secondly, the community self-built approach, which is of economic benefit to reduce the cost of building as well as socially significant; and lastly, local materials, which are employed in most of the construction and finishes. As such, it can be said that the motivation of the workshops is a regard for societal, economic and environmental issues, and sustainable community as a place where the Karen live and work for today and in the future. The professional involvement with the existing knowledge can recommend the design choices in possible ways. The PHP is therefore important not only in terms of design or building the physical houses but also in empowering processes to encourage the Karen to realise the problems and identify solutions at hand.

---

28 Moizo, 1997: 1,055

CONCLUSION

This paper has examined the change of the Karen house and how the Karen have managed to create and adapt their house under the regulations of the National Park. Investigation of the PHP has shown that contemporary features are generally found after rebuilding the houses by combining the local and industrial materials contributing to form and structural change. A key strength of the PHP approach is reciprocal learning to motivate the individual to discover the solution through building processes and find out how to deal with the rising scarcity of houses in the community. Workshops become a bridge linking the Karen and the researchers, as well as a bridge within the Karen group to share knowledge and experiences from each other's practices. The findings have a number of important implications for future practice to show that the participation of local people is significant for local development especially to strengthen human rights and sustainable resource management systems, with respect to the rights and traditional knowledge of local conditions. Further study would be valuable to compare experience of Karen communities within similar constraints of contexts and to evaluate the long-term influence of the PHP to the different communities.

ACKNOWLEDGEMENTS

I would like to express my sincere thanks to Dr Peter Kellett and Prof. Prue Chiles for their helpful criticism of this research.

BIBLIOGRAPHY

Alston, Margaret; and Bowles, Wendy. *Research for Social Workers: An Introduction to Method*. Australia: Allen & Unwin, 1998.

Areerat, Kongpob. 'About 40 Karens prosecuted for forest encroachment'. Accessed 3 December 2016. http://www.prachatai.com/english/node/4450.

Arnstein, Sherry R. 'A Ladder of Citizen Participation'. *Journal of the American Institute of Planners*, 35(4) (1969): 216–24.

Binder, Thomas; Brandt, Eva; and Gregory, Judith. 'Design Participation(-s)'. *CoDesign*, 4(1) (2008): 1–3.

Choguill, Marisa B. Guaraldo. 'A Ladder of Community Participation for Underdeveloped Countries'. *Habitat International*, 20(3) (1996): 431–44.

Community Organizations Development Institute (CODI). 'CODI History'. Accessed 4 December 2016. http://www.codi.or.th/housing/FrontpageHistory.html.

Delang, Claudio O. *Living at the Edge of Thai Society: the Karen in the highlands of northern Thailand*. London and New York: Routledge, 2003.

Erni, Christian. 'East and Southeast Asia'. In: *The Indigenous World 2001/2002*, edited by Diana Vinding, 272–8. Copenhagen: IWGIA, 2002.

Erni, Christian. 'East and Southeast Asia'. In: *The Indigenous World 2005*, edited by Diana Vinding, 329–36. Copenhagen: IWGIA, 2005.

Erni, Christian; and Nilsson, Christina. 'East and Southeast Asia'. In: *The Indigenous World*

2015, edited by Cæcilie Mikkelsen, 279–85. Copenhagen: IWGIA, 2015.

Erni, Christian; and Stidsen, Sille. 'East and Southeast Asia'. In: *The Indigenous World 2003*, edited by Diana Vinding, 257–63. Copenhagen: IWGIA, 2003.

Fals Borda, Orlando. 'Participatory (action) research in social theory: Origins and challenges'. In: *The Handbook of Action Research: Participative Inquiry and Practice*, edited by Peter Reason and Bradbury Hilary, 27–31. London: SAGE, 2000.

Hussain, Sofia. 'Empowering Marginalised Children in Developing Countries through Participatory Design Processes'. *CoDesign*, 6(2) (2010): 99–117.

Lennie, June. 'Increasing the rigour and trustworthiness of participatory evaluations: learnings from the field'. *Evaluation Journal of Australasia*, 6(1) (2006): 27–35.

Luck, Rachael. 'Dialogue in Participatory Design'. *Design Studies*, 24(6) (2003): 523–35.

Moizo, Bernard. 'Karen (Burma, Thailand)'. In: *Encyclopedia of Vernacular Architecture of the World*, edited by Paul Oliver, 1,054–5. Cambridge: Cambridge University Press, 1997.

Participation and Cultural Personnel Development Institute (PCPDI). *Policy and Implementation Principles in Restoration of Karen Subsistence*. Bangkok: Chulalongkorn University Press, 2011.

Pimentel Walker, Ana Paula. 'Self-help or Public Housing? Lessons from Co-managed Slum Upgrading via Participatory Budget'. *Habitat International*, 55 (2016): 58–66.

Ratanakul, Suriya; and Burusrat, Somsong. *The Encyclopedia of Ethnic Groups in Thailand, Sgaw Karen*. Bangkok: Sahadhammik, 1995.

Sanoff, Henry. 'Special Issue on Participatory Design'. *Design Studies*, 28(3) (2007): 213–15.

Santasombat, Yos. 'Karen Cultural Capital and the Political Economy of Symbolic Power'. *Asian Ethnicity*, 5(1) (2004): 105–20.

Schinkel, Ulrike; Angela, Jain; and Schröder, Sabine. *Local Action and Participation: Approaches and Lessons Learnt from Participatory Projects and Action Research in Future Megacities*. Future Megacities; v. 4. Berlin: Jovis, 2014.

Soen, Dan. 'Citizen and Community Participation in Urban Renewal and Rehabilitation – Comments on Theory and Practice'. *Community Development Journal*, 16(2) (1981): 105–17.

Talo, Cosimo; Mannarini, Terri; and Rochira, Alessia. 'Sense of Community and Community Participation: A Meta-Analytic Review'. *Social Indicators Research*, 117(1) (2014): 1–28.

Thai National Parks. 'Kaeng Krachan National Park'. Accessed 4 December 2016. https://www.thainationalparks.com/kaeng-krachan-national-park.

Tungittiplakorn, Waranoot. 'Highland–lowland conflict over natural resources – A case of Mae-Soi, Chaiang Mai, Thailand'. *Society and Natural Resources*, 8(4) (1995): 279–88.

Williams, John J. 'Community Participation'. *Policy Studies*, 27(3) (2006): 197–217.

Yab, Kio-Sheng. 'Promoting community participation through training: The DANIDA/UNCHS training programme'. *Habitat International*, 11(4) (1987): 77–86.

CHAPTER SIXTEEN

JACQUELINE POWER

University of Tasmania, Australia

PALAWA RESILIENCE AND RESISTANCE TO COLONIAL HOUSING AT WYBALENNA

INTRODUCTION

Colonisation of *trouwunna/lutruwita*[1] (now Tasmania) brought with it destructive processes that resulted in conflict between the European colonisers and the palawa people of the Tasmanian Aboriginal Nations.[2] The first recorded fatal conflict between colonisers and the palawa people took place on 3 May 1804 at Risdon Cove, where the settlement party fired upon "a very large group of Aboriginal people, including women and children".[3] By 1824 the colonisers reached 12,313 in number,[4] and by 1831 this

---

1   The adoption of Aboriginal language nomenclature continues to be debated and contested to varying degrees. Variations in spelling are sometimes found. For more on Aboriginal place names used today in Tasmania, see 'Aboriginal and Dual Names of Place', Tasmanian Aboriginal Centre Inc, accessed 12 December 2016, http://tacinc.com.au/official-aboriginal-and-dual-names/.

2   In the 1990s, Tasmanian Aboriginal people "called upon the name of our creation-time ancestor and declared ourselves Palawa. This, perhaps more than any other step, summoned up the cultural imprimatur to begin reclaiming traditional practices and expressions". (Lehman, 2006: 35) Highlighting its linguistic ownership, a lowercase 'p' is often used rather than the expected capitalisation so as not to adhere to English language grammatical rules.

3   Boyce, 2008: 77

4   Clements, 2013: xiii

population had swelled to 26,640.[5] This rapid increase caused "Aboriginal people… [to be] further marginalised by the expanding frontier of European expansion", leading to conflict.[6] The "resulting slaughter became known as the Black War".[7] A settlement, called Wybalenna, was established on Flinders Island off the north-east coast of Tasmania as a "palatable solution" to this conflict.[8] Wybalenna, meaning black men's houses, was occupied from February 1833 to October 1847.

This chapter will focus on the built environment of Wybalenna and its purpose to effect change. The literature upon which this chapter draws has been analysed from within the lens of the interior architecture/interior design discipline. This provides a specific reading of the settlement. However, much of the history and complexity of the settlement cannot be covered within the constraints of this chapter, nor is this attempted. This chapter is specifically focused on exploring the built environment and presents the hypothesis that the Aboriginal community residing there demonstrated varying levels of resistance to this environment.

The content of the chapter will draw predominantly on published secondary literature about the Wybalenna settlement. It also focuses on the content within the primary journals of George Augustus Robinson who was commandant at the settlement for a period of time, referenced in their published form as edited by N.J.B. (Brian) Plomley. The buildings at Wybalenna are no longer extant (except the chapel that was reconstructed in the 1970s), meaning that any reading of the site must be confined to the literature. Archaeological investigation was carried out in the 1970s and the findings from this research are also referenced.

A further caveat to the discussion must be provided. In this case, acknowledgement that the Aboriginal or palawa voice is largely absent from the historic Wybalenna record. A richer and more nuanced understanding of experience at the settlement would be gained with access to observations from the people who resided there. The discussion that follows is therefore offered as a 'reading' of the settlement. It is neither intended to be conclusive nor to form a definitive interpretation.

CONTEXT

This research arrives at a time when the wrongs of the past remain firmly in the present. Reconciliation continues to be a process that is still in progress in the Australian context.[9] In December 2016, for instance, the remains of three Aboriginal people were repatriated back to Tasmania, having previously been kept in an institution for

---

5   Ibid., 341

6   Geoffrey McLean, in discussion with the author, December 2016.

7   Lehman, 2013: 206

8   Ibid., 207

9   For more on reconciliation see: Reconciliation Australia, accessed 7 December 2016, https://www.reconciliation.org.au.

research.[10] "The Tasmanian Aboriginal Centre has campaigned for the repatriation of ancestral remains from national and international museums and other institutions for more than 40 years, in order to return the elders to their tribal lands so their spirits could be put to rest".[11] This is one example that makes clear that the colonisation of Tasmania is not a story confined to the past and that its effects continue to be felt. This research is positioned so as to add to the dialogue and generate understanding,[12] within the built environment disciplines, about this chapter of history.

THE TASMANIAN ABORIGINAL LANDSCAPE

It is now widely accepted that at least nine palawa nations existed across *trouwunna/lutruwita* at the time of European colonisation in 1803. The social structure is generally agreed to have comprised three units: "the domestic unit, or *family group* [comprising between two and eleven people]; the basic social unit, or *clan* [comprising between forty and fifty people]; and the political unit, or *nation*".[13] Population estimates range from a conservative 3,000 to 10,000.[14] Lyndall Ryan has concluded that the population was probably close to 7,000 and increasing.[15] Of particular interest to the built environment disciplines are the built expressions constructed by the palawa people. A range of building types, suited to their climatic context, were constructed across the island. These buildings presented varying degrees of enclosure, from windbreaks through to fully enclosed dome buildings. Historical accounts note that the buildings were sited close to resources such as fuel, food and fresh water, and were described as being located in "healthy situations".[16] These buildings would be in stark contrast to the habitations that would be later provided at Wybalenna.

HOUSING AS A SOLUTION TO CONFLICT

Colonisation of Van Diemen's Land (as it was re-named by colonisers, later becoming Tasmania) expanded during the 1820s into the "areas of open forest and grassland between Hobart in the south and Launceston in the north, resulting in the loss of Aboriginal hunting grounds and thus their means of living".[17] Rapid growth in the colonial population, from immigration and convict transportation, was also an

---

10   Holly Monery, 'Tasmanian Aboriginal ancestors repatriated to Launceston', *The Examiner*, 6 December 2016, http://www.examiner.com.au/story/4337863/honouring-aboriginal-rituals-photos-videos/?cs=5312.

11   Ibid.

12   This research is based on a chapter contained in the author's doctoral research, which explores Australian Indigenous buildings and their spatial arrangements (Power, 2013).

13   Ryan, 2012: 11

14   Ibid., 14

15   Ibid., 42

16   Plomley, 1966: 171

17   Reynolds, 2004: 4

exacerbating factor in the conflict – "by the height of the War the ratio of colonists to Aborigines had blown out to around 100:1".[18] Historian Nicholas Clements has explained that during the Black War "the island was the scene of horrific violence that produced at least 450 colonial casualties and all but wiped out the Aborigines".[19] He highlights that the historic record does not fully capture the extent of the conflict and that, for the "violence against Aborigines... a working estimate of 600 wartime killings in eastern Van Diemen's Land is both conservative and realistic".[20] The colonial government employed various measures in an attempt to quash the violent conflict and keep the palawa peoples away from the European-colonised areas. Although it is not possible to provide detailed background to the Black War within the constraints of this chapter, it is necessary to provide some context to this period. In November 1828, Lieutenant-Governor George Arthur declared martial law and formed six roving parties to kill or capture palawa peoples (additional roving parties were also established by colonialists themselves).[21] The period of martial law lasted from November 1828 to January 1832.[22] Martial law in the settled districts meant "the military now had the right to apprehend without warrant or to shoot on sight any Aboriginal found in the settled districts".[23] When this strategy proved unsuccessful in quelling the violence, another measure was adopted. In 1830, the Black Line operation mobilised 2,200 men in an attempt to push the Aboriginal population onto Tasman's Peninsula where they would be isolated from the colonists.[24] Despite costing "more than half the colony's annual budget", the operation was a failure.[25]

At the start of December 1829, still during the period of martial law, missionary George Augustus Robinson was granted permission by Lieutenant-Governor Arthur to travel to Port Davey in the south-west of the island "for the purpose of endeavouring to effect an amicable understanding with the aborigines in that quarter, and through them, with the tribes in the interior."[26] Robinson figures prominently in the Tasmanian Aboriginal colonisation period and is a controversial figure "often reviled by Tasmanian Aborigines, both as a colonial agent, and personally" for suspect motives.[27] Robinson travelled through the west and north-west coastal areas of Van Diemen's Land in an effort

---

18   Clements, 2013: xiii–xiv
19   Ibid., xiii
20   Ibid., 331
21   Ryan, 1996: 101–2
22   Ryan, 2012: 141
23   Ryan, 1996: 99
24   Clements, 2013: 196
25   Ryan, 2013: 3. Ryan provides a re-assessment of the significance of the Black Line in the article.
26   Colonial Secretary, 'Colonial Secretary to Robinson, 1 December 1829' in Plomley, 1966: 89.
27   Johnston and Rolls, 2008: 17

to negotiate a settlement with the palawa peoples.[28] This was the commencement of Robinson's so-called Friendly Mission journeys that took place over four years, from 1830 to 1834. The purpose of these missions was to make contact with and subsequently remove people from their homelands. The degree to which negotiation actually took place is questionable and at times Robinson seemingly used intimidation to fulfil[29] what he described as his "work of conciliation".[30] Ultimately, a settlement at Wybalenna on Flinders Island in the Bass Strait was established.

AN ISLAND HOME OR PRISON?

The palawa peoples from mainland Tasmania and a number of women residing on islands in the Bass Strait were gradually relocated to the settlement. The establishment of Wybalenna followed a series of previously failed settlements.[31] A number of commandants managed Wybalenna for the colonial government during the period of its occupation; however, much of the discussion here focuses on two periods during which William James Darling (from March 1832 to September 1834)[32] and George Augustus Robinson (from October 1835 to February 1839) were commandants. More documentation is available from these periods (Robinson, for instance, kept extensive journals) and it was also under the commands of Darling and Robinson that the two phases of building took place that characterised the island settlement.

Various pragmatic reasons lead to the decision to select Flinders Island as the site for the Wybalenna settlement. Some valuable lessons had been learned from the previous settlements and their failures. Four main factors, however, influenced the final decision. In the eyes of the colonialists the island was considered inescapable and, in addition to this, the palawa peoples would be protected from kidnap by sealers. There was also an adequate supply of food and water. In addition, Flinders Island was thought to offer opportunity for amusement, as the palawa peoples would be able to hunt for game. Finally, the island was considered to facilitate communication with the Tasmanian mainland and provide suitable anchorage for vessels.[33] The Aborigines Committee, "an advisory body composed of prominent officials", also considered Maria Island as a possible option for a settlement but these four factors swayed the decision in

---

28   Reynolds, 2004: 5
29   For example, Robinson describes in his journal entry of 21 May 1833: "I remained outside so that they could not tell where I was. This caution was necessary to be observed to intimidate them, for had only one escaped it would have thwarted my plans, for they would have at once prejudiced the minds of all the rest." (Plomley, 1966: 727)
30   Ibid., 725
31   For a brief explanation of the settlements, period of occupation and reason for their closure see: Power, 2013: 205–7.
32   Darling began his term as Commandant whilst the settlement was still located at The Lagoons site. (Plomley, 1987: 57)
33   Turnbull, 1948: 138–9

favour of Flinders Island.[34] However, after a period of occupation at the settlement, the shortcomings of Flinders Island began to be revealed. Whilst environmental factors on the island presented challenges, the building stock itself presented a different set of trials for the residents.

Wybalenna translates as *black men's houses*, thus reflecting the centrally important role the buildings would play throughout the years of occupation of the site. Permanent buildings were constructed to align with European concepts of how a building should look and the manner in which it should function. From the colonialists' perspective, the buildings were not simply to be inhabited by their residents: it was hoped that the buildings would bestow their associated European qualities on the palawa peoples. As described by Ryan, "the Aboriginal Establishment at Flinders Island was an artificially created environment which was the means of foisting one set of cultural beliefs upon another".[35] The nomenclature of the peninsula where Wybalenna was built, Civilisation Point,[36] reflects this motivation. The siting of the settlement on an island meant that the palawa peoples were kept at a distance from the European colonialists by being spatially separated. As described by Ryan, "the Aborigines were to remain out of the sight and largely out of the minds of both administrators and settlers".[37] Wybalenna reveals not only a metaphorical dislocation where the palawa peoples were placed within the new strictures of colonial authority, but also their physical removal from traditional lands and building types. Wybalenna was described in the controversial 1978 film *The Last Tasmanian*[38] as being focused on "changing 'savages' into 'respectable' citizens: clothes for the skin, agricultural food for the stomach, the English language for the tongue and Christianity for the soul".[39] Current-day Aboriginal elder Rodney Dillon has highlighted the mix of elements at Wybalenna that contributed to the alienating environment, explaining the dislocation from Country, being housed with "unfamiliar people from different tribes and [being supplied with] unfamiliar food".[40]

Criticisms of the Wybalenna 'solution' are not confined to a contemporary understanding. A newspaper article from 1838, for instance, describes the palawa people as being "imprisoned on Flinder's Island" and draws a direct comparison between their treatment and that of convict prisoners:

> Can anything be done for these injured beings? All that has been done by the Colonial Government for them, up to the present time, has been to exile them, and to order

---

34 Reynolds, 2004: 36
35 Ryan, 1975: 212
36 Roth, 1899: 4
37 Ryan, 1975: 212
38 The documentary attracted criticism for its perpetuation of the dying race myth and its failure to acknowledge the existence of contemporary Tasmanian Aboriginal peoples. For more, see Smith, 2004: 180–3.
39 Haydon and Jones, 1978
40 Dillon, 2008: 145

their confinement in a prison out of which it is impossible for them to escape, and, in fact, to do for them what has been done for prisoners of another colour – appointing a Superintendent or Commandant, to see they do not escape, and to enforce the Government orders, and a Storekeeper to serve out their clothes and rations, and a Catechist or Chaplain to instruct them; so that the Government has just done as much for the aborigines as it has done for British convicts.[41]

This article was originally published in the Launceston newspaper the *Cornwell Chronicle*. One of the roles of the paper has been described as providing "a check on government abuses".[42] This article indicates that although many of the palawa peoples had been removed to Flinders Island, they were not entirely forgotten. The treatment of Australia's Indigenous population was a particular focus of the "humanitarian network", described by Alan Lester, that communicated the "abuses that Britons were inflicting on indigenous peoples."[43] However, Lester outlines that these interactions were "never 'neutral' or 'innocent'… Both settler and humanitarian networks carried dispossessive force".[44]

HOUSING AT WYBALENNA

Housing at Wybalenna was split into two primary phases aligning with the periods that Darling and Robinson held their respective positions at the settlement. In the first phase, under the direction of Darling, wattle-and-daub cottages were constructed. The cottages were 28ft by 14ft with a central double fireplace dividing the space in two, each apartment accommodated approximately six people.[45] The overall settlement consisted of the following buildings: "living quarters for civil staff, two cottages for the military, and huts for the convict labourers. There were nine double huts for the Aborigines,[46] a large provision store".[47]

Missionaries James Backhouse and George Walker visited the settlement in the summer of 1833–4 and provided a report to the Colonial Secretary. Quaker Backhouse toured the Australian colonies between 1832 and 1838 accompanied by Quaker Walker.[48] During his travels, Backhouse was in communication with Thomas Fowell Buxton, a director of the London Missionary Society, "requesting that he lobby for legislative action. The governors of the Australian colonies also commissioned reports

41   'Flinders Island', *Sydney Monitor*, 4 May 1838: 2.
42   Bell, 1993: 132
43   Lester, 2006: 236
44   Ibid., 236–7
45   Plomley, 1987: 65
46   Ryan seems to adopt the term 'hut' in reference to Robinson's journal entries in which he uses the term, presumably in reference to the buildings constructed during Darling's period at the settlement. This presents an anachronism in relation to the type of building being referred to.
47   Ryan, 1996: 183
48   Lester, 2006: 233

from the two Quakers [Backhouse and Walker], which were printed for circulation in the colonies and in Britain".[49] Backhouse and Walker described the settlement as consisting of:

> about twenty cottages, nine of which are occupied by the Aborigines… the buildings are of wattles and plaster, white-washed both inside and out, and with thatched roofs. Being of so slight a texture, several of those inhabited by the blacks are already undergoing repairs. These are placed a few yards from each other, extending in the form of a crescent, in front of which is a garden of about an acre and half in extent. There is an interval of at least quarter of a mile between the dwellings of the Aborigines and those of the assigned servants. The cottages of the Commandant and other officers are placed in such a position as to command a full view of both sections of the settlement, an arrangement on the whole judicious.[50]

Alan Lester has described the role of settler and humanitarian communication networks that contributed to the "construction of the Christian humanitarian worldview that many missionaries shared during the early nineteenth century".[51] This assists to contextualise Backhouse and Walker's motivations for visiting the settlement and documenting their visit.

As made evident by the previous description, the housing constructed in this first phase of the settlement soon fell into a state of disrepair and by 1836 one visitor commented that "to induce these people to become domesticated you must provide them with the means of internal comfort".[52] This quote captures two key ideas. One, that the housing was being used as a mechanism through which to change cultural practices, and two, that the interior spaces of the buildings were unsatisfactory from a 'comfort' standpoint. The unsatisfactory comfort was believed to have been a causal factor in the poor health of the residents and a link was thought to exist between the peoples' ill health and the housing, prompting calls to the government to provide improved housing.[53]

It is somewhat difficult to ascertain what "improved housing" would have meant to the Aboriginal residents at Wybalenna, but Robinson's arrival at the settlement was followed by a second phase of housing construction. In this phase of building, terraced brick apartments were constructed (visible in Figure 2). The building works were "an undertaking which he considered vital because he attributed [the palawa peoples'] poor health to bad housing".[54] This second phase of building did not commence until March 1837, although Robinson arrived in October 1835.[55] Ryan has suggested

---

49   Ibid., 234

50   James Backhouse and George Washington Walker, 'Backhouse and Walker's Report Summer 1833–1834' in Plomley, 1987: 269.

51   Lester, 2006: 231

52   Plomley, 1987: 635

53   Ibid., 635

54   Ibid., 92

55   Ibid.

that Robinson "had every reason to believe that both he and the entire Aboriginal Establishment would soon be relocated to South Australia", meaning that Wybalenna was treated as a "transit camp".[56]

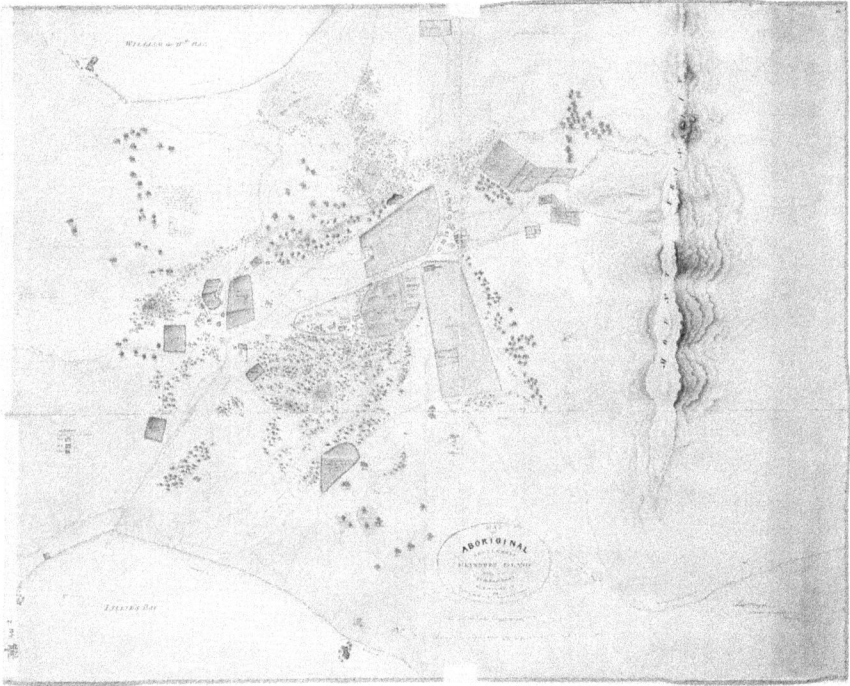

Figure 1. Map of Wybalenna believed to be based on Robinson's 1838 map.
(T.S. Edgar, 1838, Mitchell Library, State Library of NSW – Call no. Z / M4 889.1/1838/1)

In an attempt to improve the existing housing, Robinson undertook some provisional works in 1835, which included relocating the entrance doors in an effort to stop westerly winds blowing directly into the interiors.[57] In addition, Robinson had workmen adapt "the further native hut for a school and chapel" that would allow him to instruct the palawa peoples in Christianity and instigate European teaching pedagogy.[58] The new chapel was completed on the 2 December 1835 and the first of the palawa peoples were moved into their renovated accommodation on this date.[59]

---

56 Ryan, 2012: 219
57 Plomley, 1987: 92
58 Ibid., 309
59 Ibid., 311

Robinson eventually erected a brick L-shaped terrace containing twenty apartments, each accommodating two families, with brick or wooden floors and thatched roofs.[60] These were of a similar type to those erected in Britain "for rural labourers, with stone exterior and brick partition walls".[61] In addition, some existing buildings on the site were improved and new ones constructed, such as the bathing house.[62] Today, the chapel is the only building left standing at the site, re-constructed by the National Trust of Australia (Tasmania) in the 1970s.

Figure 2. View of Wybalenna showing the terraces from Robinson's era.
(John Skinner Prout, Residences of the Aborigines Flinders Island, 1846, Record ID 100956, Allport Library and Museum of Fine Arts, Tasmanian Archive and Heritage Office)

---

60   Ibid., 92
61   Birmingham, 1992: 31
62   "The bathing house is very strongly built of logs and wattled with teatree and thatched with grass, with rustic seats and table; is about 9 by 9, thus". Robinson follows this description in his journal with both a plan and perspective view of the building. (Plomley, 1987: 535)

HEALTH IMPACT OF THE HOUSING

Due to the high number of mortalities at Wybalenna, the interiors of the terraces have been linked to the procession of death at the settlement. The question of genocide has even been raised.[63] Ryan has described the terraces as a place:

> where the Aborigines would privately become transformed into white Christian people. But of course in the terraces was where they became sick because they were closed in. Because they had no fresh air or very little fresh air, they became very damp. Many people died in those terraces and in a sense the terraces are a kind of death camp.[64]

A death camp these terraces did seem to become, for when Robinson arrived at the settlement "in October 1835... 123 Aborigines greeted him, [whereas by] his departure three and a half years later, fifty-nine of them had died, eleven others were born or arrived separately, and fifteen accompanied him to Port Phillip. Only sixty Aborigines remained at Wybalenna".[65] In Robinson's journals, the deaths are recorded along with an indicative map of the burial locations.

However, Reynolds has commented that whilst "many writers have suggested that Flinders Island was a particularly unhealthy environment", a member of the medical staff residing there "judged it more salubrious than mainland Tasmania".[66] Reynolds' observation is important as it suggests health ramifications did not necessarily result from a poor standard of accommodation. Reynolds points out that during the period between "September 1833 and May 1837 only one of the seventy convicts died of disease", whilst forty palawa residents passed away.[67] The notion that the housing was not necessarily constructed to a poor European standard (although it must be said that poor maintenance regimes resulted in dilapidation, particularly in the later years of the settlement) points to the negative *effect* of European buildings on the palawa residents – both physical and psychological.

RESISTANCE TO THE HOUSING

Although Wybalenna figures as an overwhelmingly negative chapter in Australian history, it is also important to acknowledge as part of this history the "adaptability and resourcefulness of the [palawa] community, the continuing zest for life, the

---

63   Historian Henry Reynolds has stated that whilst the number of deaths at Wybalenna did fall within the UN draft convention concerning genocide in death camps, where 30–40% of the camp population is reduced in number annually, "there is no available evidence at all to suggest that it was the intention of the colonial government to effect the extinction of the Tasmanians." (Reynolds, 2001: 85)

64   Lyndall Ryan in Thomas, Moore and Open Channel Co-operative, 1992

65   Ryan, 2012: 239

66   Reynolds, 2001: 84

67   Ibid.

political passion" that still found expression.[68] This was manifest in the observance of cultural practices, such as ceremonial dancing at night, and hunting expeditions for muttonbirds and shellfish.[69] Reynolds explains that "They pleased themselves, refusing to work, demanding better conditions and rations, coming and going as they wished and often spending long periods out in the bush on hunting expeditions. They regarded the settlement as theirs".[70] A significant example of resilience and resistance takes the form of the 1846 petition that was signed by eight of the palawa people living at Wybalenna. The petition stemmed from concern about the possible return of Dr Jeanneret to the settlement and his previous poor treatment of the residents and neglect of their living conditions. The petition has been analysed in detail by Reynolds, who explains the significance of the signatories' description of themselves as "the free Aborigines Inhabitants of Van Diemen's Land now living upon Flinders Island" and the reference that is made to an "agreement" made between the palawa people and Robinson and Colonel Arthur.[71] The petition itself is testament to the political resilience and agency of the palawa people despite their confinement at Wybalenna. Although the buildings themselves were not the catalyst for the petition, the totality of the Wybalenna environment – the living conditions, the authority imposed, the agreement that was made that led to Wybalenna – forms the backdrop to the writing of the petition. Another example of resilience, adaptability and perhaps political expression can be found in the examples of resistance to the accommodation that were recorded by Robinson.

The hypothesis proposed here is that the palawa peoples displayed various methods of resistance to occupation of the houses. This demonstrates both a positive continuity of culture, as well as the subversion of the strictures imposed. Several instances of this have been identified and are provided as initial support for this thinking. These instances range from interaction with the built environment, including adaptation and destruction of the spaces, to selective inhabitation of the spaces.

One instance that challenged European expectations of inhabitation was the intersection of the interior spaces with cultural expression – specifically, drawing upon the whitewashed walls. Robinson recorded in his journal entry of 26 December 1835: "In several huts are to be seen rude drawings on the walls of ships, others of letters and a variety of devices and hieroglyphics such as they had been accustomed to make in their own country".[72] It is not clear from this description what medium was used for these drawings or how frequently this practice took place at Wybalenna. Traditionally, paintings and incised images were made on interior walls, particularly in buildings

---

68   Reynolds notes that writers often "tell a simple story – sentimental and sad – which has no room for complexity. It would be spoilt if it encompassed the view of Walter Arthur and his friends that the Tasmanians were a free people." (Reynolds, 2004: 189)
69   Ryan, 1996: 196–7
70   Reynolds, 2001: 84
71   Reynolds, 2004: 7–8
72   Plomley, 1987: 329

intended for use for a lengthy duration on the west coast.[73] When viewed through a European lens, the painting of the whitewashed walls could be considered a form of vandalism of the building and therefore illustrative of resistance. However, perhaps what the undertaking of the practice better highlights is an attempt by the palawa residents to adapt the buildings and continue cultural practices, and to make the interior spaces feel more 'familiar'.

Physical damage to the buildings reveals another form of resistance. In August 1836, walls of the catechist's house were knocked down by twelve of the boys. Robinson recorded in his journal that "the boys broke the house and beat down the walls".[74] This event could be considered the result of ill-behaved youth or, alternatively, as a symbolic attack on Christianity and its attempts to transform cultural and religious practices. The catechist was unpopular at Wybalenna according to Robinson,[75] who describes him as "very querulous and litigious".[76] It is possible the catechist had behaved in a manner that gave offence, thus resulting in retaliation or 'pay-back'.[77] The likelihood of this seems increased when considered in the context of several fires at the catechist's quarters. In the case of "the outbuildings at the catechist's quarters" being burnt to the ground in December 1836, Robinson suspects the cause of the fire was "the native boys, and if not intentionally must have been gross carelessness".[78] In the case of the incident in which the walls were knocked down, whatever motivated the action of the boys, the specific target was a building. It suggests that the built environment was significant as providing a focus for expression and communication.

A further illustration of resistance to the housing is demonstrated by the distribution of artefacts uncovered during archaeological investigations that took place at the site in 1971. The excavation revealed a quantity of animal bone and shells, and small amounts of European artefacts such as bowls, buttons and bottle glass.[79] The distribution of the artefacts suggests a particular inhabitation of the spaces that was unexpected. As explained by archaeologist Judy Birmingham, the artefacts:

> were scattered both inside and outside the two cottages, and it was their distribution which initially raised the spectre of the interpretive dilemma. In Eurocentric terms, while the finds were those familiarly found on nineteenth-century colonial sites globally, their distribution on investigation related oddly to the stone and brick cottages.[80]

---

73   For a discussion of palawa building types see: Power, 2016.
74   Plomley, 1987: 371
75   In contrast to Robinson's description, historian Lyndall Ryan describes the catechist Robert Clark, who was at the settlement from 1834 to 1839 and later returned in this role at Oyster Cove, as someone "who had long been their champion." (Ryan, 2012: 246; 252)
76   Plomley, 1987: 460
77   Geoffrey McLean, in discussion with the author, December 2016.
78   Plomley, 1987: 399
79   Birmingham, 1992: 31
80   Ibid.

Arguably, the distribution of the artefacts reveals a resistance to the spatial constructs established by the buildings – of inside–outside space. The palawa peoples were not governed by the buildings' fabric that separated inside and outside space – traditional 'outside' elements were uncovered during the archaeological investigation inside, including flora and fauna.[81] Accounts of traditional palawa buildings note the bones of small animals being found around the deserted fire-places.[82] Traditional palawa dome-building interiors were often decorated with feathers.[83] It is perhaps then unsurprising that according to Birmingham there was "no simple, European style recognition of the household contents' paradigm visible in the overall distribution of artefacts"[84] at Wybalenna. This suggests that the spatial organisation established by the buildings did not dictate how they were inhabited.

The several examples of resistance to the buildings presented here are not necessarily an exhaustive account. The instances demonstrate the *effect* of the built environment and the interaction with it by the people who resided there. It suggests that the housing stock was an important element of the Wybalenna story, not just for its general purpose at a macro scale but also for the micro-scale interactions with it by the inhabitants. The built environment was just one element of a framework established by officialdom to transform culture and generate new practices. However, the built environment enables an understanding of not only the restrictions of the settlement but also the desire to modify, challenge and reorganise the spatial experiences provided.

THE CLOSURE OF THE SETTLEMENT

Eventually, Wybalenna was abandoned and the inhabitants were relocated to another settlement at Oyster Cove on the Tasmanian mainland. A number of factors contributed to the decision to abandon Wybalenna, including the protests by the palawa peoples of their cruel treatment by Commandant Dr Henry Jeanneret, whose command at the settlement was terminated in May 1847.[85]

In 1847, the remaining forty-seven palawa people at Wybalenna made the journey to the ex-convict penal station at Oyster Cove,[86] which had been "abandoned in 1844 when it

---

81 Judy Birmingham refers to previous investigation of the faunal matter both in and around Cottage 7 and 8. This investigation unearthed quite an abundance of brush wallaby, pademelon and brush-tailed possum remains, and in lesser quantity, ring-tailed possum, wombat, brown bandicoot and potoroo remains. For more detail regarding their distribution see ibid., 32.

82 Roth, 1899: 87

83 Plomley, 1966: 722

84 Birmingham, 1992: 33

85 Ryan, 2012: 251

86 The group was comprised of fifteen men, twenty-two women and ten children. (Ryan, 1996: 203)

failed to meet convict health standards".[87] A very similar housing formula was applied despite it having shown considerable negative consequences at Wybalenna. Historian Greg Lehman explains that "Oyster Cover was only abandoned when its inhabitants, left to die in miserable conditions, had reduced to a single woman".[88]

CONCLUSION

The settlement of Wybalenna on Flinders Island provides an historical example of the provision of housing provided against a complex backdrop of social and political agendas. The inhabitation of the settlement followed the removal of the palawa peoples from their homelands as a result of Robinson's "friendly missions". Ryan has summed up that the "The forced removal of the South West and North West nations remains one of the most shameful episodes in Australian history".[89] The settlement of Wybalenna formed the focal point following this undertaking and was used by officialdom in an attempt to transform culture and undertake assimilation. However, this paper has shown that the palawa peoples demonstrated resistance to the accommodation provided and sought to maintain culture whilst housed at Wybalenna. The resilience and resistance demonstrated at Wybalenna continued to be expressed during the activist period of the 1970s, ultimately leading in 2004 to Wybalenna being returned to the Tasmanian Aboriginal community under the *Aboriginal Lands Act 1995 (Tas)*.[90] Today, Wybalenna is Aboriginal land.

ACKNOWLEDGEMENT

My thanks are extended to Geoffrey McLean, Aboriginal historian and lecturer at Riawunna Centre for Aboriginal and Torres Strait Islander Higher Education at the University of Tasmania, for his generous feedback and advice on the text.

BIBLIOGRAPHY

Bell, Jane. '"An Extremely Scurrilous Paper": The Cornwell Chronicle: 1835–47'. Master's thesis, University of Tasmania, 1993.

Birmingham, Judy. 'Meaning from Artefacts: a question of scale'. *Australasian Historical Archaeology*, 10 (1992): 30–5.

Boyce, James. 'What business have you here?' In: *First Australians: An Illustrated History*, edited by Rachel Perkins and Marcia Langton, 65–113. Carlton, VIC: The Miegunyah Press, 2008.

---

87   Ryan, 1975: 272
88   Lehman, 2013: 207
89   Ryan, 2012: 216
90   For more on land rights in Tasmania see: Alison Alexander, 'Aboriginal Land Rights', *The Companion to Tasmanian History*, accessed 14 December 2016, http://www.utas.edu. au/library/companion_to_tasmanian_history/A/Aboriginal%20land%20rights.htm.

Clements, Nicholas. 'Frontier Conflict in Van Diemen's Land'. PhD diss., University of Tasmania, 2013.

Dillon, Rodney. 'Community Voices'. In: *Reading Robinson: Companion Essays to Friendly Mission*, edited by Anna Johnston and Mitchell Rolls, 143–5. Hobart: Quintus Publishing, 2008.

Haydon, Tom; and Jones, Rhys. *The Last Tasmanian*. Avalon Beach, NSW: Maxwell's Collection [distributor], 1978. Videocassette (VHS), 104 min.

Johnston, Anna; and Rolls, Mitchell. 'Reading Friendly Mission in the Twenty-First Century: An Introduction'. In: *Reading Robinson: Companion Essays to Friendly Mission*, edited by Anna Johnston and Mitchell Rolls, 13–25. Hobart: Quintus Publishing, 2008.

Lehman, Greg. 'Being Here: authenticity and presence in Tasmanian Aboriginal art'. In: *Keeping Culture: Aboriginal Tasmania*, edited by Amanda Jane Reynolds, 33–43. Canberra: National Museum of Australia Press, 2006.

Lehman, Greg. 'Tasmanian Gothic: the art of Australia's forgotten war'. *GriffithREVIEW*, Autumn (2013): 201–12.

Lester, Alan. 'Colonial Networks, Australian Humanitarianism and the History Wars'. *Geographical Research*, 44(3) (2006): 229–41.

Plomley, N.J.B., ed. *Friendly Mission: The Tasmanian Journals and Papers of George Augustus Robinson, 1829–1834*. Hobart: Tasmanian Historical Research Association, 1966.

Plomley, N.J.B., ed. *Weep in Silence: A History of the Flinders Island Aboriginal Settlement; with the Flinders Island Journal of George Augustus Robinson, 1835–1839*. Sandy Bay, TAS: Blubber Head Press, 1987.

Power, Jacqueline. 'South-East Australian Indigenous Space and its Cosmological Origins'. PhD diss., University of New South Wales, 2013.

Power, Jacqueline. 'Australian palawa Buildings: rethinking interiors and their representation'. *Journal of Interior Design*, 41(3) (2016): 15–32.

Reynolds, Henry. *An Indelible Stain? The Question of Genocide in Australia's History*. Ringwood, VIC: Viking, 2001.

Reynolds, Henry. *Fate of a Free People*, rev. ed. Camberwell, VIC: Penguin, 2004.

Roth, H. Ling. *The Aborigines of Tasmania*, 1899. Facsimile of the 2nd ed. Hobart: Fullers Bookshop, 1899.

Ryan, Lyndall. 'The Aborigines in Tasmania, 1800–1974 and their Problems with the Europeans'. PhD diss., Macquarie University, 1975.

Ryan, Lyndall. *The Aboriginal Tasmanians*, 2nd ed. St. Leonards, NSW: Allen & Unwin, 1996.

Ryan, Lyndall. *Tasmanian Aborigines: A History since 1803*. Sydney: Allen & Unwin, 2012.

Ryan, Lyndall. 'The Black Line in Van Diemen's Land: Success or Failure?' *Journal of Australian Studies*, 37(1) (2013): 3–18.

Smith, Laurajane. *Archaeological Theory and the Politics of Cultural Heritage*. London: Routledge, 2004.

Thomas, Steve; Moore, John; and Open Channel Co-operative. *Black Man's Houses*. Fitzroy, VIC: A Steve Thomas/Open Channel Production, 1992. Videocassette (VHS), 58 min.

Turnbull, Clive. *Black War: The Extermination of the Tasmanian Aborigines*. Melbourne: F.W. Cheshire, 1948.

GRAHAM CAIRNS

AFTERWORD

HOUSING – CRITICAL FUTURES

By way of a brief afterword, it is useful to return to what was laid out in the foreword: that housing is not only a complex problem that takes on many forms in the variegated contexts it exists in – basically everywhere there is human habitation – but that, in addition, it is for many an absolutely 'critical issue'. What makes it critical is itself diverse. For some it is a question of financial security, for others it is a public health issue. In some cases, as discussed in this book, it is a question of political allegiance or the survival of traditional values and cultures. Whatever the case, it is clear that the design of housing in and of itself is not enough to address the problems at hand. That said, design of housing for the future must remain at the top of the agenda for those concerned with housing – whether its function is to be as a utopian goal to strive for, or as a practical model we can implement as soon as specific political or financial criteria are met.

The *Housing the Future* book series by Libri Publishing has attempted to underline this role for design whilst keeping in mind that it is only a single facet of a bigger problem. In the first of the books in the series, *Housing the Future – Alternative Approaches for Tomorrow (2015)*, projects from the United Kingdom, Spain, Italy, Canada, Germany, the United States, Cyprus, Greece and several Latin American contexts were included. They dealt with *planning and strategic approaches* that considered legal, financial and planning issues; *urban design initiatives* that contemplated the inevitable urban implications of housing large numbers of people in specific locations; *sustainable house initiatives* that considered housing at the level of the individual building or on a social platform; *renovating for life considerations* that underlined creative and practical ideas on how to re-use existing housing – or other building stock – to meet modern housing needs, and much more.

In the second book of the series, *Housing Solutions through Design* (2017), a mainly Western European perspective was evident and several common features emerged as issues of specific concern in that region: the need for appropriate construction that is durable, well built, empowers the inhabitant and offers the opportunity for sustainable reuse. In that book, a number of these issues were brought to the fore only to remerge again in this final book in the series. One of those arguments echoes strongly ideas laid out by Herman Hertzberger, not only in his contribution to this series but in his work over decades: the importance of designing *for* and *with* people, ensuring that the 'users' of the buildings we construct become their 'dwellers'. Nowhere is this more important than in the housing we design and build, and nothing has been more important to this book and the Libri series than this central argument. As we face the critical issues of housing supply and affordability, it is essential to remember this. The quality of the homes we create will, in the long run, be as important as the number of houses we build.

www.ingramcontent.com/pod-product-compliance
Lightning Source LLC
Chambersburg PA
CBHW070924030426
42336CB00014BA/2527